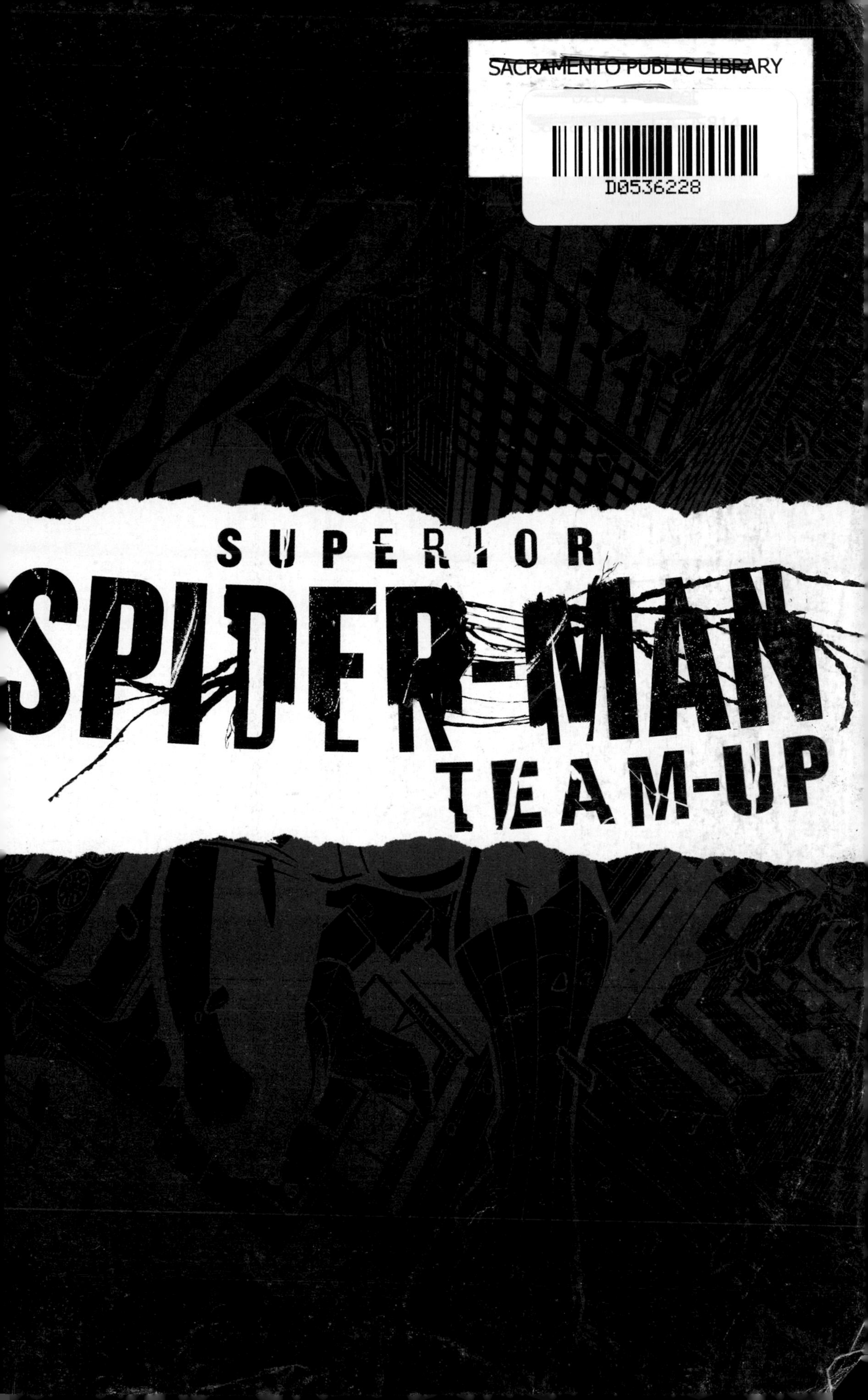
SUPERIOR
SPIDER-MAN
TEAM-UP

# SUPERIOR
# SPIDER-MAN
## TEAM-UP
## SUPERIORITY COMPLEX

### WRITER
# CHRIS YOST

**PENCILER, #15.1 & #16-17**
## PACO MEDINA

**ARTIST, #18-19**
## MARCO CHECCHETTO

**INKER, #15.1 & #16-17**
### JUAN VLASCO

**COLORIST, #15.1 & #16-17**
### DAVID CURIEL

**COLOR ARTIST, #18-19**
### RACHELLE ROSENBERG

**LETTERER**
### VC'S JOE CARAMAGNA

**COVER ART**
### PAOLO RIVERA (#15.1, #16-17 & #19) & MARCO CHECCHETTO (#18)

**ASSISTANT EDITOR**
### ELLIE PYLE

**ASSISTANT EDITOR**
### SANA AMANAT

**EDITOR**
### STEPHEN WACKER

**EXECUTIVE EDITOR**
### TOM BREVOORT

Collection Editor: **Cory Levine** • Assistant Editors: **Alex Starbuck & Nelson Ribeiro**
Editors, Special Projects: **Jennifer Grünwald & Mark D. Beazley** • Senior Editor, Special Projects: **Jeff Youngquist**
SVP of Print & Digital Publishing Sales: **David Gabriel** • Book Design: **Jeff Powell**

Editor in Chief: **Axel Alonso** • Chief Creative Officer: **Joe Quesada** • Publisher: **Dan Buckley** • Executive Producer: **Alan Fine**

**SUPERIOR SPIDER-MAN TEAM-UP: SUPERIORITY COMPLEX.** Contains material originally published in magazine form as AVENGING SPIDER-MAN #16-19 and #15.1. First printing 2013. ISBN# 978-0-7851-6536-1. Published by MARVEL WORLDWIDE, INC., a subsidiary of MARVEL ENTERTAINMENT, LLC. OFFICE OF PUBLICATION: 135 West 50th Street, New York, NY 10020. Copyright © 2012 and 2013 Marvel Characters, Inc. All rights reserved. All characters featured in this issue and the distinctive names and likenesses thereof, and all related indicia are trademarks of Marvel Characters, Inc. No similarity between any of the names, characters, persons, and/or institutions in this magazine with those of any living or dead person or institution is intended, and any such similarity which may exist is purely coincidental. **Printed in the U.S.A.** ALAN FINE, EVP - Office of the President, Marvel Worldwide, Inc. and EVP & CMO Marvel Characters B.V.; DAN BUCKLEY, Publisher & President - Print, Animation & Digital Divisions; JOE QUESADA, Chief Creative Officer; TOM BREVOORT, SVP of Publishing; DAVID BOGART, SVP of Operations & Procurement, Publishing; C.B. CEBULSKI, SVP of Creator & Content Development; DAVID GABRIEL, SVP of Print & Digital Publishing Sales; JIM O'KEEFE, VP of Operations & Logistics; DAN CARR, Executive Director of Publishing Technology; SUSAN CRESPI, Editorial Operations Manager; ALEX MORALES, Publishing Operations Manager; STAN LEE, Chairman Emeritus. For information regarding advertising in Marvel Comics or on Marvel.com, please contact Niza Disla, Director of Marvel Partnerships, at ndisla@marvel.com. For Marvel subscription inquiries, please call 800-217-9158. **Manufactured between 5/22/2013 and 6/24/2013 by QUAD/GRAPHICS, VERSAILLES, KY, US.**

10 9 8 7 6 5 4 3 2 1

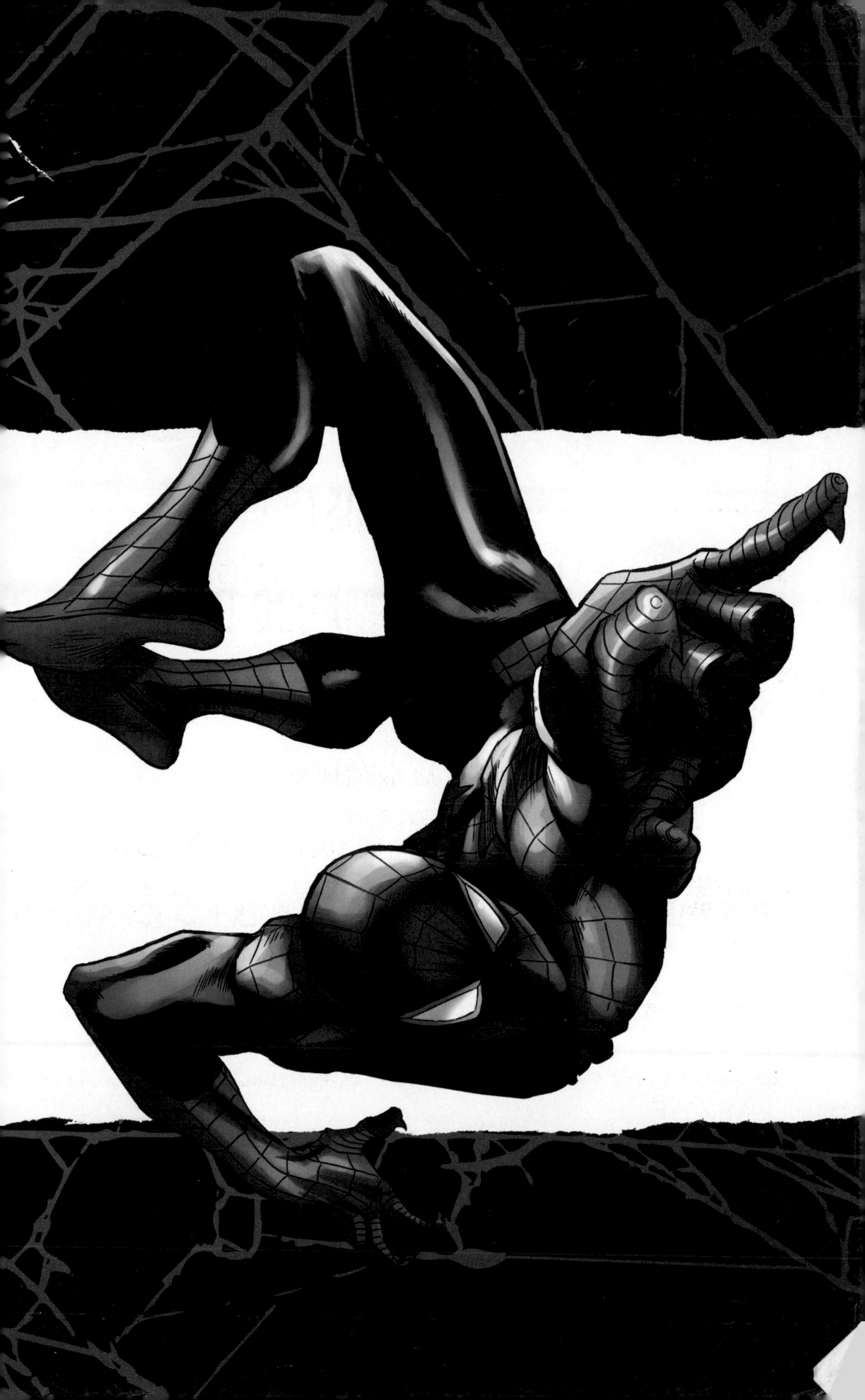

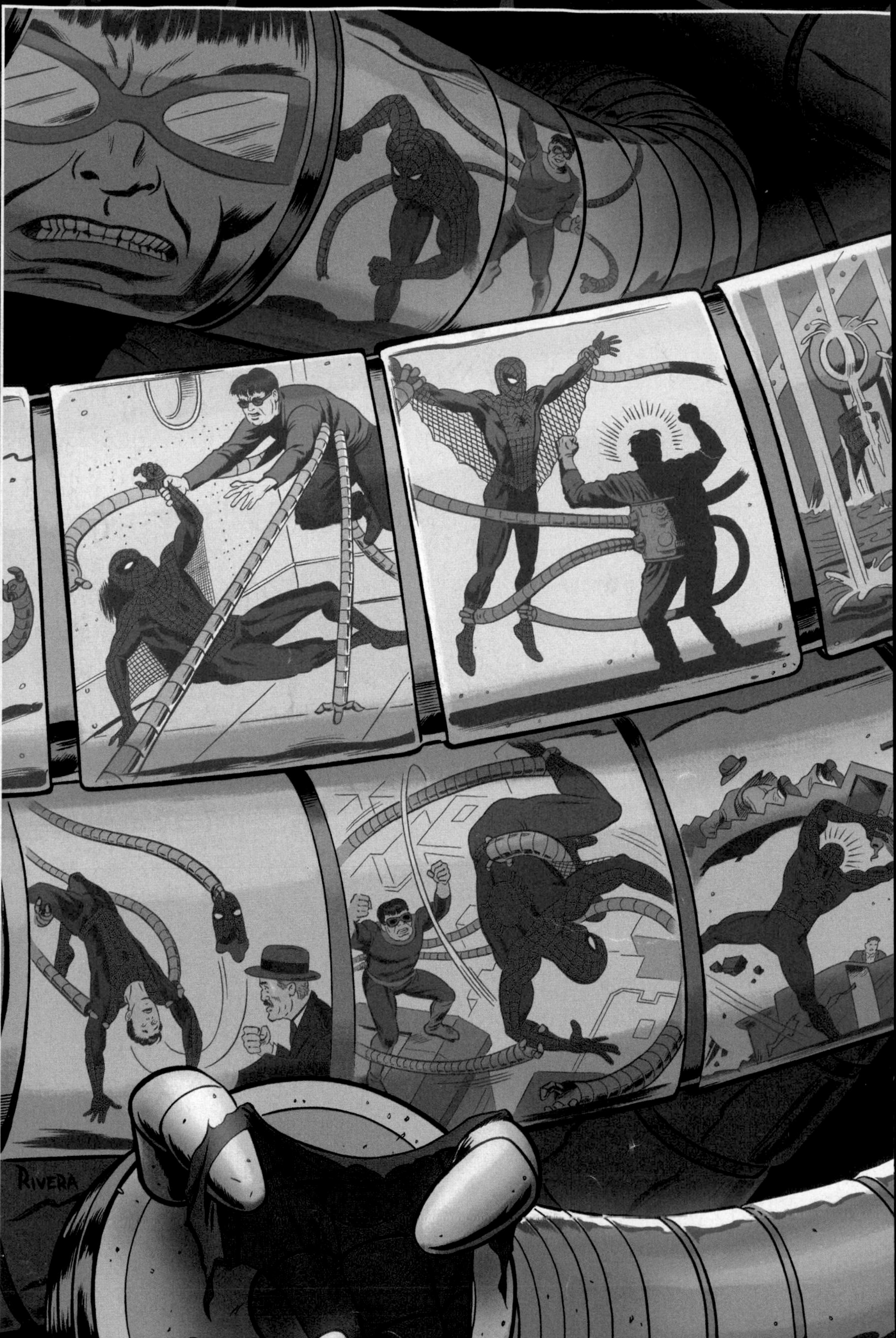
RIVERA

AVENGING SPIDER-MAN 15.1

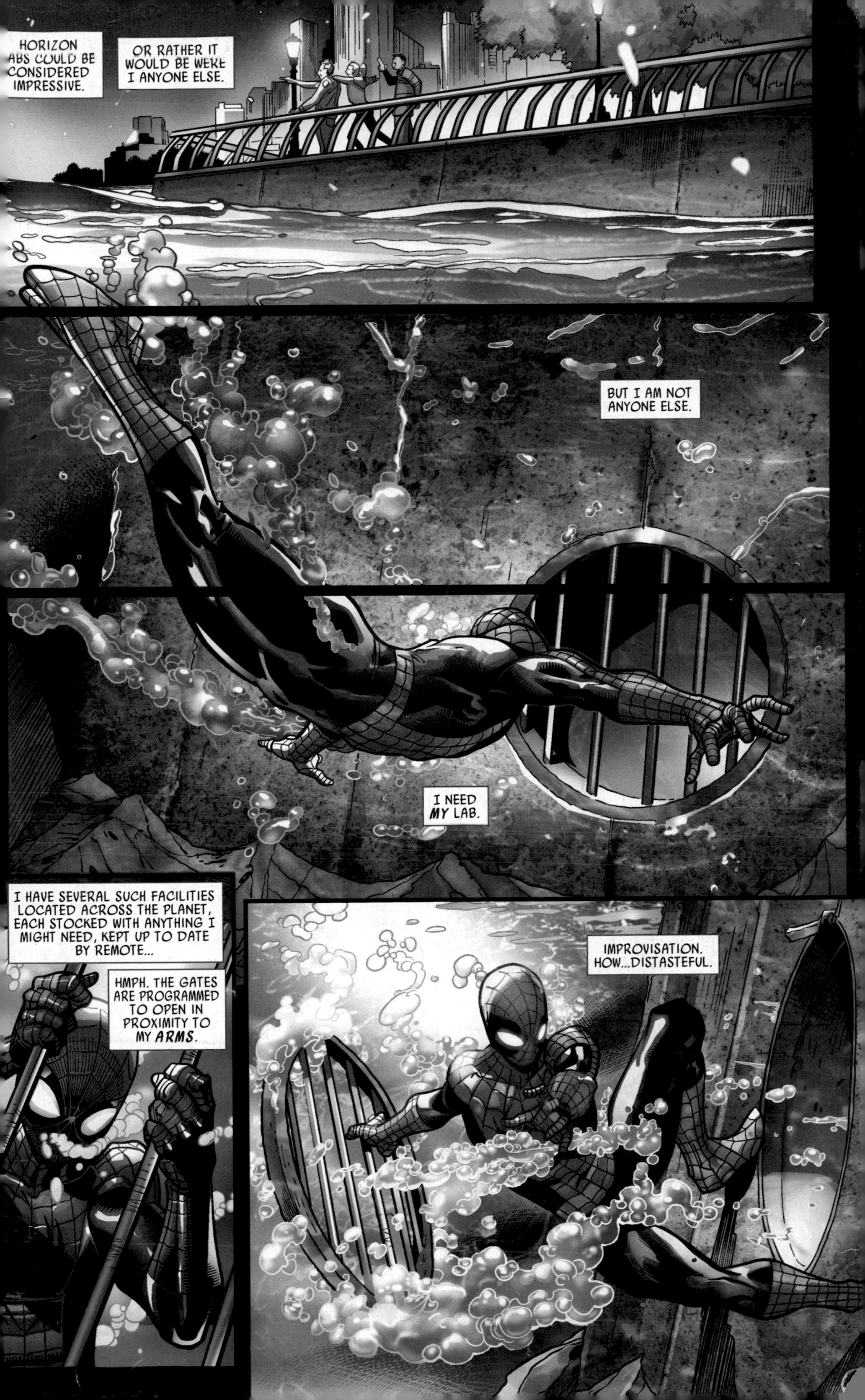

HORIZON ABS COULD BE CONSIDERED IMPRESSIVE.
OR RATHER IT WOULD BE WERE I ANYONE ELSE.
BUT I AM NOT ANYONE ELSE.
I NEED *MY* LAB.
I HAVE SEVERAL SUCH FACILITIES LOCATED ACROSS THE PLANET, EACH STOCKED WITH ANYTHING I MIGHT NEED, KEPT UP TO DATE BY REMOTE...
HMPH. THE GATES ARE PROGRAMMED TO OPEN IN PROXIMITY TO MY *ARMS*.
IMPROVISATION. HOW...DISTASTEFUL.

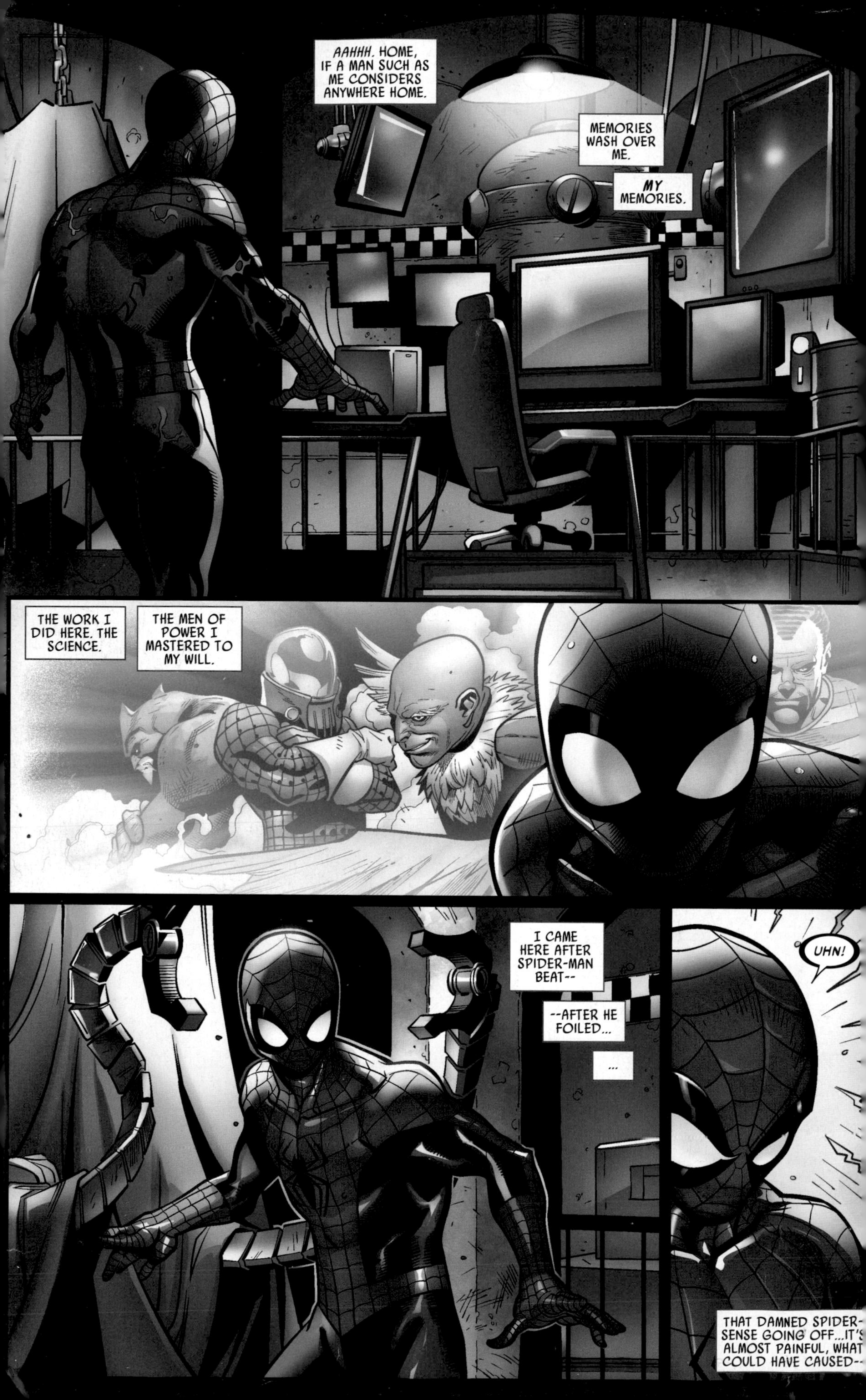
AAHHH. HOME, IF A MAN SUCH AS ME CONSIDERS ANYWHERE HOME.
MEMORIES WASH OVER ME.
MY MEMORIES.
THE WORK I DID HERE. THE SCIENCE.
THE MEN OF POWER I MASTERED TO MY WILL.
I CAME HERE AFTER SPIDER-MAN BEAT--
--AFTER HE FOILED...
...
UHN!
THAT DAMNED SPIDER-SENSE GOING OFF...IT'S ALMOST PAINFUL, WHAT COULD HAVE CAUSED--

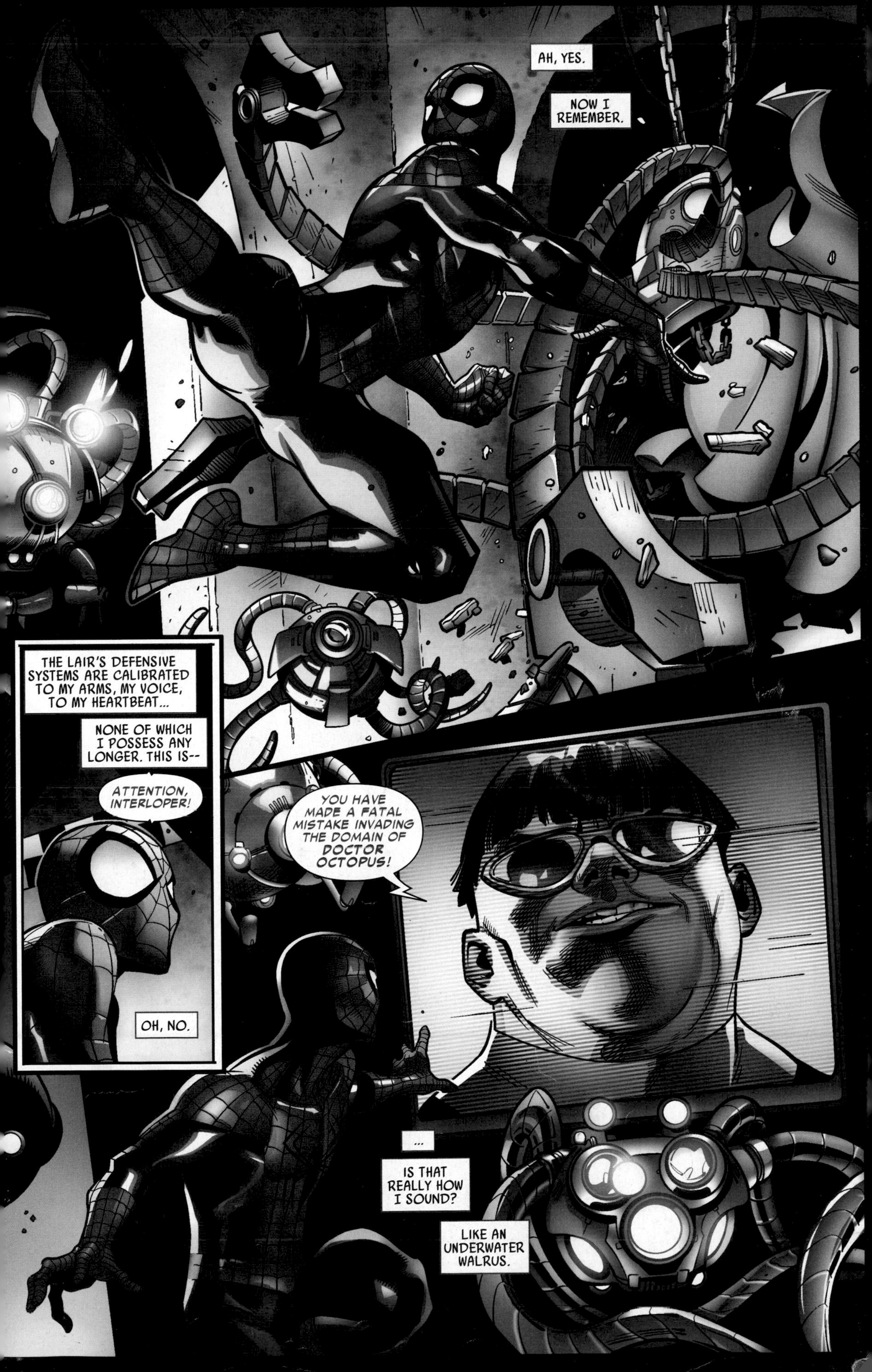
AH, YES.
NOW I REMEMBER.
THE LAIR'S DEFENSIVE SYSTEMS ARE CALIBRATED TO MY ARMS, MY VOICE, TO MY HEARTBEAT...
NONE OF WHICH I POSSESS ANY LONGER. THIS IS--
ATTENTION, INTERLOPER!
OH, NO.
YOU HAVE MADE A FATAL MISTAKE INVADING THE DOMAIN OF DOCTOR OCTOPUS!
...
IS THAT REALLY HOW I SOUND?
LIKE AN UNDERWATER WALRUS.

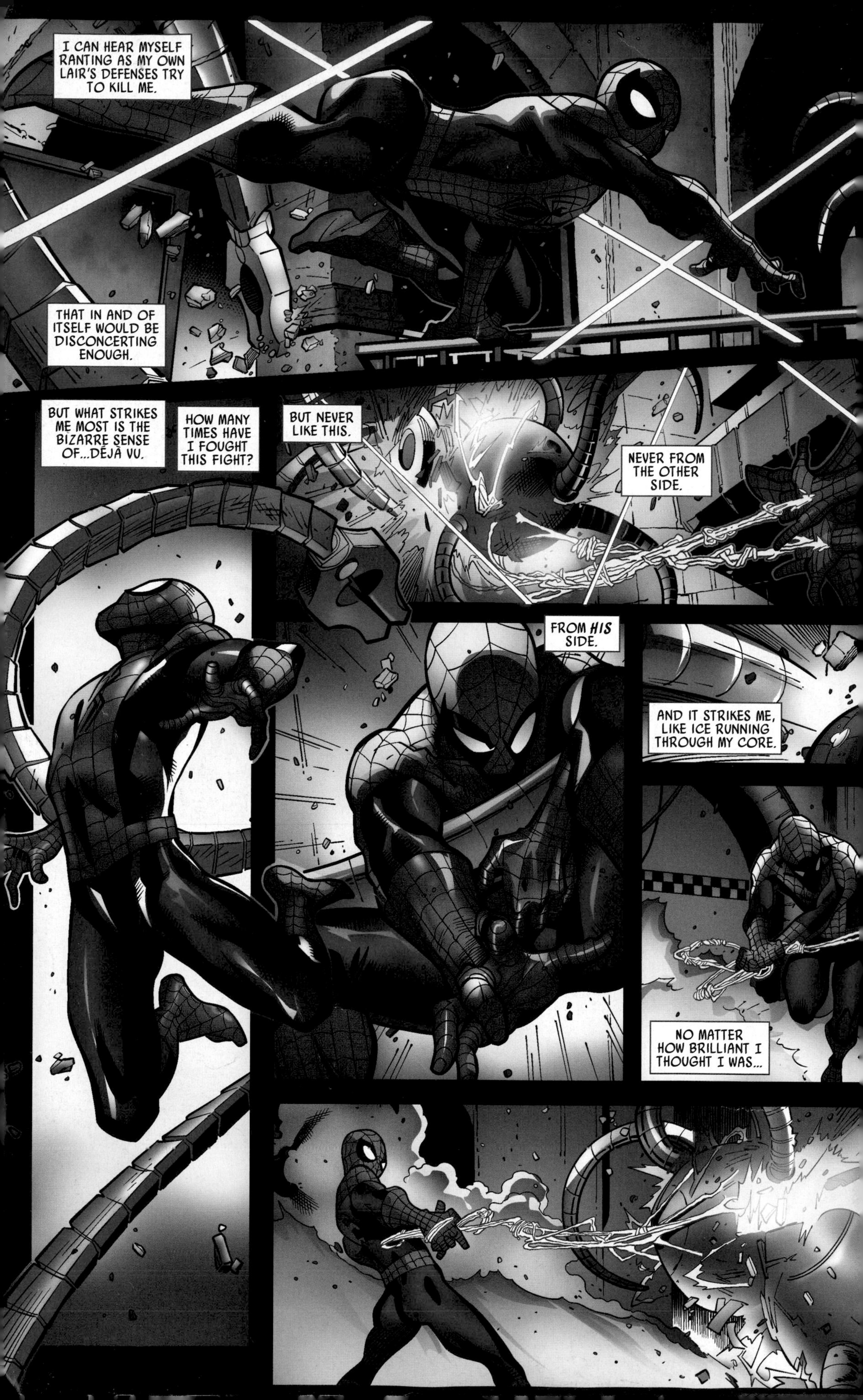
I CAN HEAR MYSELF RANTING AS MY OWN LAIR'S DEFENSES TRY TO KILL ME.
THAT IN AND OF ITSELF WOULD BE DISCONCERTING ENOUGH.
BUT WHAT STRIKES ME MOST IS THE BIZARRE SENSE OF...DÉJÀ VU.
HOW MANY TIMES HAVE I FOUGHT THIS FIGHT?
BUT NEVER LIKE THIS.
NEVER FROM THE OTHER SIDE.
FROM *HIS* SIDE.
AND IT STRIKES ME, LIKE ICE RUNNING THROUGH MY CORE.
NO MATTER HOW BRILLIANT I THOUGHT I WAS...

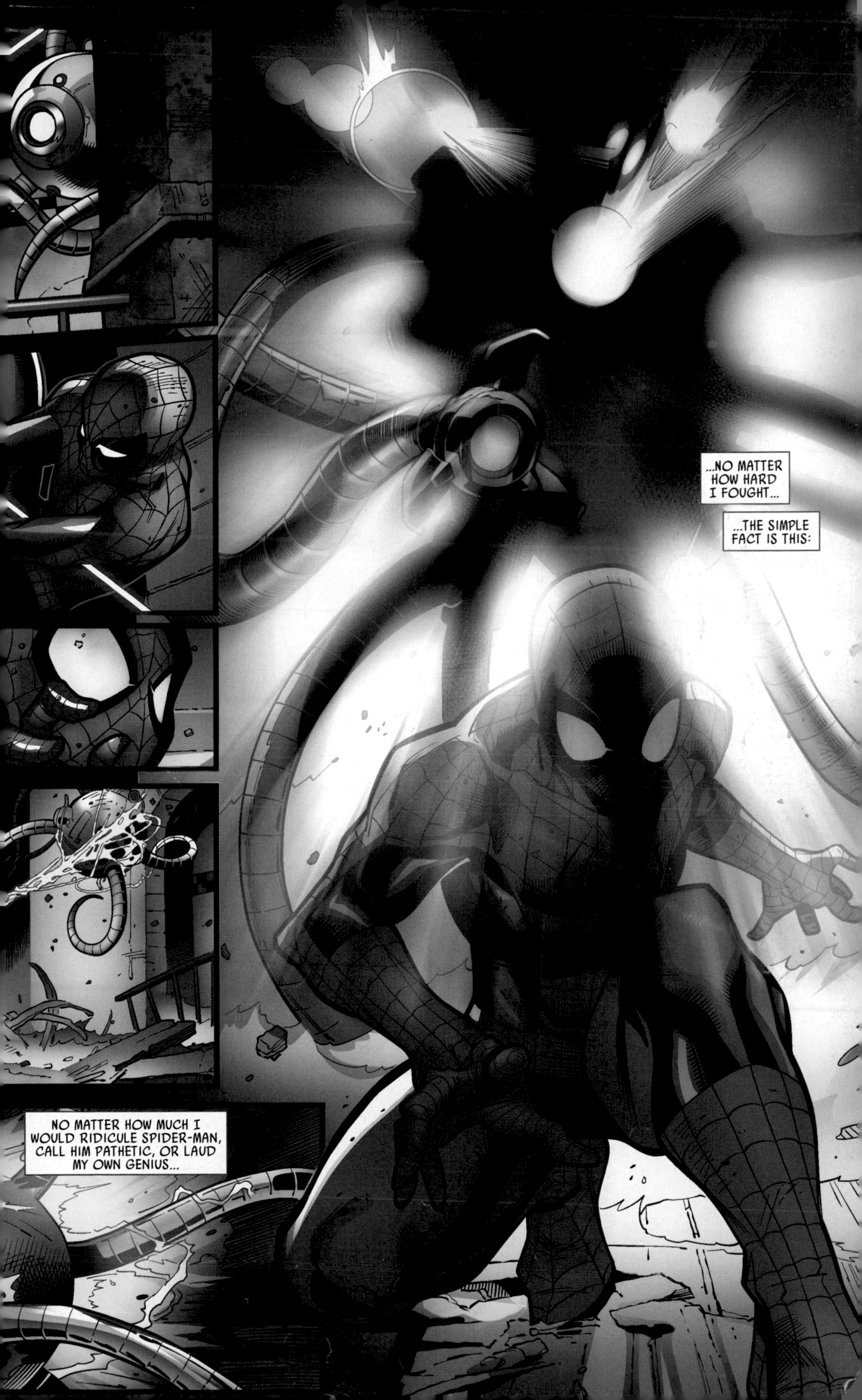
...NO MATTER HOW HARD I FOUGHT...
...THE SIMPLE FACT IS THIS:
NO MATTER HOW MUCH I WOULD RIDICULE SPIDER-MAN, CALL HIM PATHETIC, OR LAUD MY OWN GENIUS...

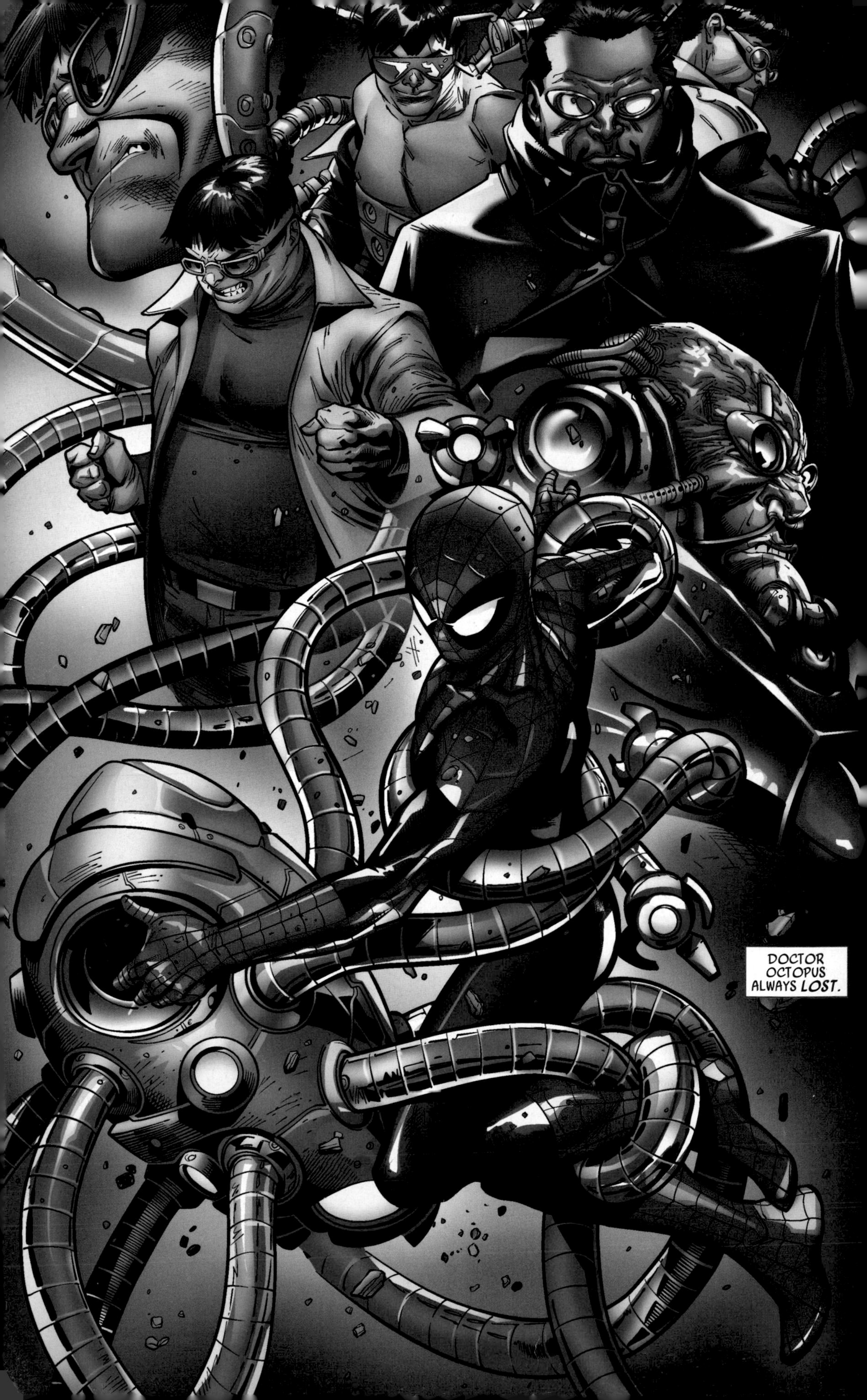
DOCTOR OCTOPUS ALWAYS LOST.

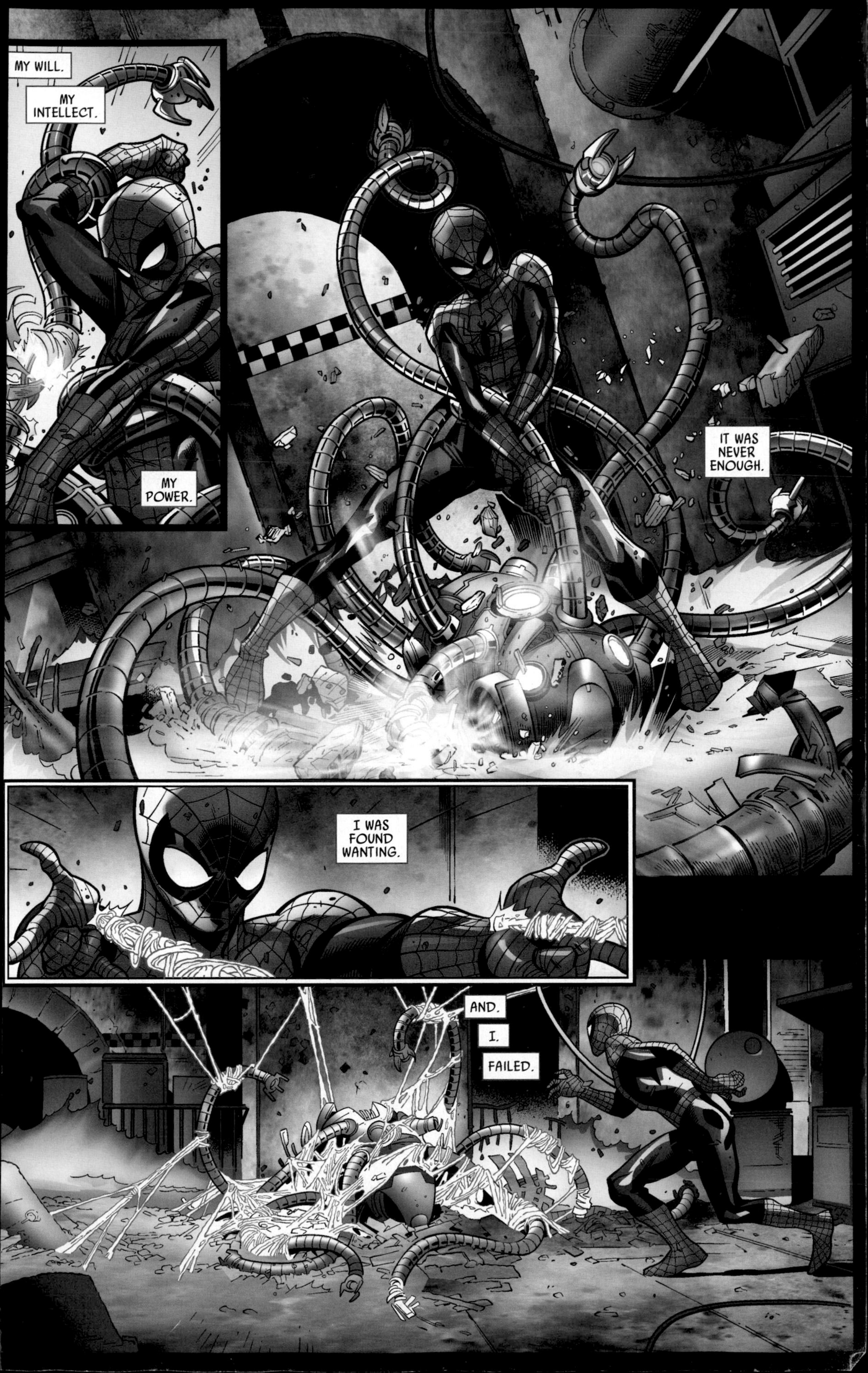
MY WILL.
MY INTELLECT.
MY POWER.
IT WAS NEVER ENOUGH.
I WAS FOUND WANTING.
AND.
I.
FAILED.

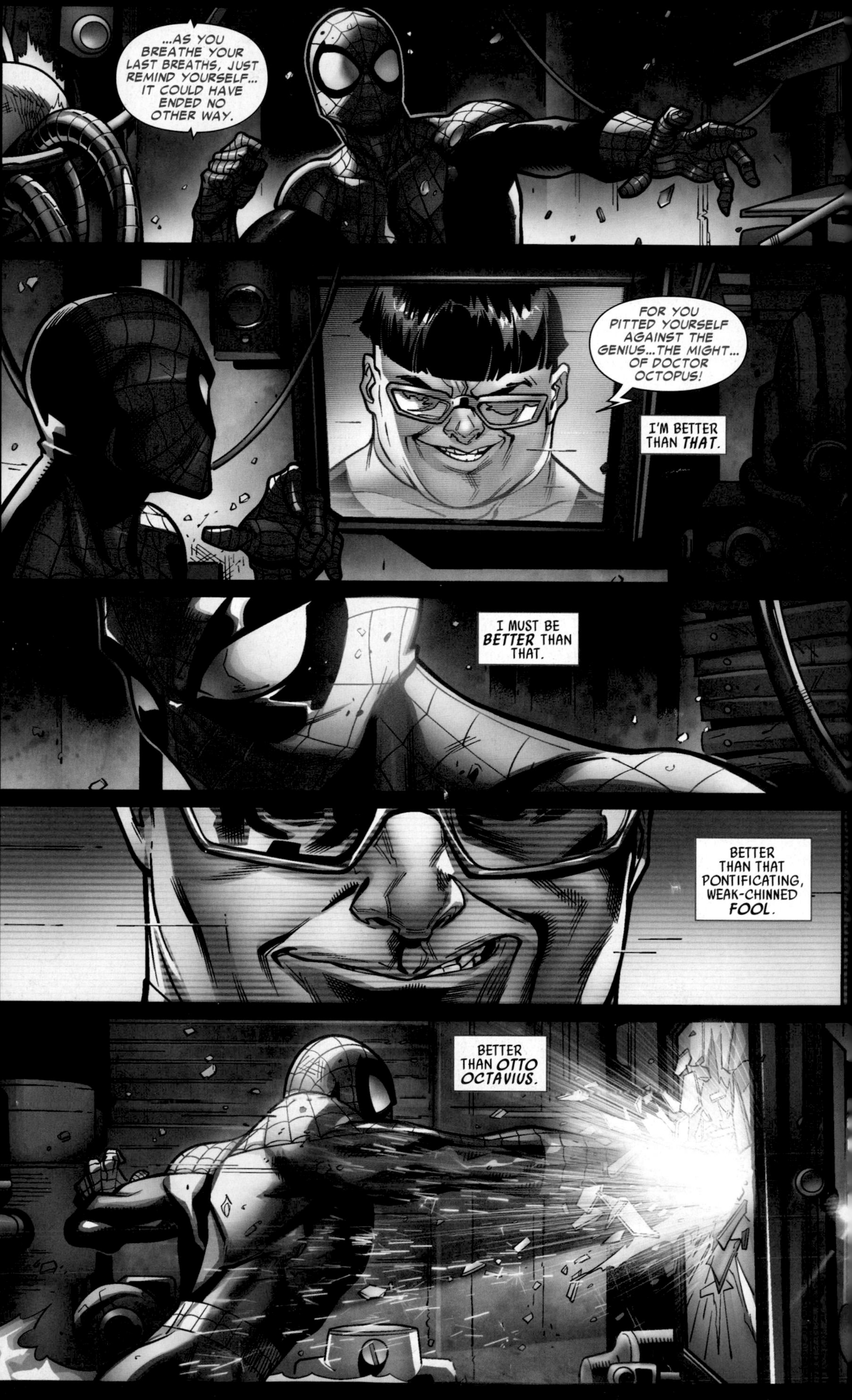
...AS YOU BREATHE YOUR LAST BREATHS, JUST REMIND YOURSELF... IT COULD HAVE ENDED NO OTHER WAY.
FOR YOU PITTED YOURSELF AGAINST THE GENIUS...THE MIGHT... OF DOCTOR OCTOPUS!
I'M BETTER THAN *THAT*.
I MUST BE *BETTER* THAN THAT.
BETTER THAN THAT PONTIFICATING, WEAK-CHINNED *FOOL*.
BETTER THAN *OTTO OCTAVIUS*.

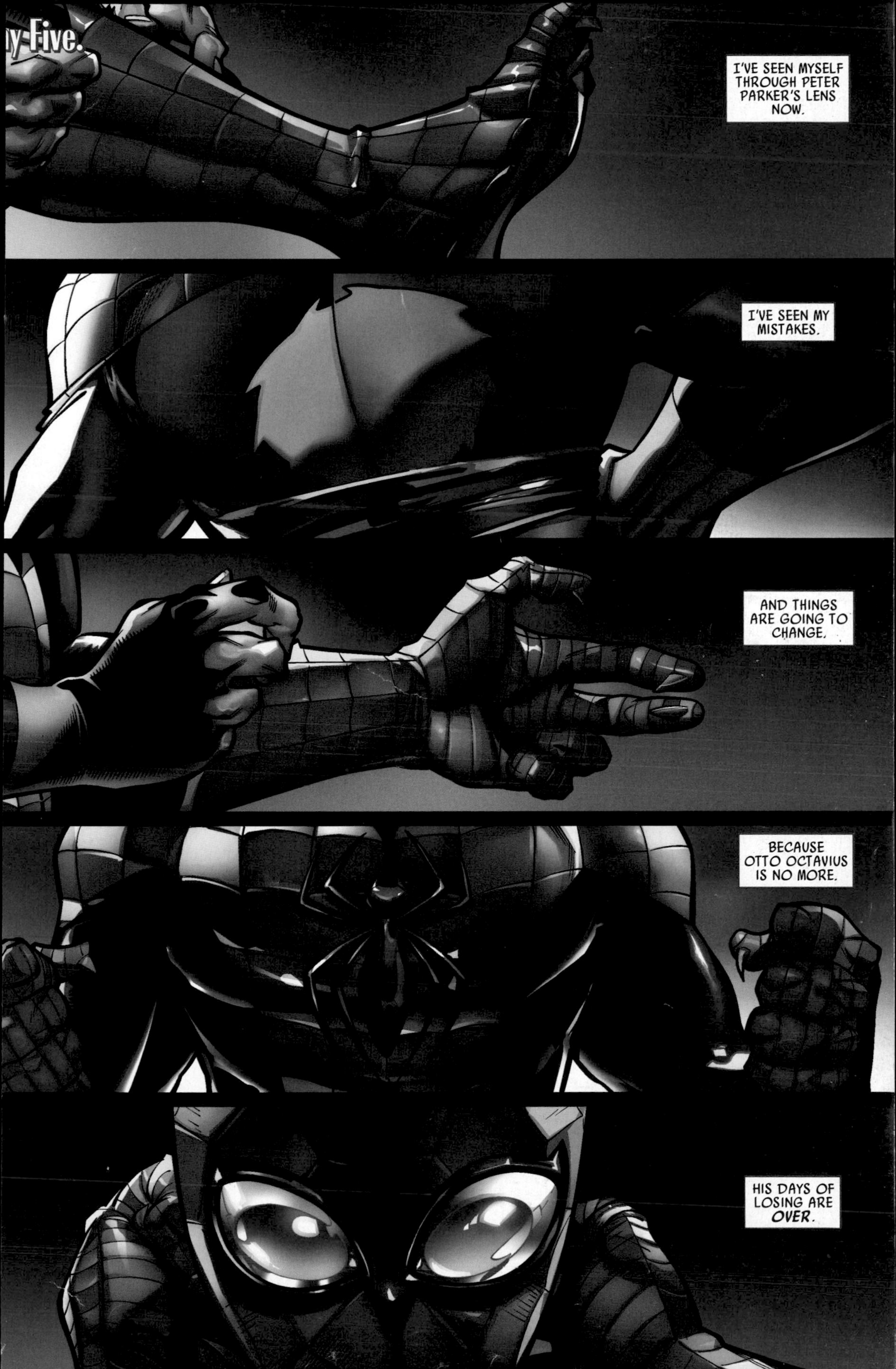
I'VE SEEN MYSELF THROUGH PETER PARKER'S LENS NOW.
I'VE SEEN MY MISTAKES.
AND THINGS ARE GOING TO CHANGE.
BECAUSE OTTO OCTAVIUS IS NO MORE.
HIS DAYS OF LOSING ARE *OVER*.

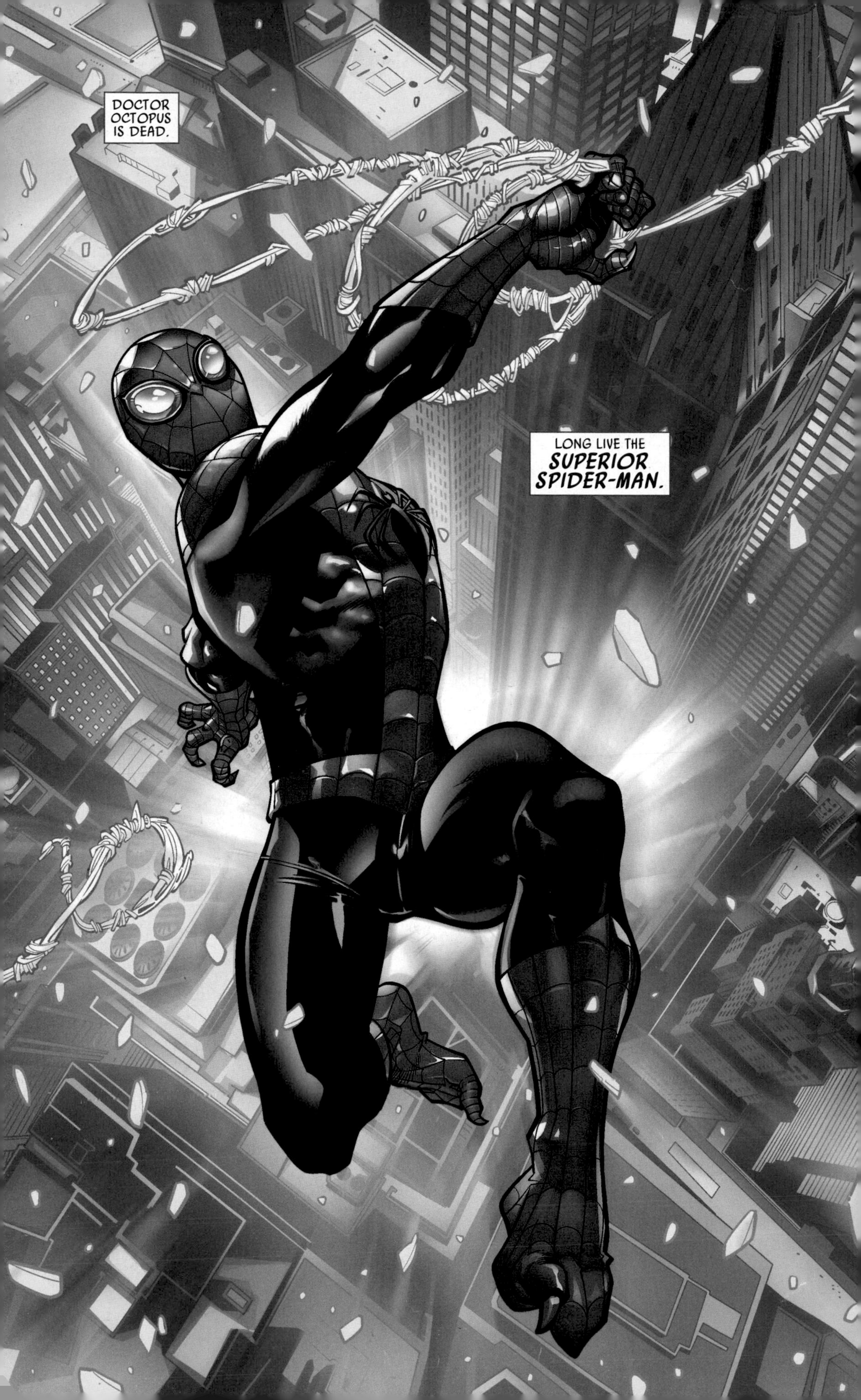
DOCTOR OCTOPUS IS DEAD.
LONG LIVE THE SUPERIOR SPIDER-MAN.

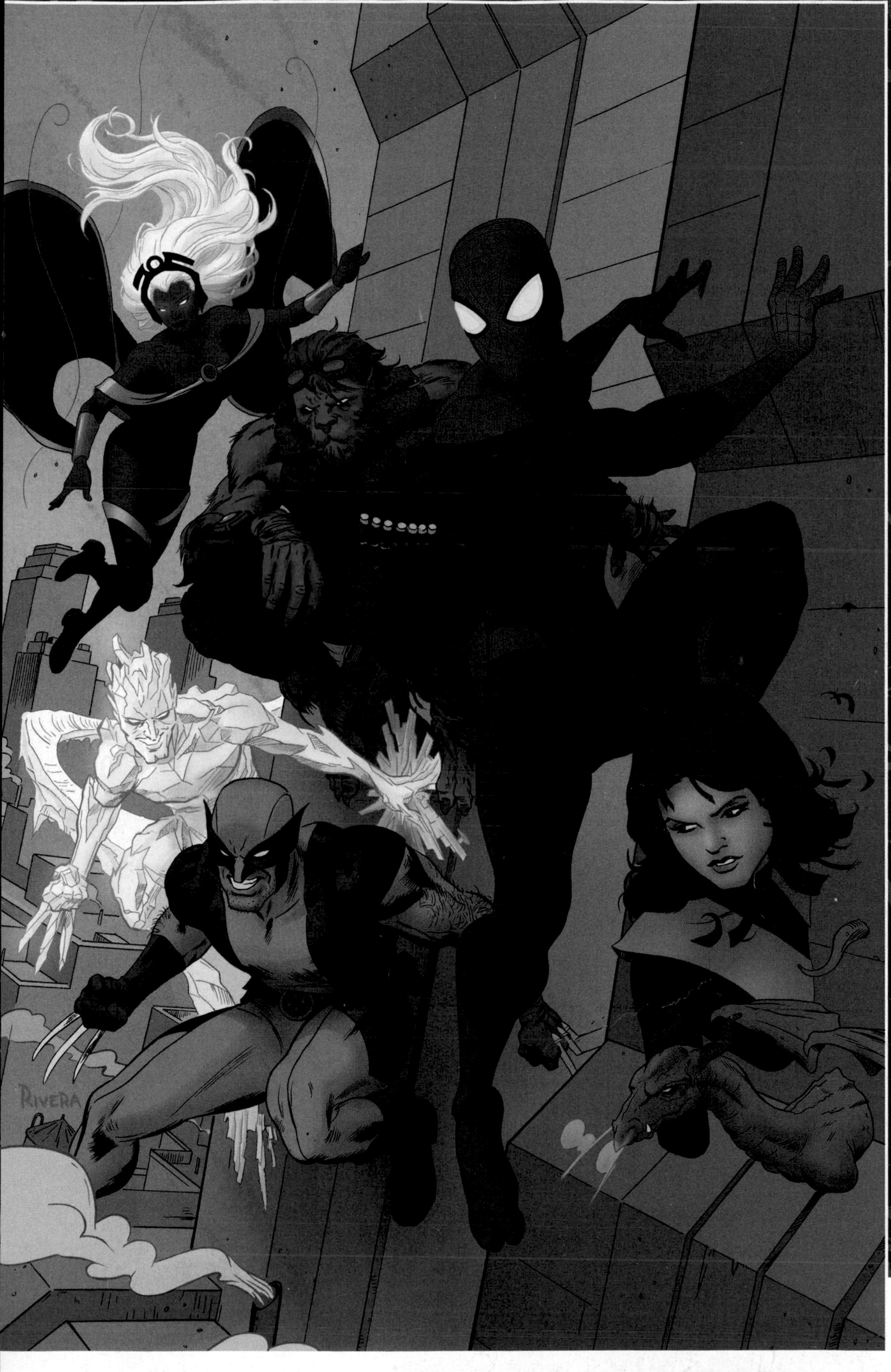
RIVERA

AVENGING SPIDER-MAN 16

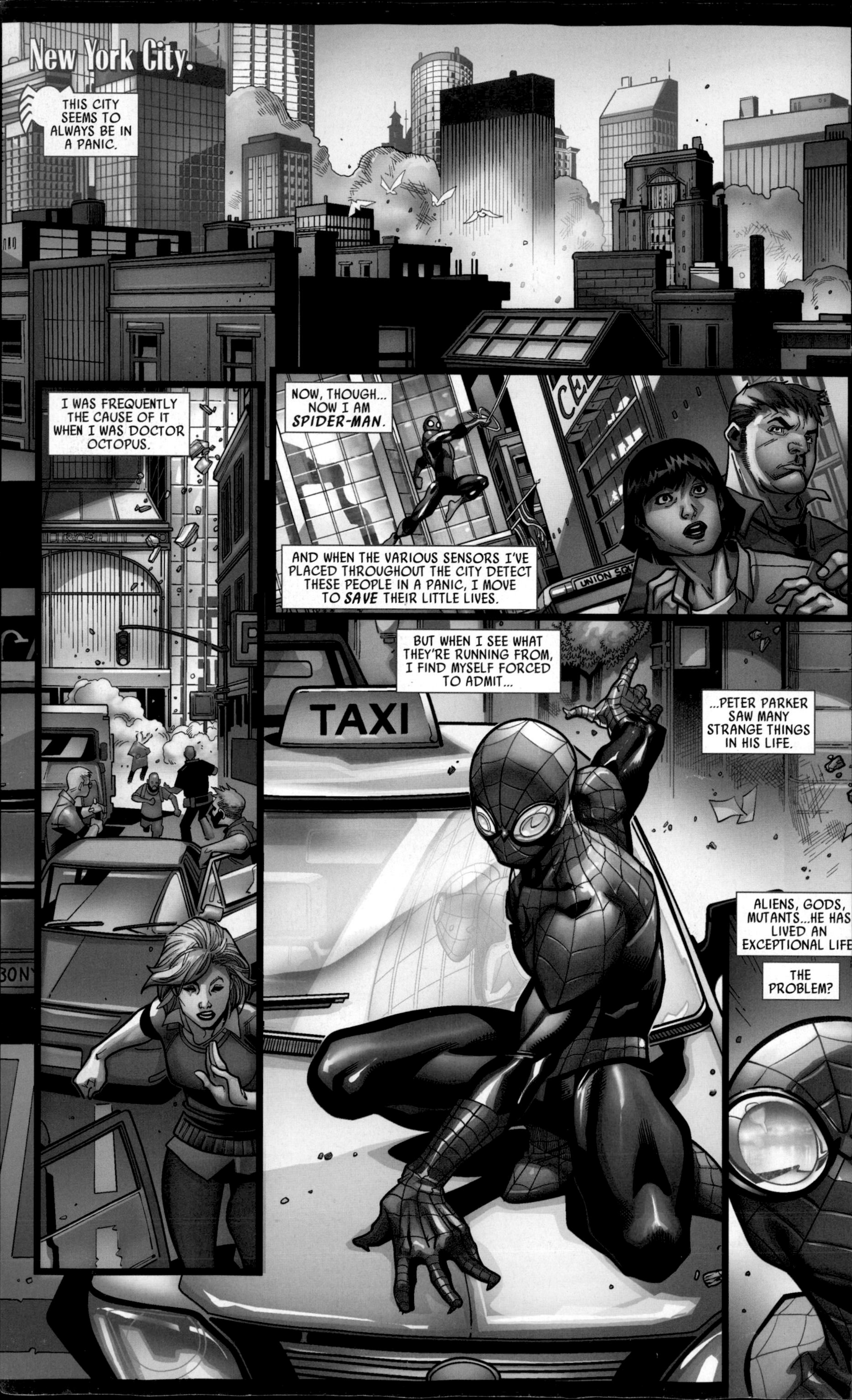

New York City.
THIS CITY SEEMS TO ALWAYS BE IN A PANIC.
I WAS FREQUENTLY THE CAUSE OF IT WHEN I WAS DOCTOR OCTOPUS.
NOW, THOUGH... NOW I AM SPIDER-MAN.
AND WHEN THE VARIOUS SENSORS I'VE PLACED THROUGHOUT THE CITY DETECT THESE PEOPLE IN A PANIC, I MOVE TO SAVE THEIR LITTLE LIVES.
BUT WHEN I SEE WHAT THEY'RE RUNNING FROM, I FIND MYSELF FORCED TO ADMIT...
TAXI
...PETER PARKER SAW MANY STRANGE THINGS IN HIS LIFE.
ALIENS, GODS, MUTANTS...HE HAS LIVED AN EXCEPTIONAL LIFE
THE PROBLEM?

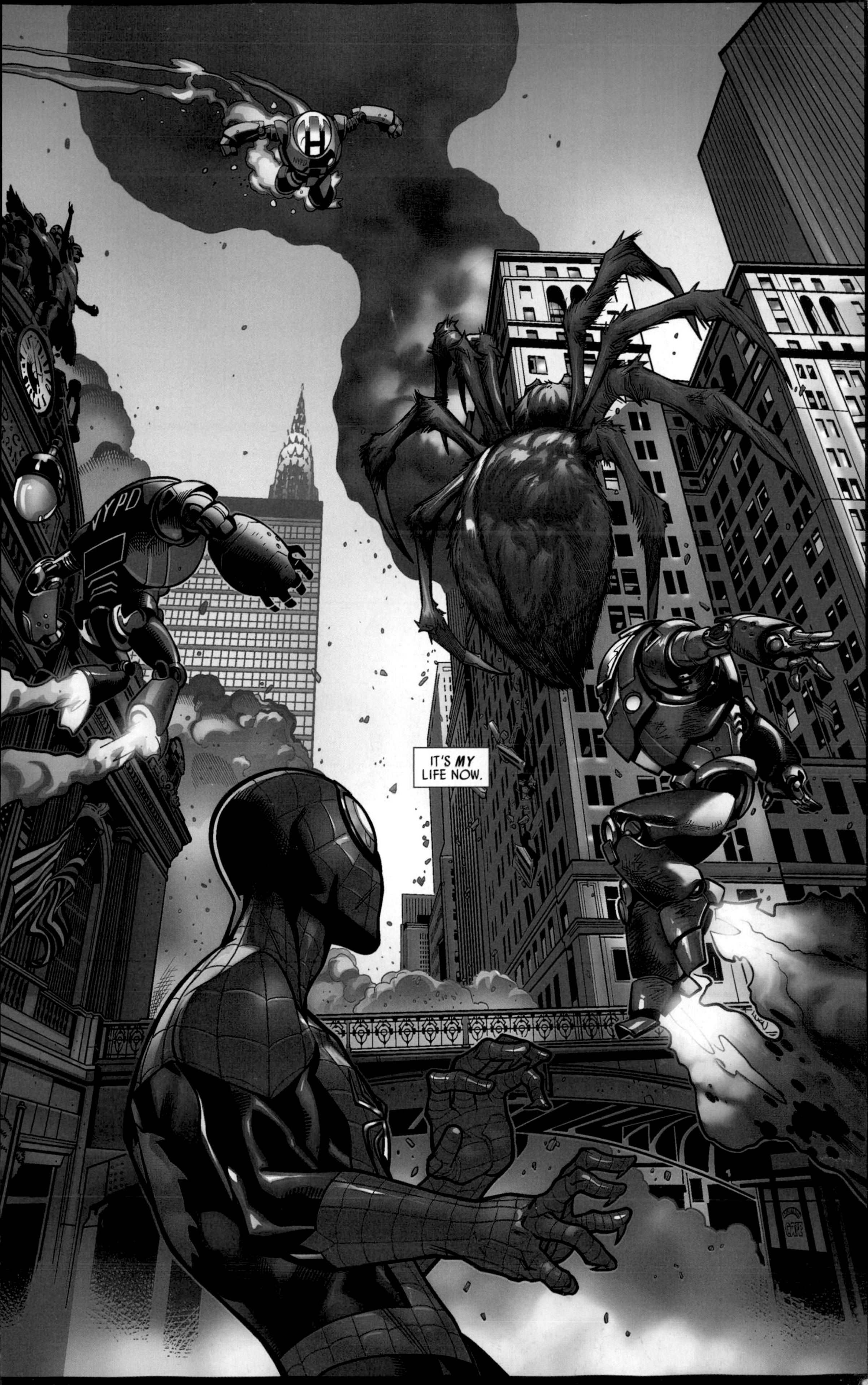
IT'S *MY* LIFE NOW.

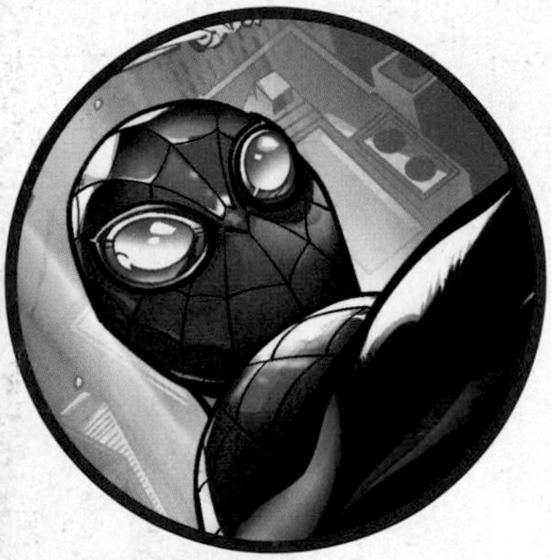

OTTO OCTAVIUS, the villain known as DOCTOR OCTOPUS, was dying. In order to cheat death, he used his skills as a mad scientist to swap minds with his greatest enemy, PETER PAR the spectacular SPIDER-MAN.

However, the transfer gave Octavius MORE than just SPIDER-MAN'S great powers, it gave hi PARKER'S experiences as well... including the lesson of great responsibility! Now Otto Octaviu beginning a NEW life as a hero—possibly the greatest hero of all. He is the--

# THE SUPERIOR SPIDER-MAN

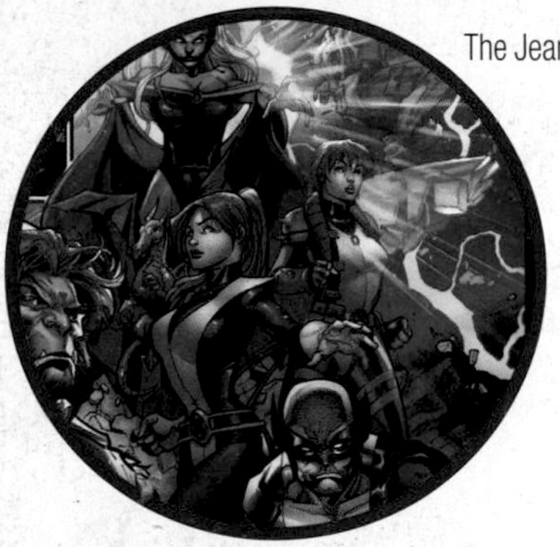

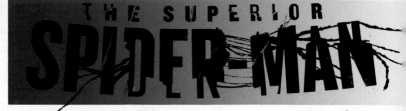

The Jean Grey School for Higher Learning was founded to teach mutants born with superpowers how to survi in a world that fears and hates them. Those heroic teachers are

# WOLVERINE and the X-MEN

# AVENGING SPIDER-MAN

**_PREVIOUSLY..._**

Peter Parker died and no one knows Doc Ock is now Spider-Man in Peter Parker's body. He's trying to be a hero. Mutants were almost extinct. Now they aren't.

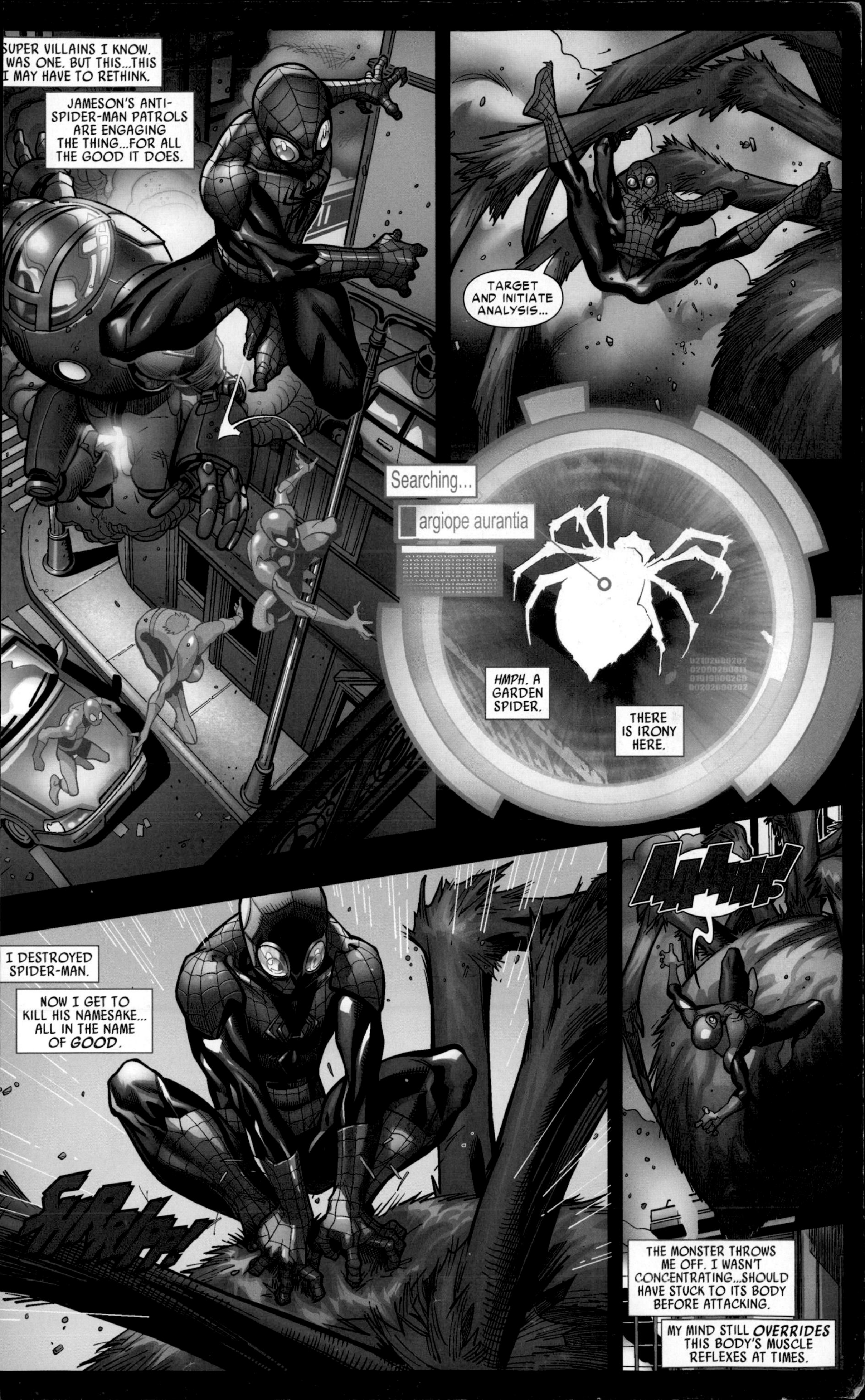
SUPER VILLAINS I KNOW. I WAS ONE. BUT THIS...THIS I MAY HAVE TO RETHINK.
JAMESON'S ANTI-SPIDER-MAN PATROLS ARE ENGAGING THE THING...FOR ALL THE GOOD IT DOES.
TARGET AND INITIATE ANALYSIS...
Searching...
argiope aurantia
HMPH. A GARDEN SPIDER.
THERE IS IRONY HERE.
I DESTROYED SPIDER-MAN.
NOW I GET TO KILL HIS NAMESAKE... ALL IN THE NAME OF GOOD.
THE MONSTER THROWS ME OFF. I WASN'T CONCENTRATING...SHOULD HAVE STUCK TO ITS BODY BEFORE ATTACKING.
MY MIND STILL OVERRIDES THIS BODY'S MUSCLE REFLEXES AT TIMES.

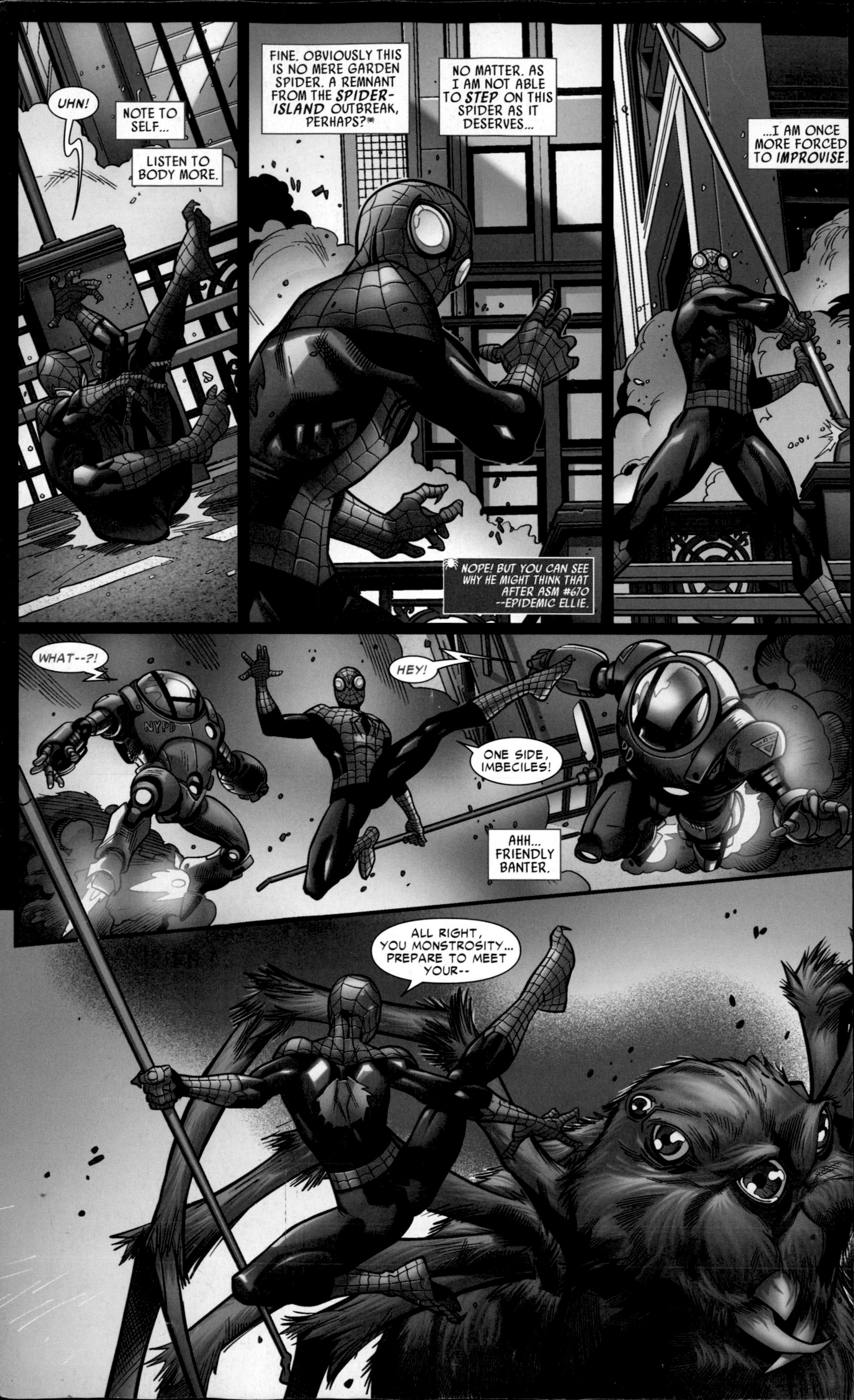
UHN!
NOTE TO SELF...
LISTEN TO BODY MORE.
FINE. OBVIOUSLY THIS IS NO MERE GARDEN SPIDER. A REMNANT FROM THE SPIDER-ISLAND OUTBREAK, PERHAPS?*
NO MATTER. AS I AM NOT ABLE TO STEP ON THIS SPIDER AS IT DESERVES...
...I AM ONCE MORE FORCED TO IMPROVISE.
*NOPE! BUT YOU CAN SEE WHY HE MIGHT THINK THAT AFTER ASM #670 --EPIDEMIC ELLIE.
WHAT--?!
HEY!
ONE SIDE, IMBECILES!
AHH... FRIENDLY BANTER.
ALL RIGHT, YOU MONSTROSITY... PREPARE TO MEET YOUR--

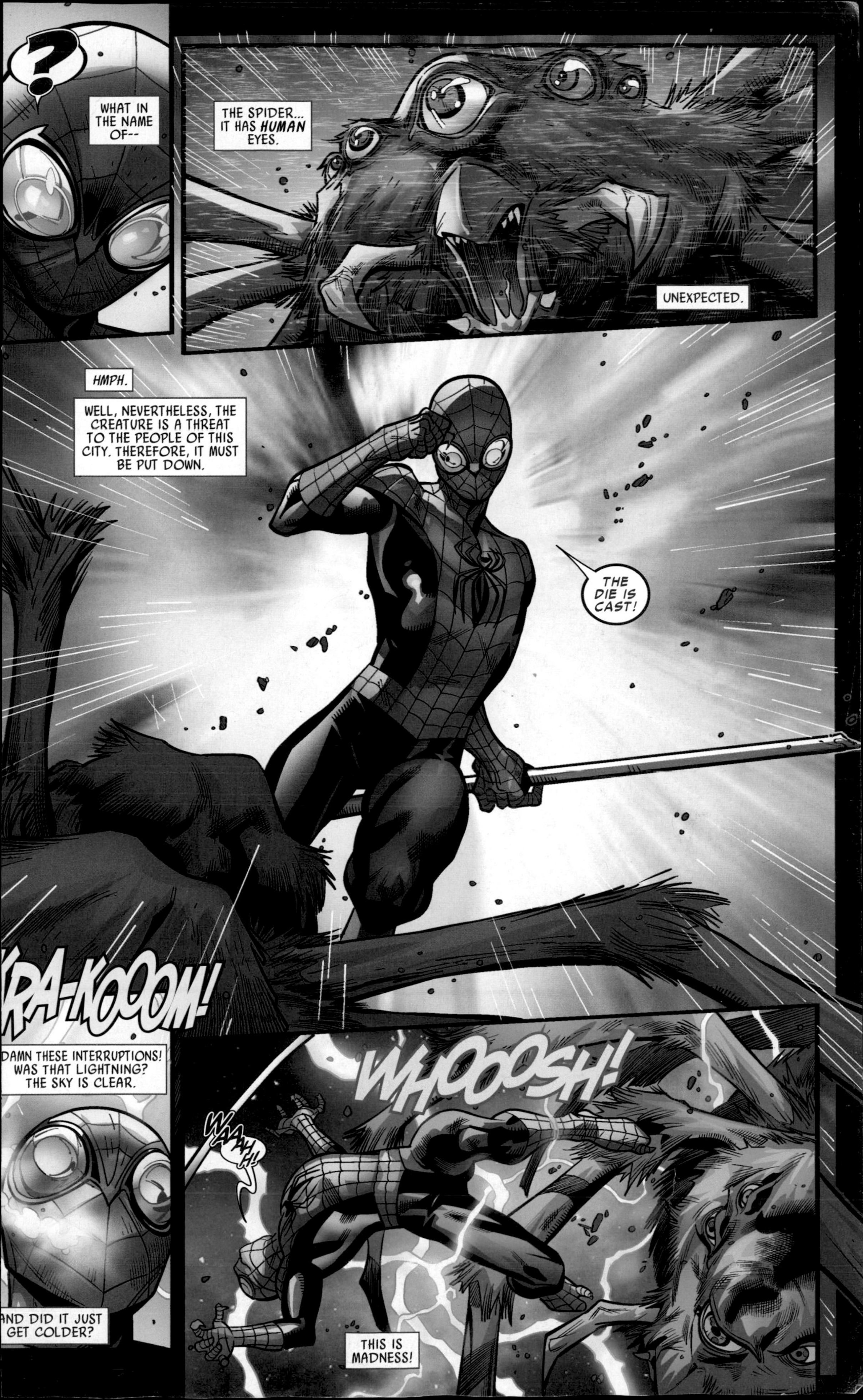
?
WHAT IN THE NAME OF--
THE SPIDER... IT HAS HUMAN EYES.
UNEXPECTED.
HMPH.
WELL, NEVERTHELESS, THE CREATURE IS A THREAT TO THE PEOPLE OF THIS CITY. THEREFORE, IT MUST BE PUT DOWN.
THE DIE IS CAST!
RA-KOOOM!
DAMN THESE INTERRUPTIONS! WAS THAT LIGHTNING? THE SKY IS CLEAR.
AND DID IT JUST GET COLDER?
WHOOOSH!
WAAAH!
THIS IS MADNESS!

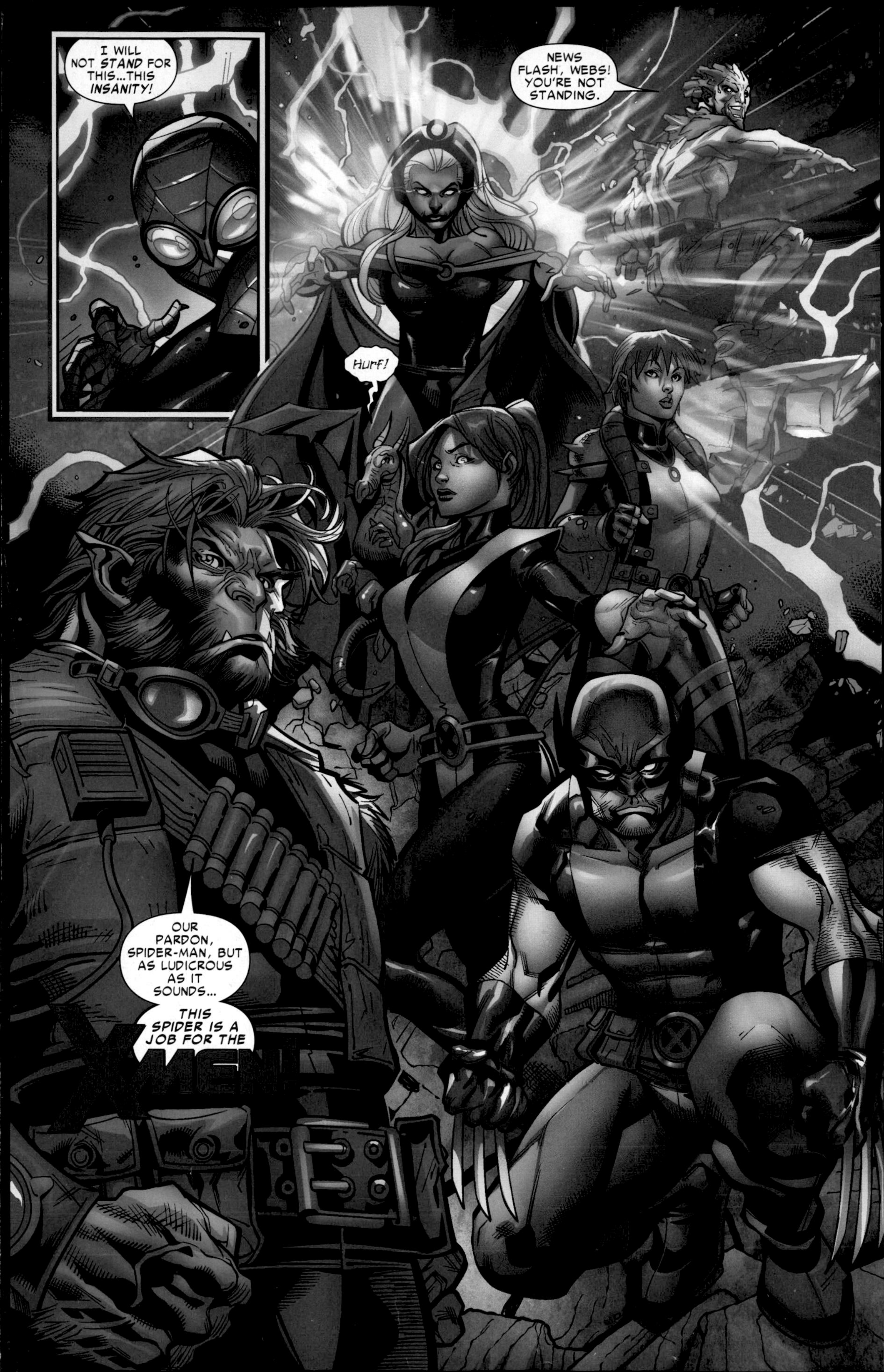
I WILL NOT STAND FOR THIS...THIS INSANITY!
NEWS FLASH, WEBS! YOU'RE NOT STANDING.
Hurf!
OUR PARDON, SPIDER-MAN, BUT AS LUDICROUS AS IT SOUNDS...
THIS SPIDER IS A JOB FOR THE
X-MEN!

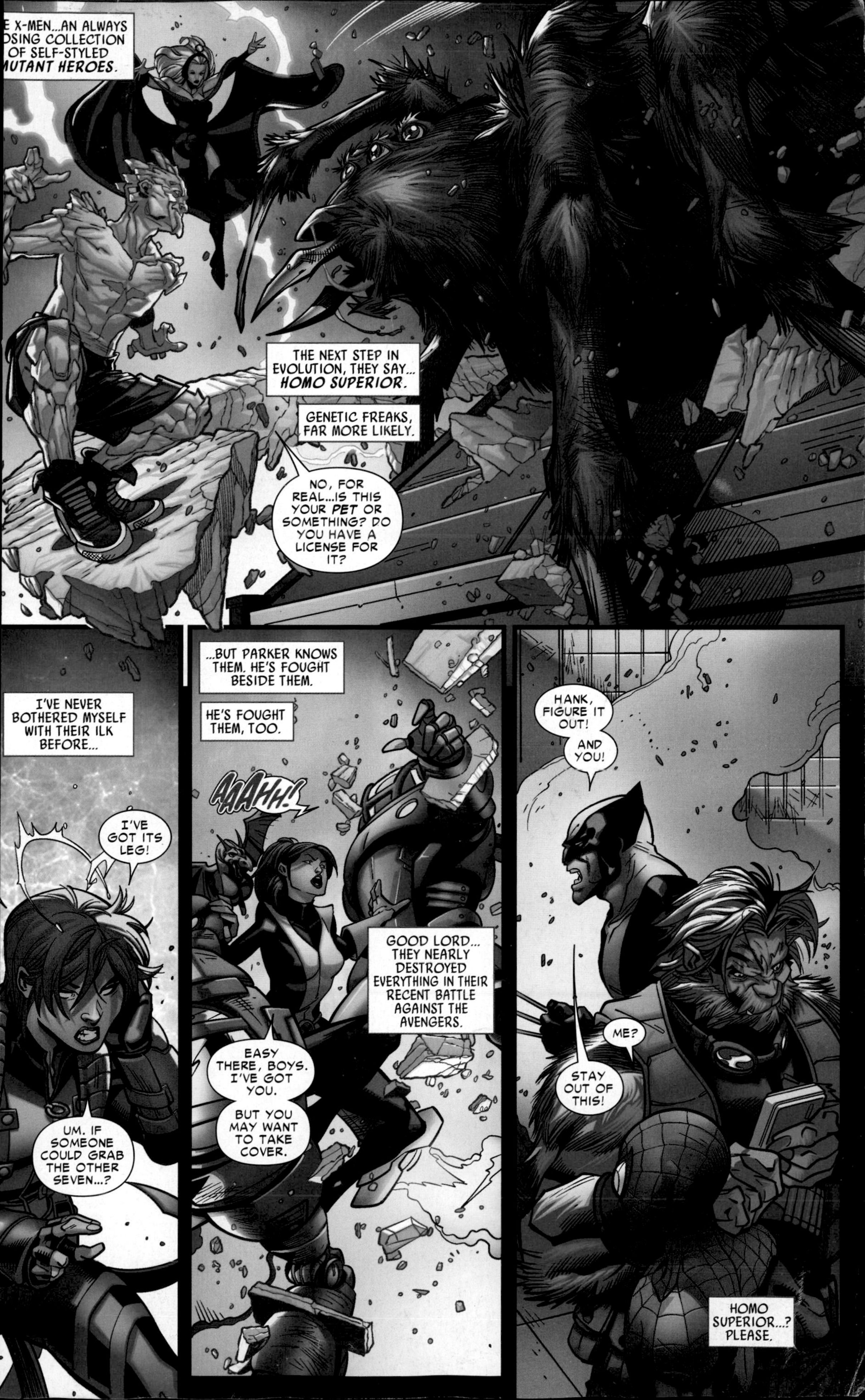
E X-MEN...AN ALWAYS
OSING COLLECTION
OF SELF-STYLED
MUTANT HEROES.
THE NEXT STEP IN EVOLUTION, THEY SAY... HOMO SUPERIOR.
GENETIC FREAKS, FAR MORE LIKELY.
NO, FOR REAL...IS THIS YOUR PET OR SOMETHING? DO YOU HAVE A LICENSE FOR IT?
I'VE NEVER BOTHERED MYSELF WITH THEIR ILK BEFORE...
I'VE GOT ITS LEG!
UM. IF SOMEONE COULD GRAB THE OTHER SEVEN...?
...BUT PARKER KNOWS THEM. HE'S FOUGHT BESIDE THEM.
HE'S FOUGHT THEM, TOO.
AAAHH!
GOOD LORD... THEY NEARLY DESTROYED EVERYTHING IN THEIR RECENT BATTLE AGAINST THE AVENGERS.
EASY THERE, BOYS. I'VE GOT YOU.
BUT YOU MAY WANT TO TAKE COVER.
HANK, FIGURE IT OUT!
AND YOU!
ME?
STAY OUT OF THIS!
HOMO SUPERIOR...? PLEASE.

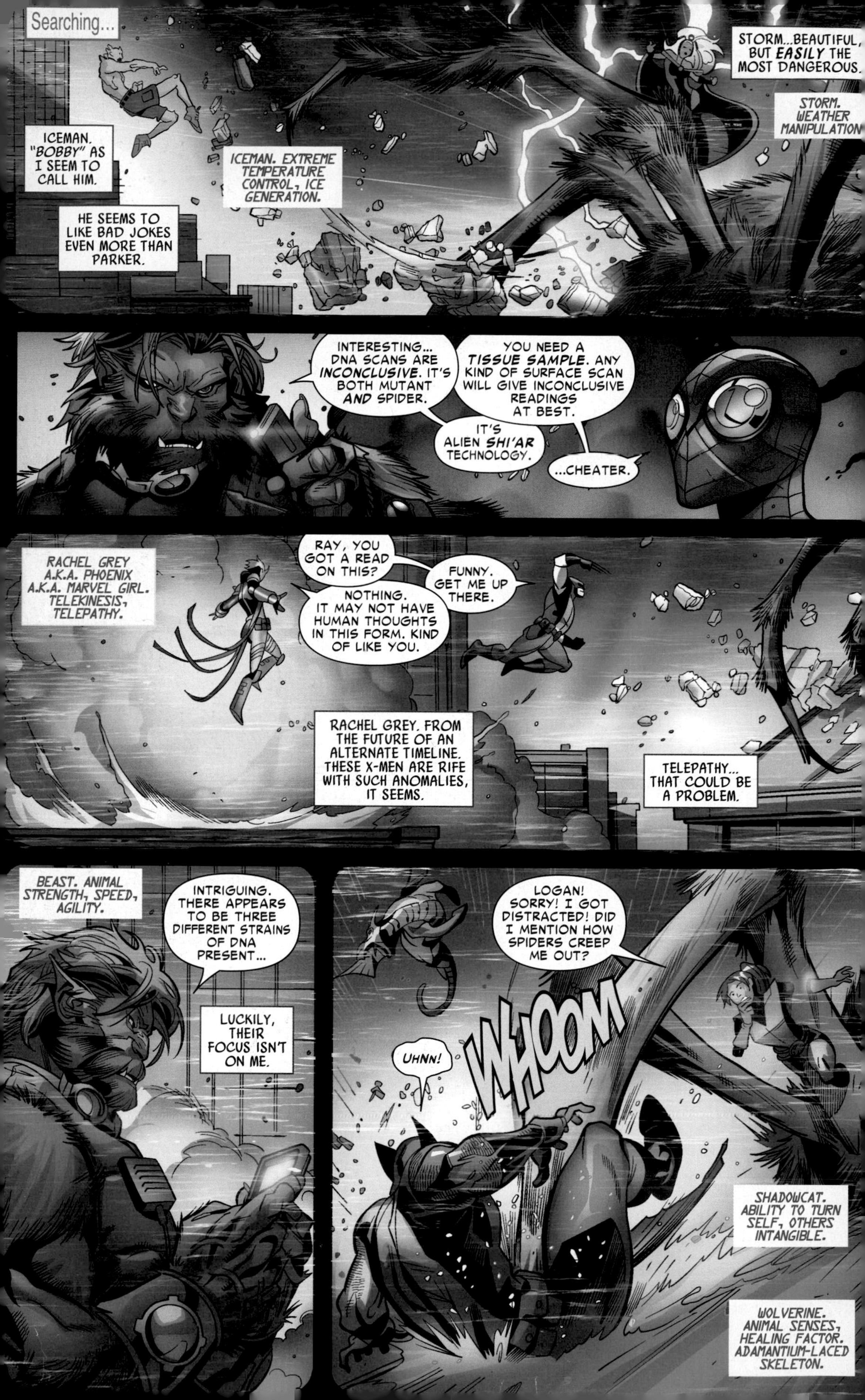
Searching...
STORM...BEAUTIFUL, BUT EASILY THE MOST DANGEROUS.
STORM. WEATHER MANIPULATION
ICEMAN. "BOBBY" AS I SEEM TO CALL HIM.
ICEMAN. EXTREME TEMPERATURE CONTROL, ICE GENERATION.
HE SEEMS TO LIKE BAD JOKES EVEN MORE THAN PARKER.
INTERESTING... DNA SCANS ARE INCONCLUSIVE. IT'S BOTH MUTANT AND SPIDER.
YOU NEED A TISSUE SAMPLE. ANY KIND OF SURFACE SCAN WILL GIVE INCONCLUSIVE READINGS AT BEST.
IT'S ALIEN SHI'AR TECHNOLOGY.
...CHEATER.
RACHEL GREY A.K.A. PHOENIX A.K.A. MARVEL GIRL. TELEKINESIS, TELEPATHY.
RAY, YOU GOT A READ ON THIS?
NOTHING. IT MAY NOT HAVE HUMAN THOUGHTS IN THIS FORM. KIND OF LIKE YOU.
FUNNY. GET ME UP THERE.
RACHEL GREY. FROM THE FUTURE OF AN ALTERNATE TIMELINE. THESE X-MEN ARE RIFE WITH SUCH ANOMALIES, IT SEEMS.
TELEPATHY... THAT COULD BE A PROBLEM.
BEAST. ANIMAL STRENGTH, SPEED, AGILITY.
INTRIGUING. THERE APPEARS TO BE THREE DIFFERENT STRAINS OF DNA PRESENT...
LUCKILY, THEIR FOCUS ISN'T ON ME.
LOGAN! SORRY! I GOT DISTRACTED! DID I MENTION HOW SPIDERS CREEP ME OUT?
UHNN!
WHOOM
SHADOWCAT. ABILITY TO TURN SELF, OTHERS INTANGIBLE.
WOLVERINE. ANIMAL SENSES, HEALING FACTOR. ADAMANTIUM-LACED SKELETON.

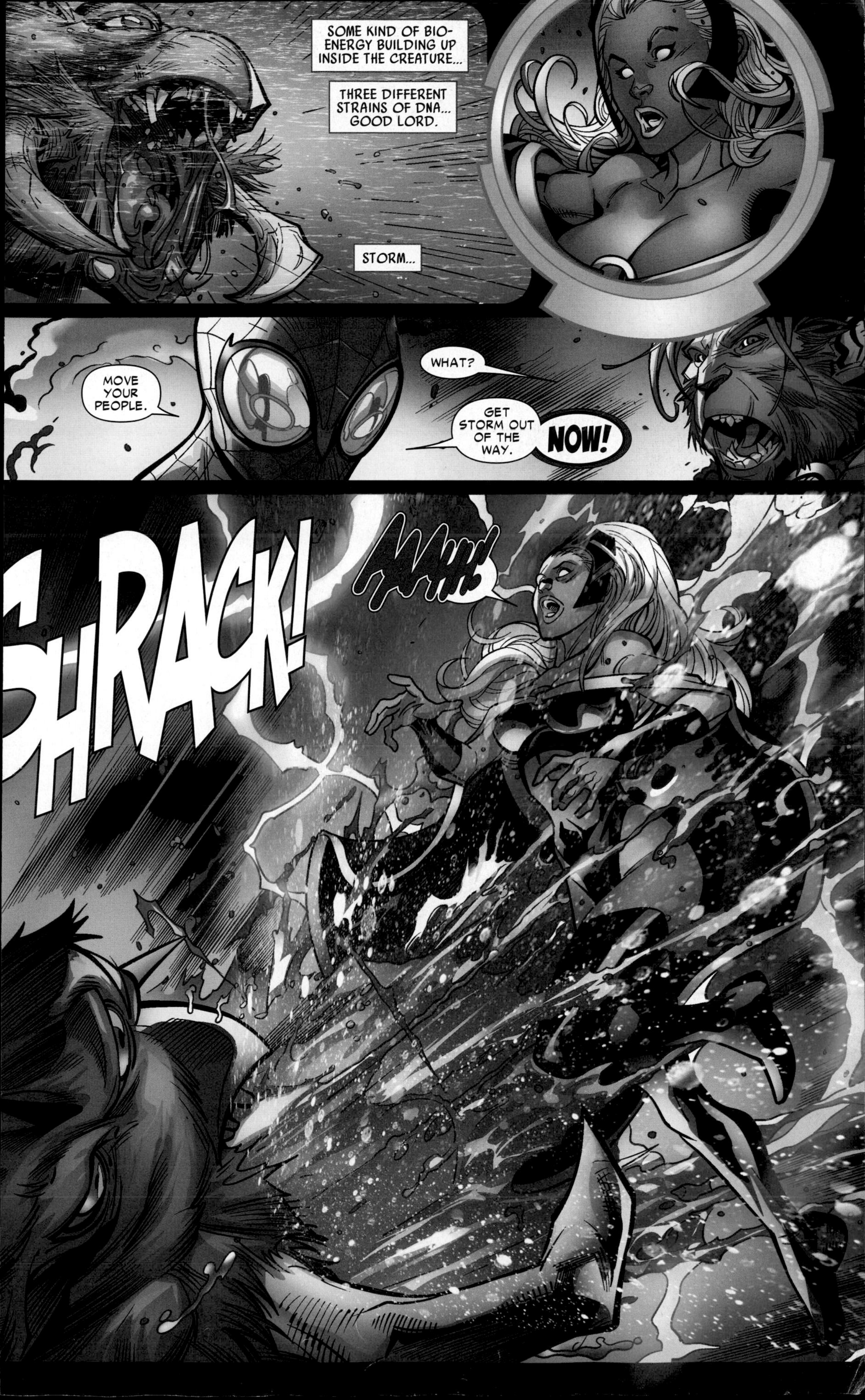
SOME KIND OF BIO-ENERGY BUILDING UP INSIDE THE CREATURE...
THREE DIFFERENT STRAINS OF DNA... GOOD LORD.
STORM...
MOVE YOUR PEOPLE.
WHAT?
GET STORM OUT OF THE WAY.
NOW!
SHRACK!

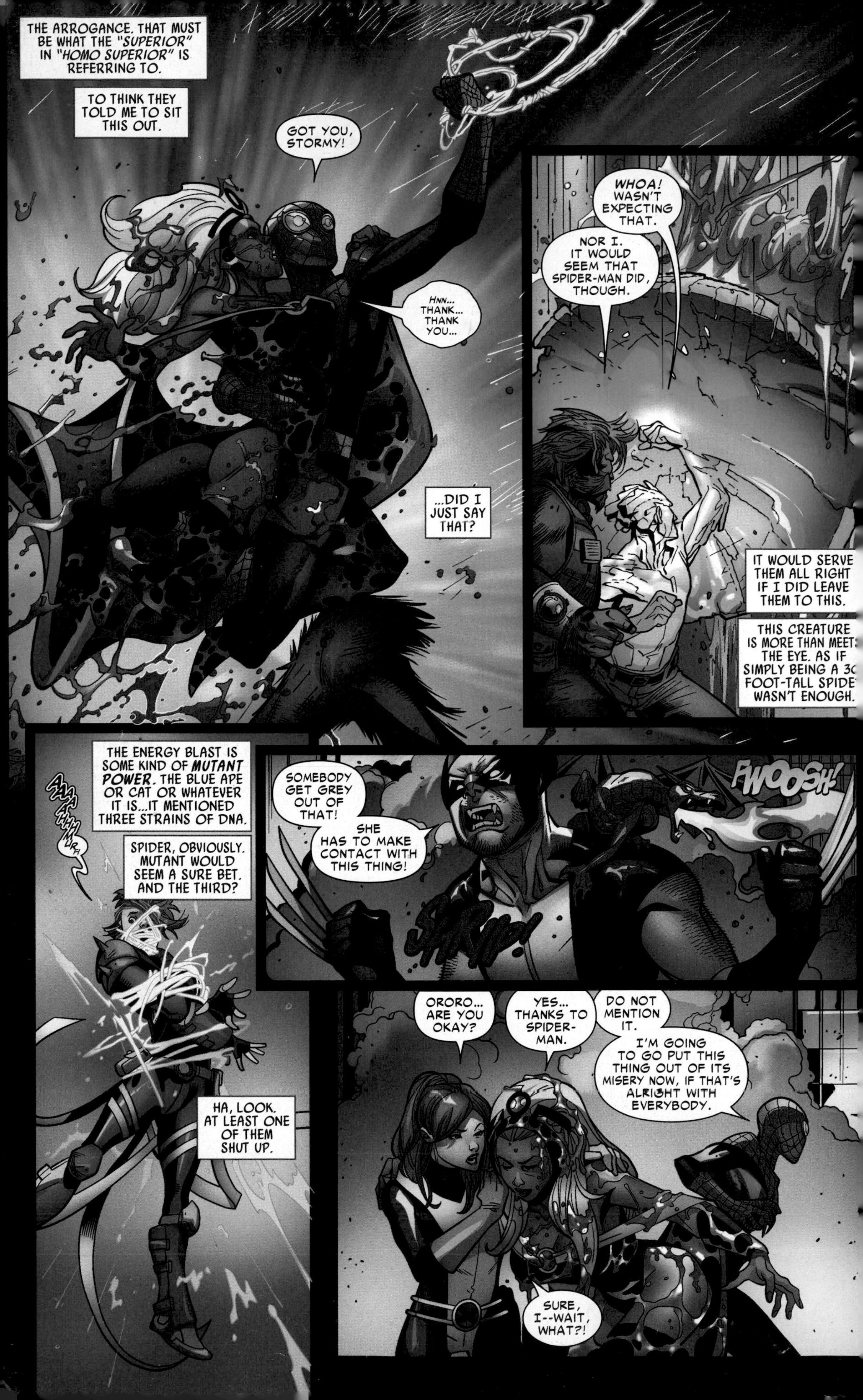

THE ARROGANCE. THAT MUST BE WHAT THE "SUPERIOR" IN "HOMO SUPERIOR" IS REFERRING TO.
TO THINK THEY TOLD ME TO SIT THIS OUT.
GOT YOU, STORMY!
HNN... THANK... THANK YOU...
...DID I JUST SAY THAT?
WHOA! WASN'T EXPECTING THAT.
NOR I. IT WOULD SEEM THAT SPIDER-MAN DID, THOUGH.
IT WOULD SERVE THEM ALL RIGHT IF I DID LEAVE THEM TO THIS.
THIS CREATURE IS MORE THAN MEETS THE EYE. AS IF SIMPLY BEING A 3C FOOT-TALL SPIDE WASN'T ENOUGH.
THE ENERGY BLAST IS SOME KIND OF MUTANT POWER. THE BLUE APE OR CAT OR WHATEVER IT IS...IT MENTIONED THREE STRAINS OF DNA.
SPIDER, OBVIOUSLY. MUTANT WOULD SEEM A SURE BET. AND THE THIRD?
SOMEBODY GET GREY OUT OF THAT!
SHE HAS TO MAKE CONTACT WITH THIS THING!
FWOOSH!
HA, LOOK. AT LEAST ONE OF THEM SHUT UP.
ORORO... ARE YOU OKAY?
YES... THANKS TO SPIDER-MAN.
DO NOT MENTION IT.
I'M GOING TO GO PUT THIS THING OUT OF ITS MISERY NOW, IF THAT'S ALRIGHT WITH EVERYBODY.
SURE, I--WAIT, WHAT?!

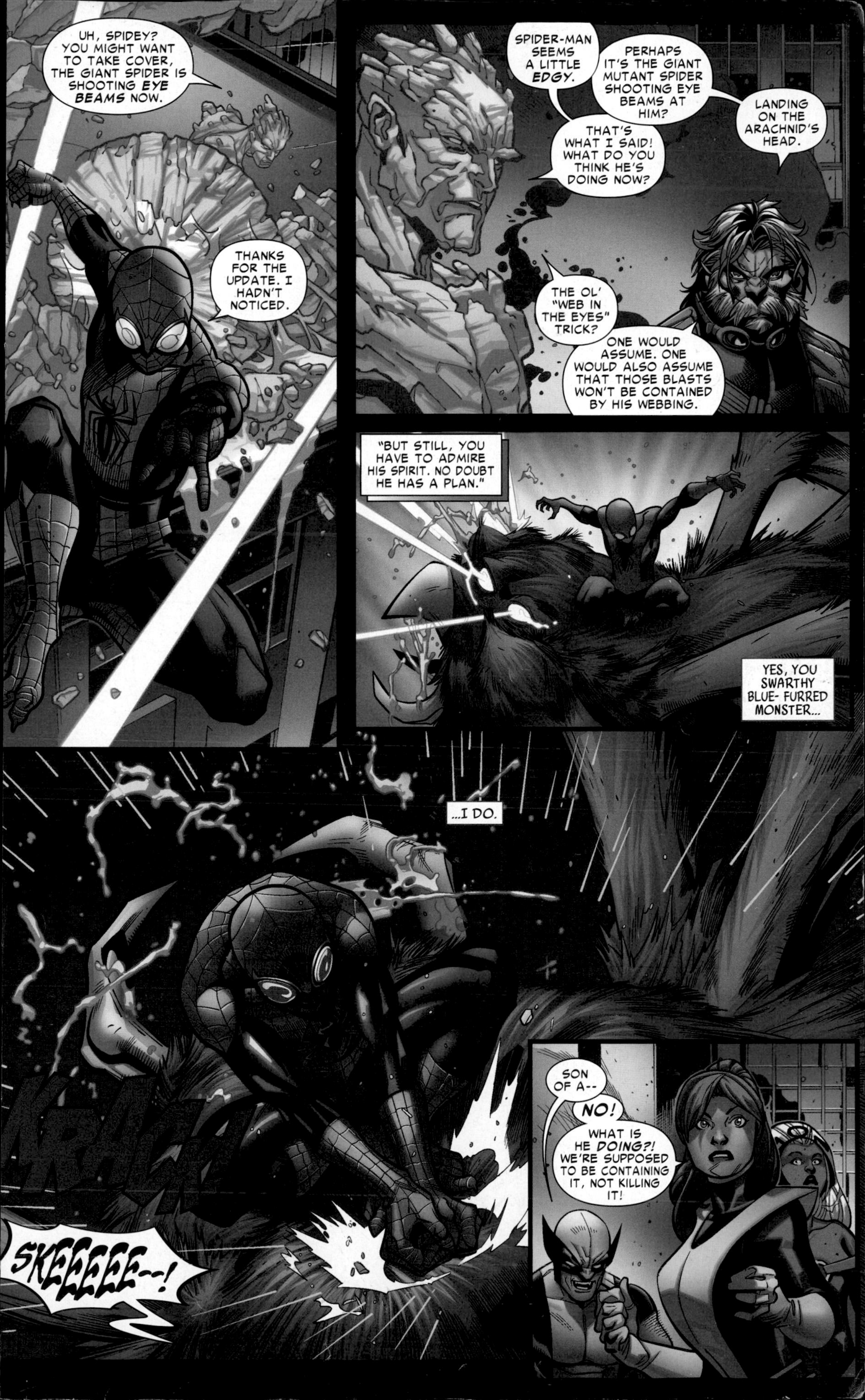
UH, SPIDEY? YOU MIGHT WANT TO TAKE COVER, THE GIANT SPIDER IS SHOOTING EYE BEAMS NOW.
THANKS FOR THE UPDATE. I HADN'T NOTICED.
SPIDER-MAN SEEMS A LITTLE EDGY.
PERHAPS IT'S THE GIANT MUTANT SPIDER SHOOTING EYE BEAMS AT HIM?
THAT'S WHAT I SAID! WHAT DO YOU THINK HE'S DOING NOW?
LANDING ON THE ARACHNID'S HEAD.
THE OL' "WEB IN THE EYES" TRICK?
ONE WOULD ASSUME. ONE WOULD ALSO ASSUME THAT THOSE BLASTS WON'T BE CONTAINED BY HIS WEBBING.
"BUT STILL, YOU HAVE TO ADMIRE HIS SPIRIT. NO DOUBT HE HAS A PLAN."
YES, YOU SWARTHY BLUE- FURRED MONSTER...
...I DO.
SKEEEEE--!
SON OF A--
NO!
WHAT IS HE DOING?! WE'RE SUPPOSED TO BE CONTAINING IT, NOT KILLING IT!

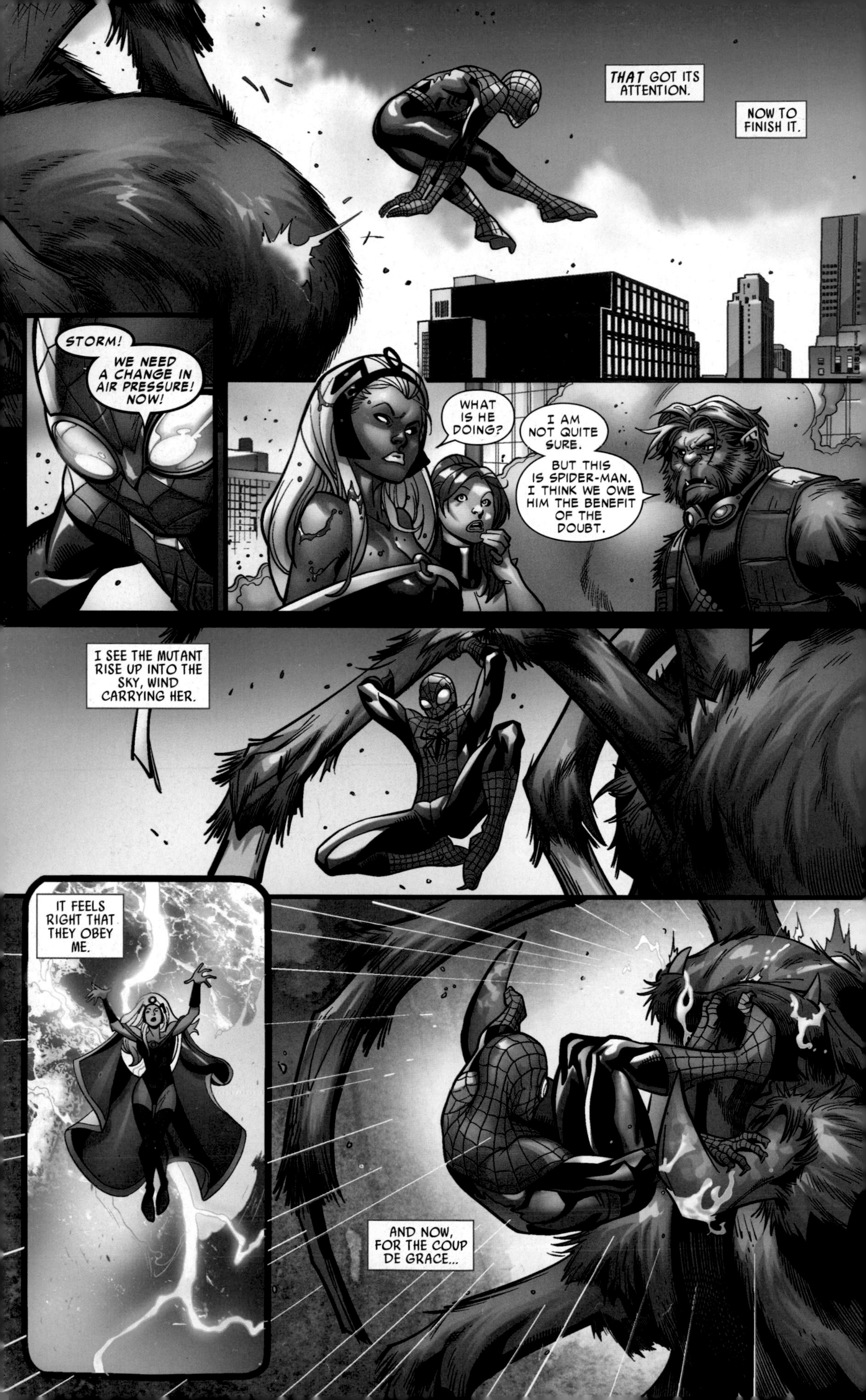

THAT GOT ITS ATTENTION.
NOW TO FINISH IT.
STORM!
WE NEED A CHANGE IN AIR PRESSURE! NOW!
WHAT IS HE DOING?
I AM NOT QUITE SURE.
BUT THIS IS SPIDER-MAN. I THINK WE OWE HIM THE BENEFIT OF THE DOUBT.
I SEE THE MUTANT RISE UP INTO THE SKY, WIND CARRYING HER.
IT FEELS RIGHT THAT THEY OBEY ME.
AND NOW, FOR THE COUP DE GRACE...

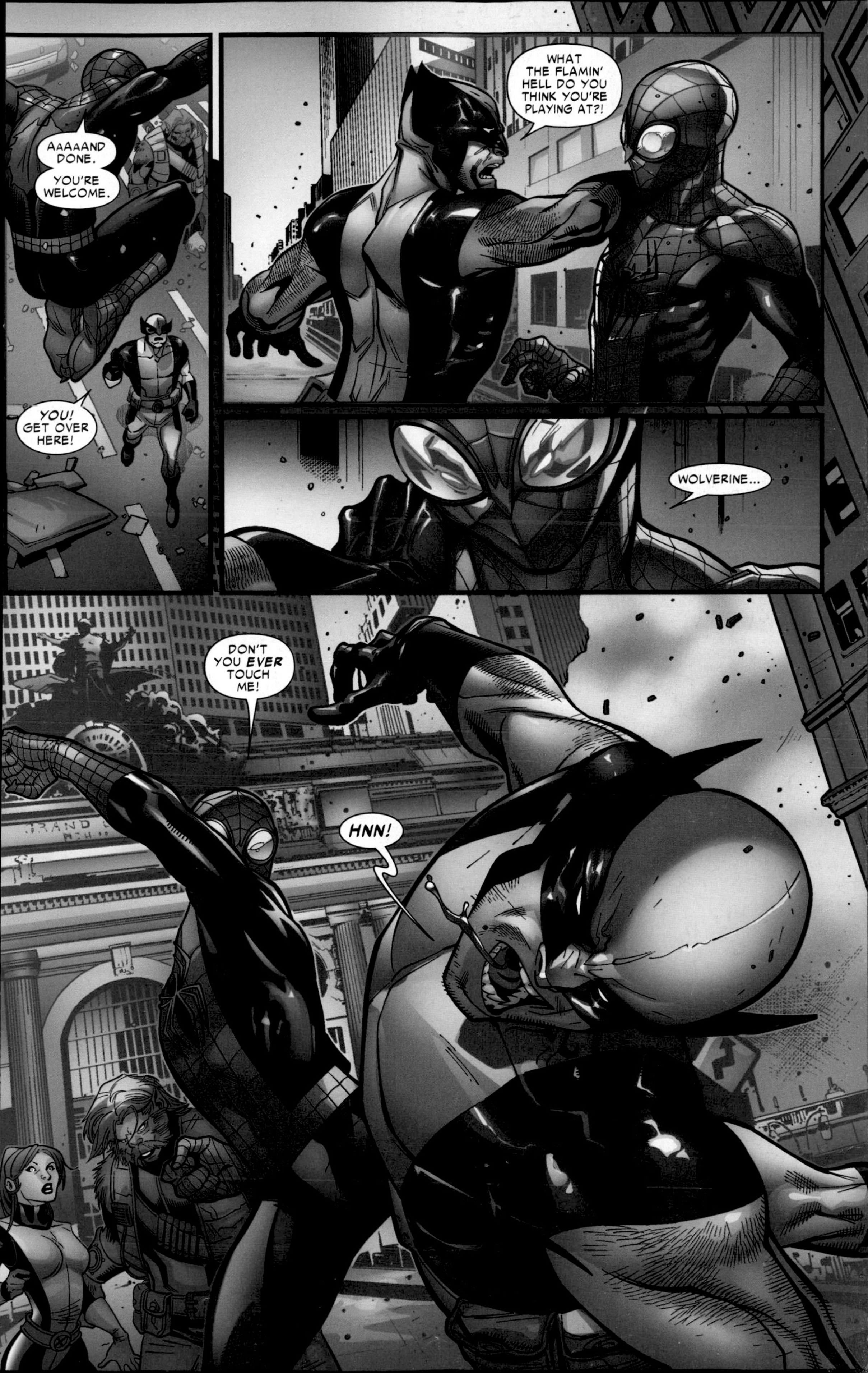
AAAAAND DONE.
YOU'RE WELCOME.
YOU! GET OVER HERE!
WHAT THE FLAMIN' HELL DO YOU THINK YOU'RE PLAYING AT?!
WOLVERINE...
DON'T YOU EVER TOUCH ME!
HNN!

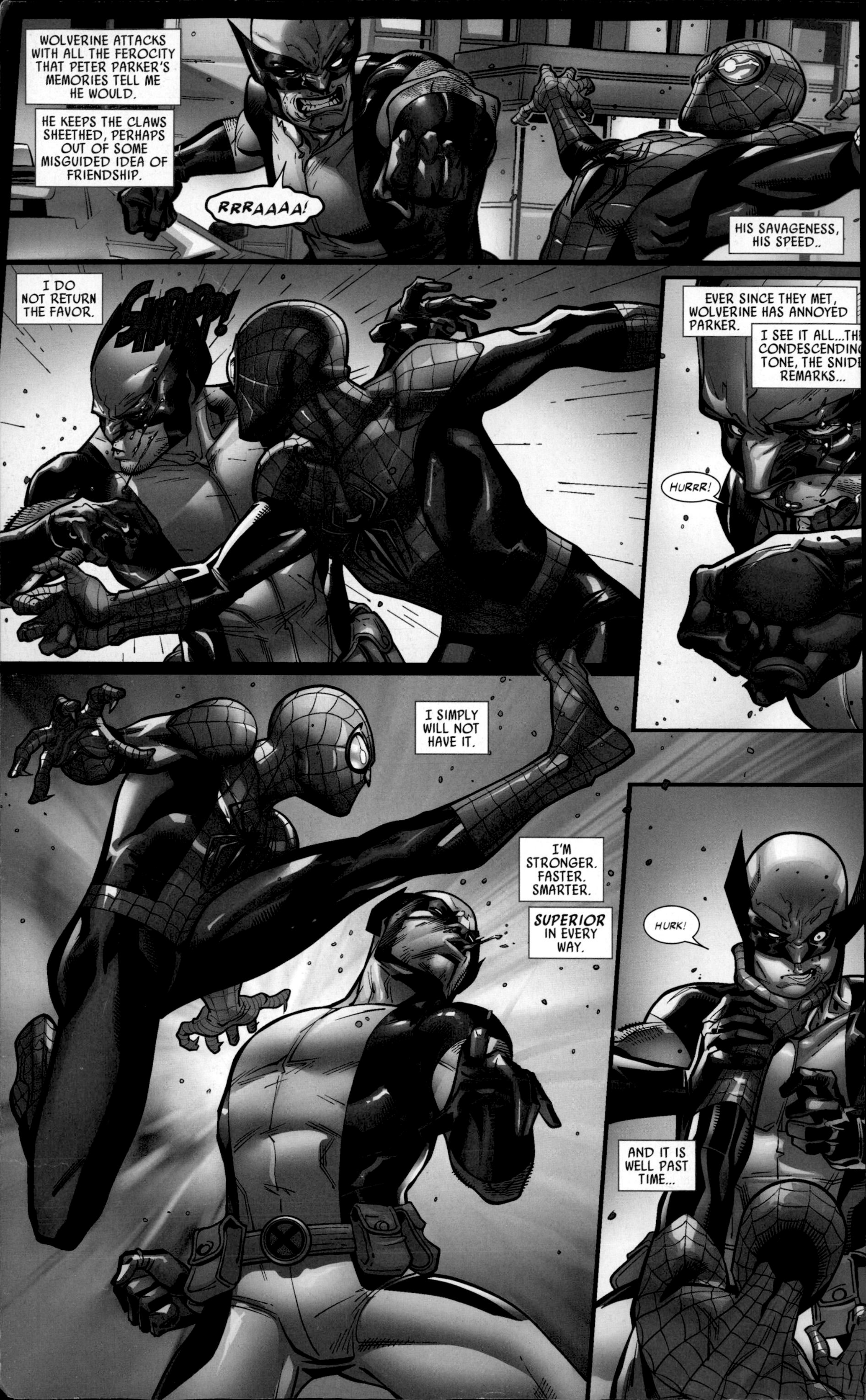
WOLVERINE ATTACKS WITH ALL THE FEROCITY THAT PETER PARKER'S MEMORIES TELL ME HE WOULD.
HE KEEPS THE CLAWS SHEATHED, PERHAPS OUT OF SOME MISGUIDED IDEA OF FRIENDSHIP.
RRRAAAA!
HIS SAVAGENESS, HIS SPEED..
I DO NOT RETURN THE FAVOR.
EVER SINCE THEY MET, WOLVERINE HAS ANNOYED PARKER.
I SEE IT ALL...TH CONDESCENDIN TONE, THE SNID REMARKS...
HURRR!
I SIMPLY WILL NOT HAVE IT.
I'M STRONGER. FASTER. SMARTER.
SUPERIOR IN EVERY WAY.
HURK!
AND IT IS WELL PAST TIME...

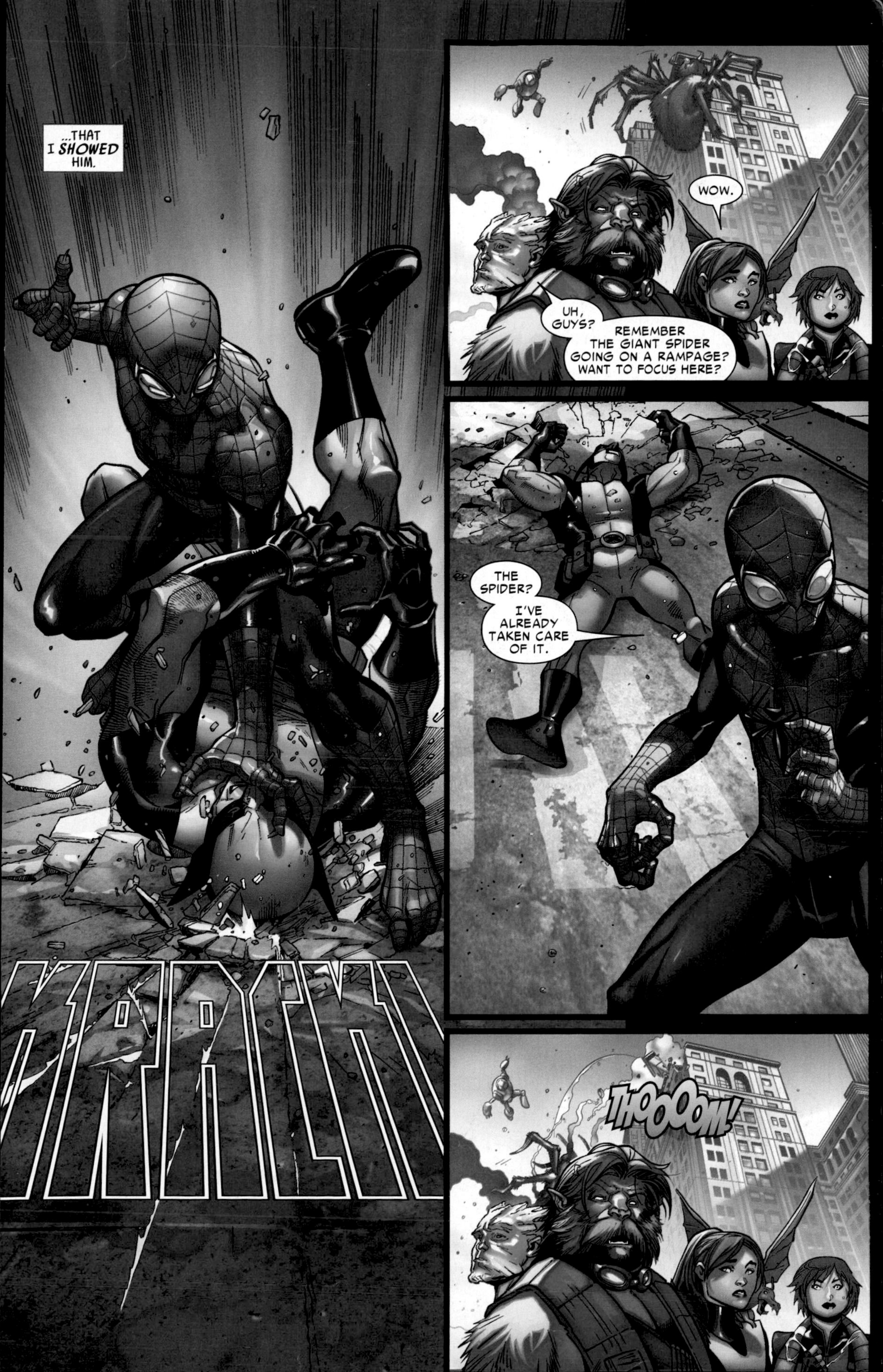
...THAT I SHOWED HIM.
KRRZKK
WOW.
UH, GUYS?
REMEMBER THE GIANT SPIDER GOING ON A RAMPAGE? WANT TO FOCUS HERE?
THE SPIDER?
I'VE ALREADY TAKEN CARE OF IT.
THOOOOM!

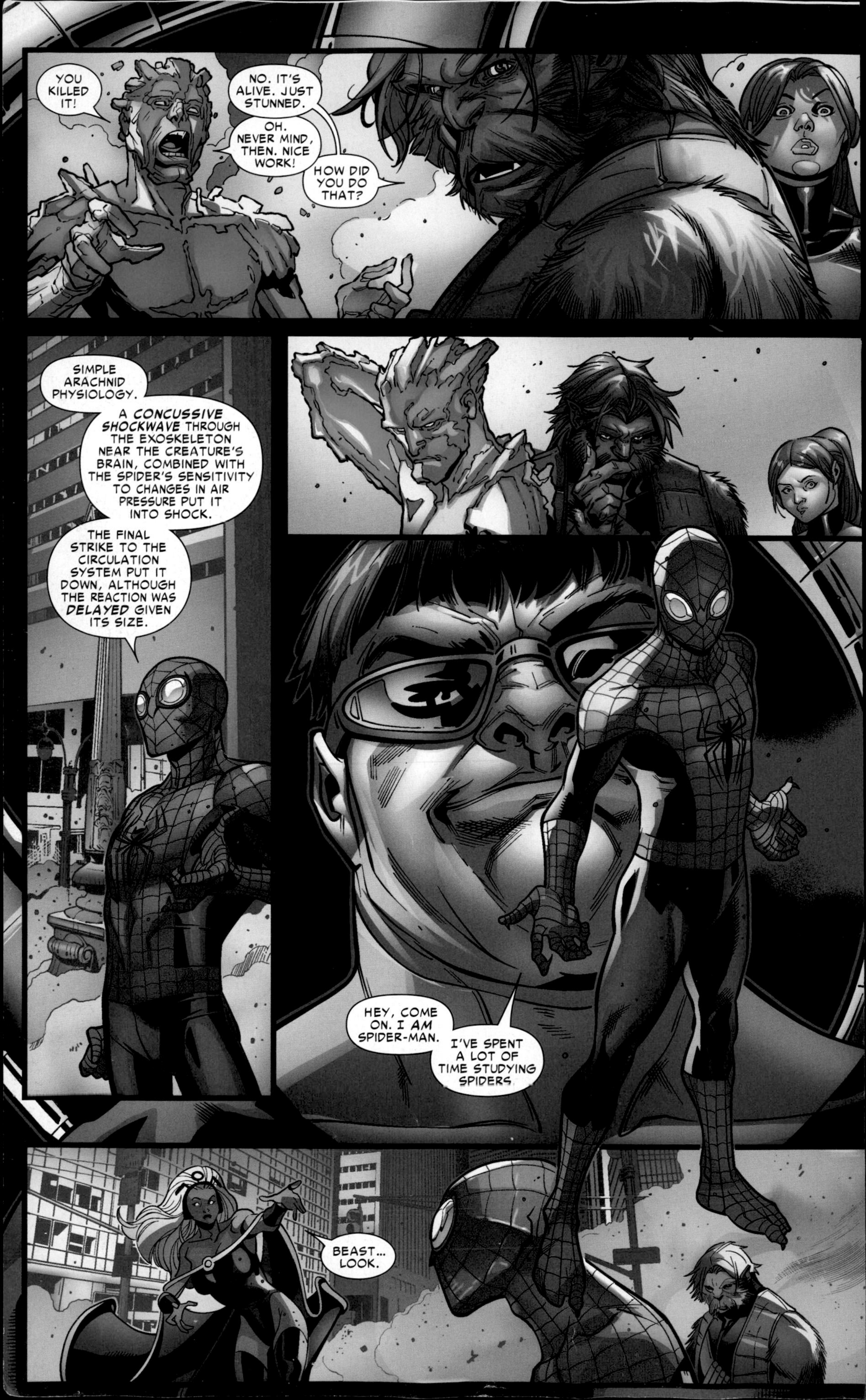
YOU KILLED IT!
NO. IT'S ALIVE. JUST STUNNED.
OH. NEVER MIND, THEN. NICE WORK!
HOW DID YOU DO THAT?
SIMPLE ARACHNID PHYSIOLOGY.
A CONCUSSIVE SHOCKWAVE THROUGH THE EXOSKELETON NEAR THE CREATURE'S BRAIN, COMBINED WITH THE SPIDER'S SENSITIVITY TO CHANGES IN AIR PRESSURE PUT IT INTO SHOCK.
THE FINAL STRIKE TO THE CIRCULATION SYSTEM PUT IT DOWN, ALTHOUGH THE REACTION WAS DELAYED GIVEN ITS SIZE.
HEY, COME ON. I AM SPIDER-MAN.
I'VE SPENT A LOT OF TIME STUDYING SPIDERS.
BEAST... LOOK.

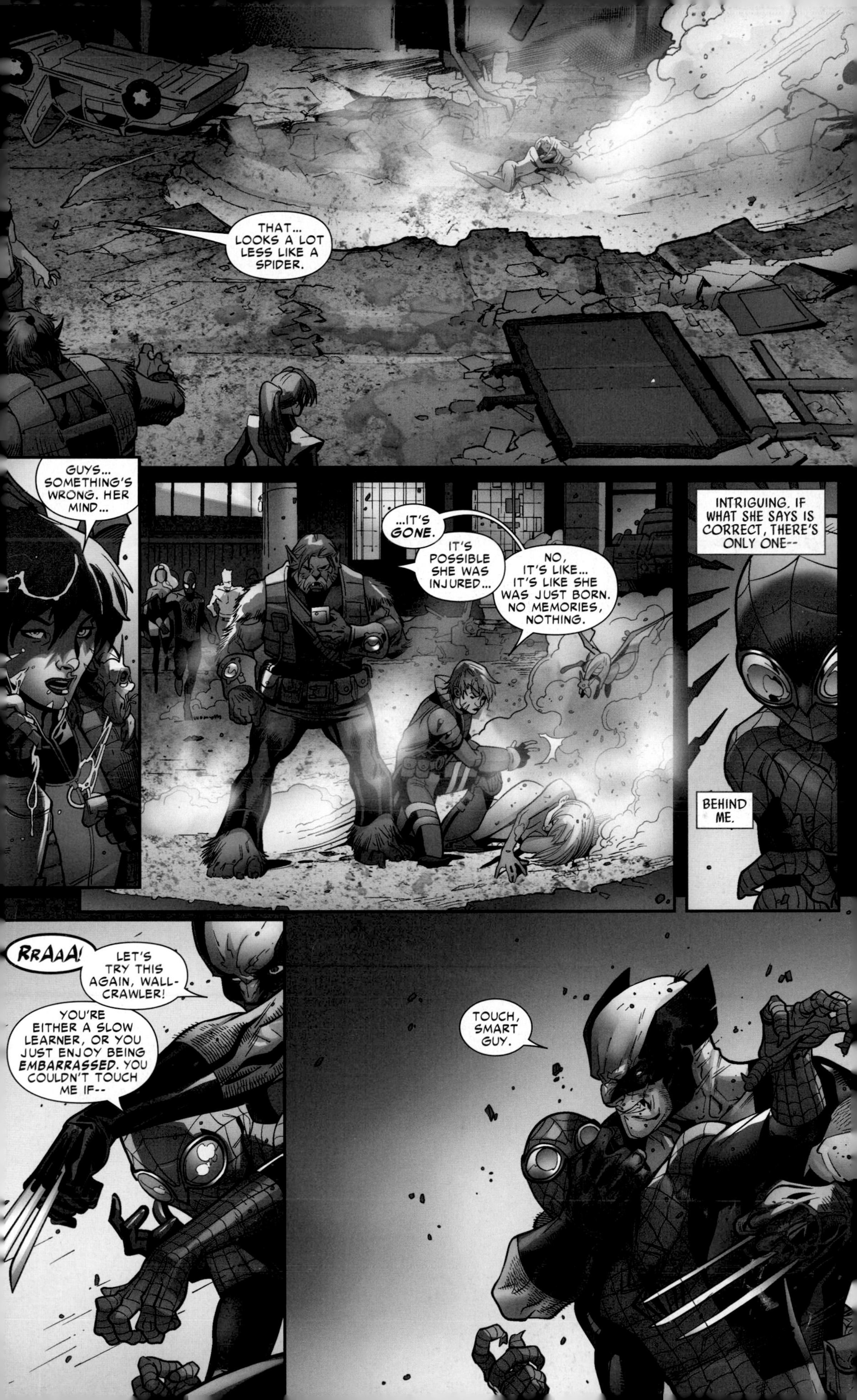
THAT... LOOKS A LOT LESS LIKE A SPIDER.
GUYS... SOMETHING'S WRONG. HER MIND...
...IT'S GONE.
IT'S POSSIBLE SHE WAS INJURED...
NO, IT'S LIKE... IT'S LIKE SHE WAS JUST BORN. NO MEMORIES, NOTHING.
INTRIGUING. IF WHAT SHE SAYS IS CORRECT, THERE'S ONLY ONE--
BEHIND ME.
RRAAA!
LET'S TRY THIS AGAIN, WALL-CRAWLER!
YOU'RE EITHER A SLOW LEARNER, OR YOU JUST ENJOY BEING EMBARRASSED. YOU COULDN'T TOUCH ME IF--
TOUCH, SMART GUY.

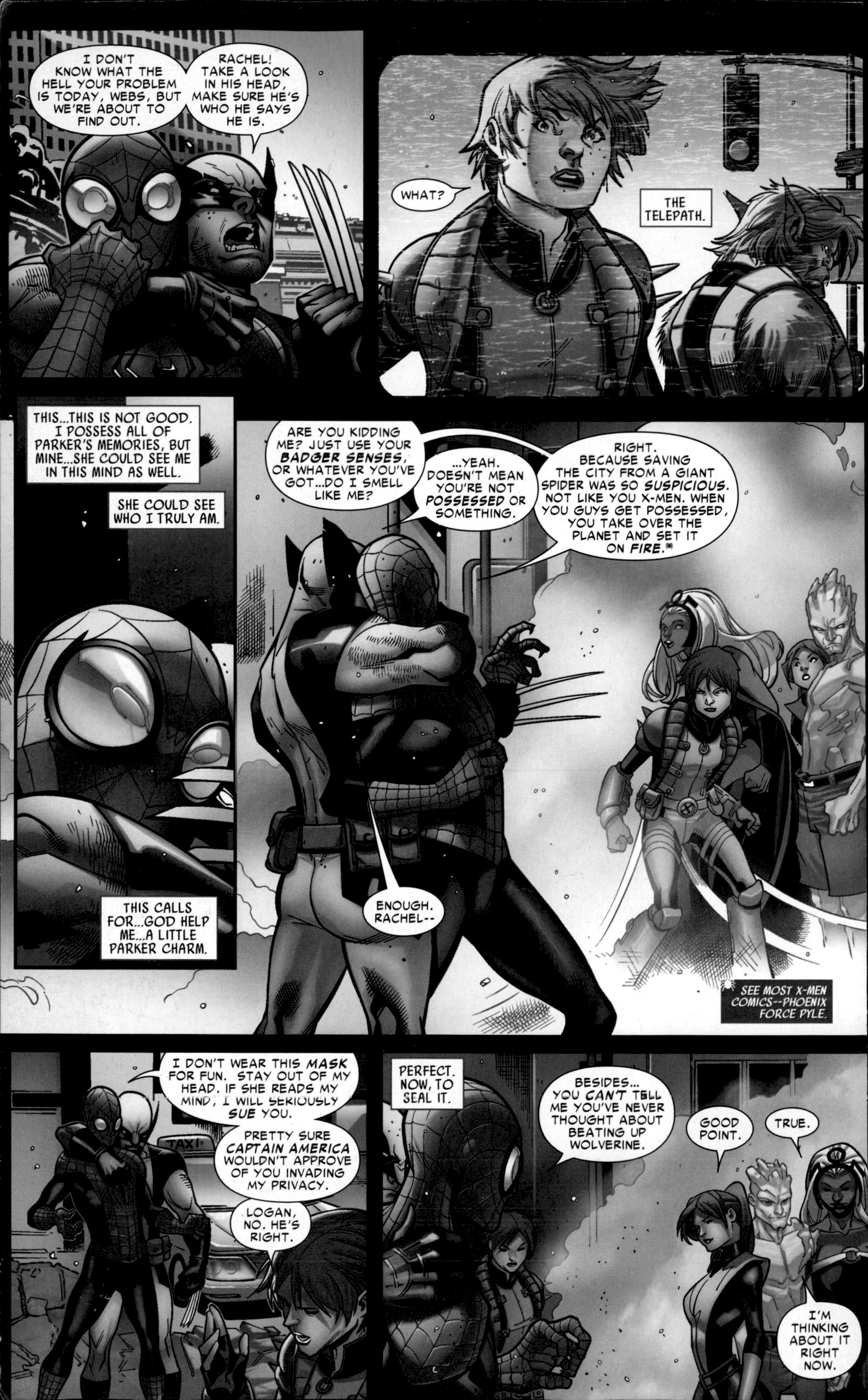
I DON'T KNOW WHAT THE HELL YOUR PROBLEM IS TODAY, WEBS, BUT WE'RE ABOUT TO FIND OUT.
RACHEL! TAKE A LOOK IN HIS HEAD, MAKE SURE HE'S WHO HE SAYS HE IS.
WHAT?
THE TELEPATH.
THIS...THIS IS NOT GOOD. I POSSESS ALL OF PARKER'S MEMORIES, BUT MINE...SHE COULD SEE ME IN THIS MIND AS WELL.
SHE COULD SEE WHO I TRULY AM.
THIS CALLS FOR...GOD HELP ME...A LITTLE PARKER CHARM.
ARE YOU KIDDING ME? JUST USE YOUR BADGER SENSES, OR WHATEVER YOU'VE GOT...DO I SMELL LIKE ME?
...YEAH. DOESN'T MEAN YOU'RE NOT POSSESSED OR SOMETHING.
RIGHT. BECAUSE SAVING THE CITY FROM A GIANT SPIDER WAS SO SUSPICIOUS. NOT LIKE YOU X-MEN. WHEN YOU GUYS GET POSSESSED, YOU TAKE OVER THE PLANET AND SET IT ON FIRE.*
ENOUGH. RACHEL--
*SEE MOST X-MEN COMICS--PHOENIX FORCE PYLE.
I DON'T WEAR THIS MASK FOR FUN. STAY OUT OF MY HEAD. IF SHE READS MY MIND, I WILL SERIOUSLY SUE YOU.
PRETTY SURE CAPTAIN AMERICA WOULDN'T APPROVE OF YOU INVADING MY PRIVACY.
LOGAN, NO. HE'S RIGHT.
TAXI
PERFECT. NOW, TO SEAL IT.
BESIDES... YOU CAN'T TELL ME YOU'VE NEVER THOUGHT ABOUT BEATING UP WOLVERINE.
GOOD POINT.
TRUE.
I'M THINKING ABOUT IT RIGHT NOW.

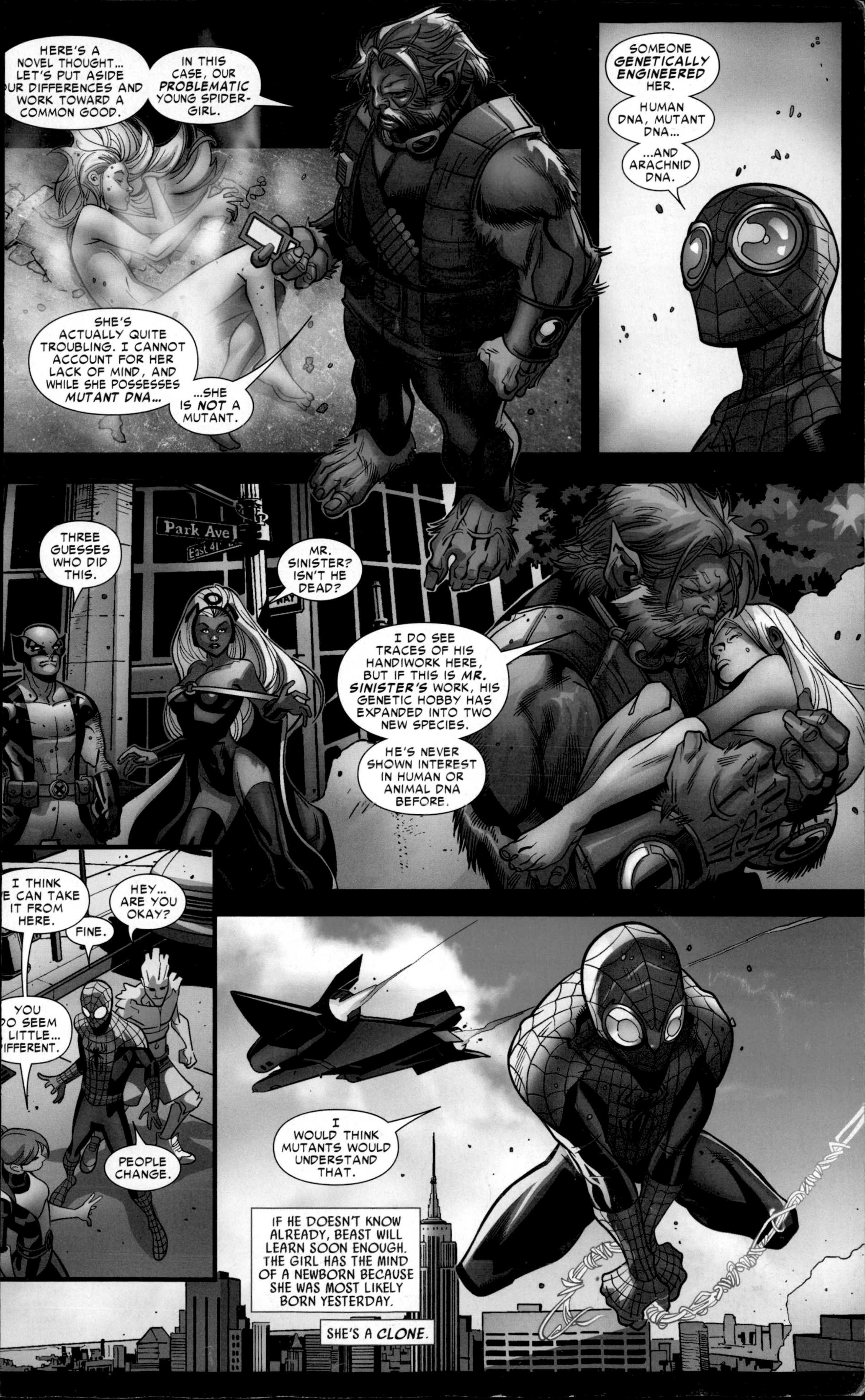

HERE'S A NOVEL THOUGHT... LET'S PUT ASIDE UR DIFFERENCES AND WORK TOWARD A COMMON GOOD.
IN THIS CASE, OUR PROBLEMATIC YOUNG SPIDER-GIRL.
SHE'S ACTUALLY QUITE TROUBLING. I CANNOT ACCOUNT FOR HER LACK OF MIND, AND WHILE SHE POSSESSES MUTANT DNA...
...SHE IS NOT A MUTANT.
SOMEONE GENETICALLY ENGINEERED HER.
HUMAN DNA, MUTANT DNA...
...AND ARACHNID DNA.
Park Ave
East 41
THREE GUESSES WHO DID THIS.
MR. SINISTER? ISN'T HE DEAD?
I DO SEE TRACES OF HIS HANDIWORK HERE, BUT IF THIS IS MR. SINISTER'S WORK, HIS GENETIC HOBBY HAS EXPANDED INTO TWO NEW SPECIES.
HE'S NEVER SHOWN INTEREST IN HUMAN OR ANIMAL DNA BEFORE.
I THINK E CAN TAKE IT FROM HERE.
HEY... ARE YOU OKAY?
FINE.
YOU O SEEM LITTLE... IFFERENT.
PEOPLE CHANGE.
I WOULD THINK MUTANTS WOULD UNDERSTAND THAT.
IF HE DOESN'T KNOW ALREADY, BEAST WILL LEARN SOON ENOUGH. THE GIRL HAS THE MIND OF A NEWBORN BECAUSE SHE WAS MOST LIKELY BORN YESTERDAY.
SHE'S A CLONE.

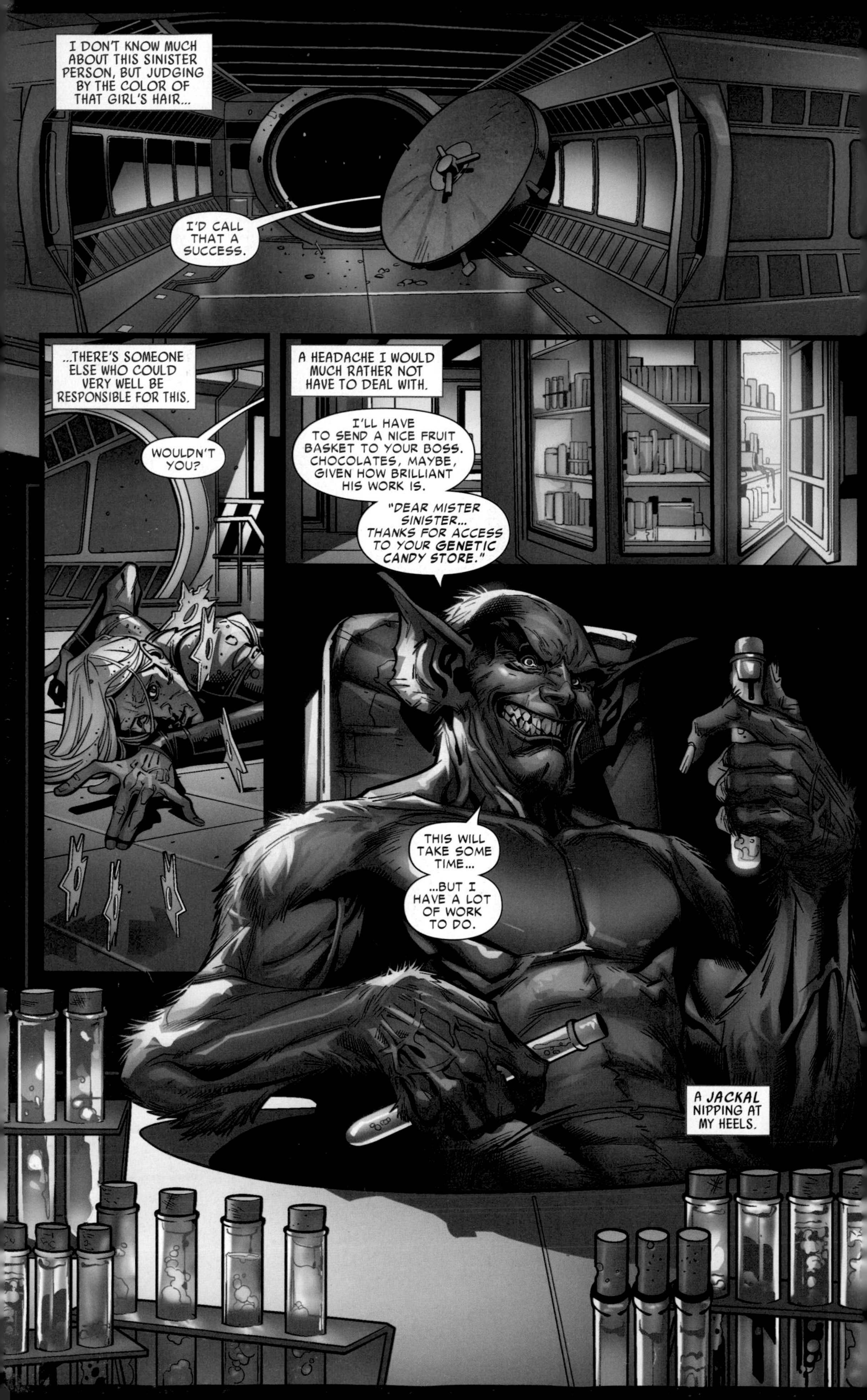
I DON'T KNOW MUCH ABOUT THIS SINISTER PERSON, BUT JUDGING BY THE COLOR OF THAT GIRL'S HAIR...
I'D CALL THAT A SUCCESS.
...THERE'S SOMEONE ELSE WHO COULD VERY WELL BE RESPONSIBLE FOR THIS.
WOULDN'T YOU?
A HEADACHE I WOULD MUCH RATHER NOT HAVE TO DEAL WITH.
I'LL HAVE TO SEND A NICE FRUIT BASKET TO YOUR BOSS. CHOCOLATES, MAYBE, GIVEN HOW BRILLIANT HIS WORK IS.
"DEAR MISTER SINISTER... THANKS FOR ACCESS TO YOUR GENETIC CANDY STORE."
THIS WILL TAKE SOME TIME...
...BUT I HAVE A LOT OF WORK TO DO.
A JACKAL NIPPING AT MY HEELS.

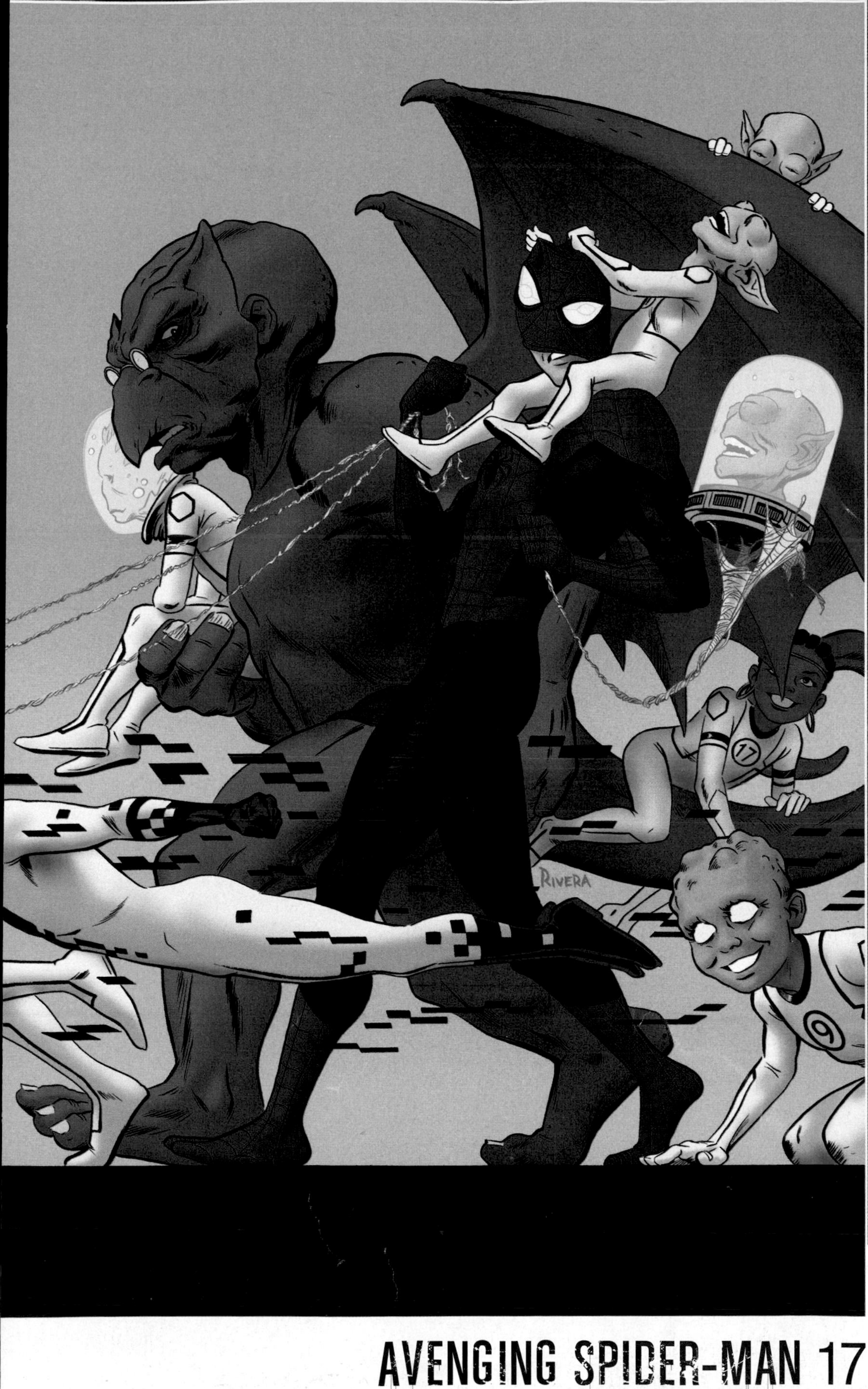
RIVERA

AVENGING SPIDER-MAN 17

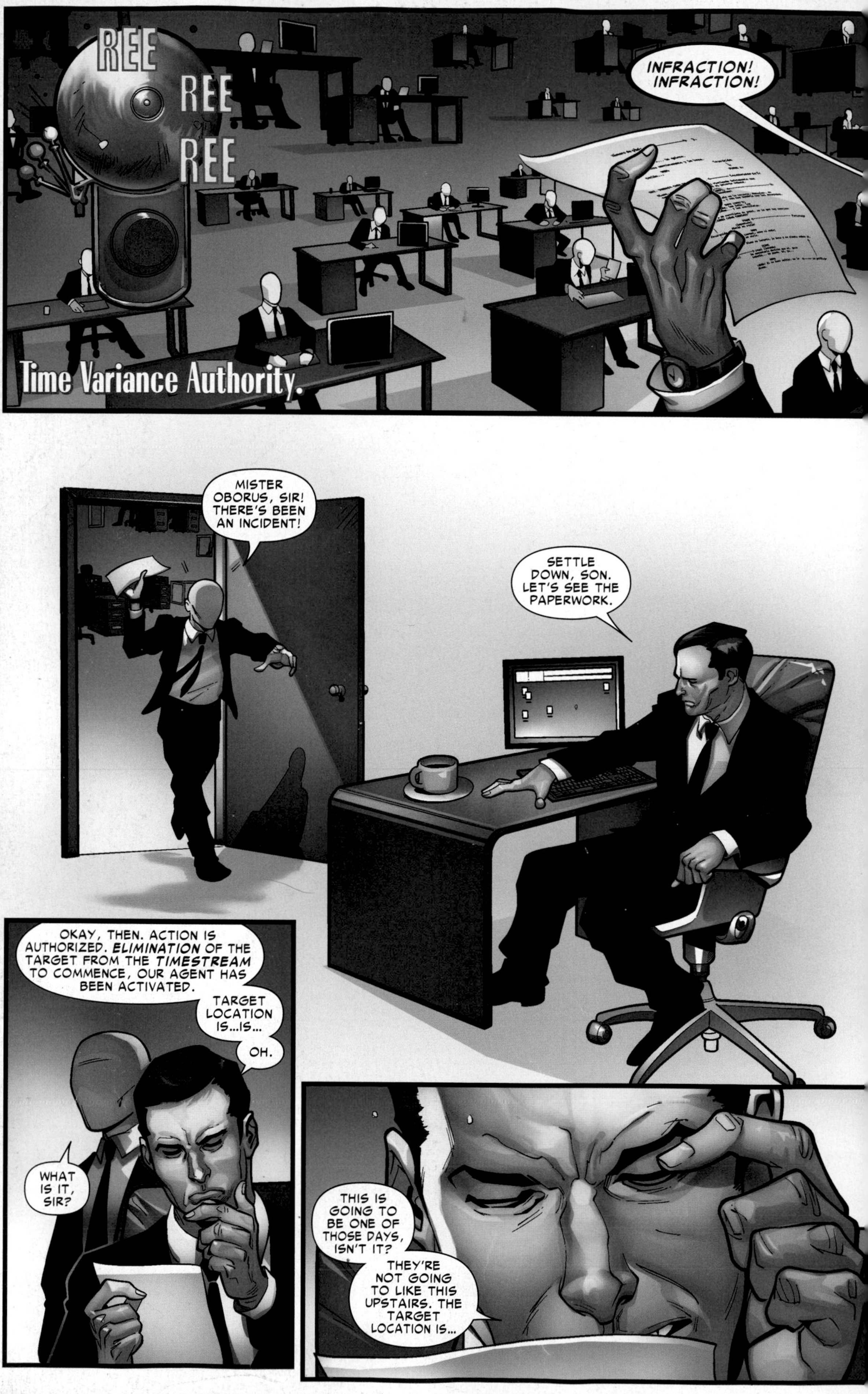
REE
REE
REE
INFRACTION! INFRACTION!
Time Variance Authority.
MISTER OBORUS, SIR! THERE'S BEEN AN INCIDENT!
SETTLE DOWN, SON. LET'S SEE THE PAPERWORK.
OKAY, THEN. ACTION IS AUTHORIZED. ELIMINATION OF THE TARGET FROM THE TIMESTREAM TO COMMENCE, OUR AGENT HAS BEEN ACTIVATED.
TARGET LOCATION IS...IS...
OH.
WHAT IS IT, SIR?
THIS IS GOING TO BE ONE OF THOSE DAYS, ISN'T IT?
THEY'RE NOT GOING TO LIKE THIS UPSTAIRS. THE TARGET LOCATION IS...

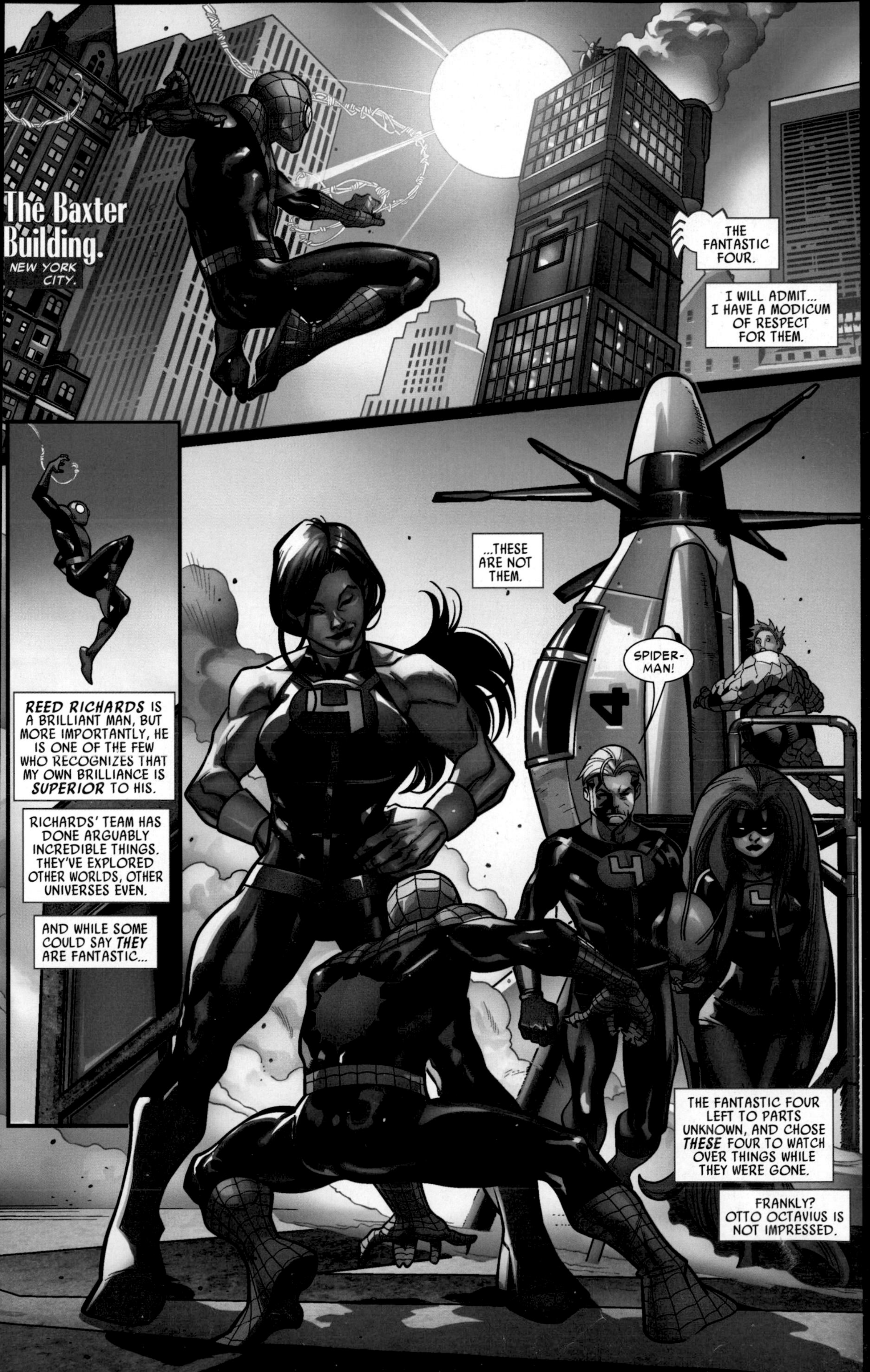
The Baxter Building.
NEW YORK CITY.
THE FANTASTIC FOUR.
I WILL ADMIT... I HAVE A MODICUM OF RESPECT FOR THEM.
...THESE ARE NOT THEM.
REED RICHARDS IS A BRILLIANT MAN, BUT MORE IMPORTANTLY, HE IS ONE OF THE FEW WHO RECOGNIZES THAT MY OWN BRILLIANCE IS SUPERIOR TO HIS.
RICHARDS' TEAM HAS DONE ARGUABLY INCREDIBLE THINGS. THEY'VE EXPLORED OTHER WORLDS, OTHER UNIVERSES EVEN.
AND WHILE SOME COULD SAY THEY ARE FANTASTIC...
SPIDER-MAN!
THE FANTASTIC FOUR LEFT TO PARTS UNKNOWN, AND CHOSE THESE FOUR TO WATCH OVER THINGS WHILE THEY WERE GONE.
FRANKLY? OTTO OCTAVIUS IS NOT IMPRESSED.

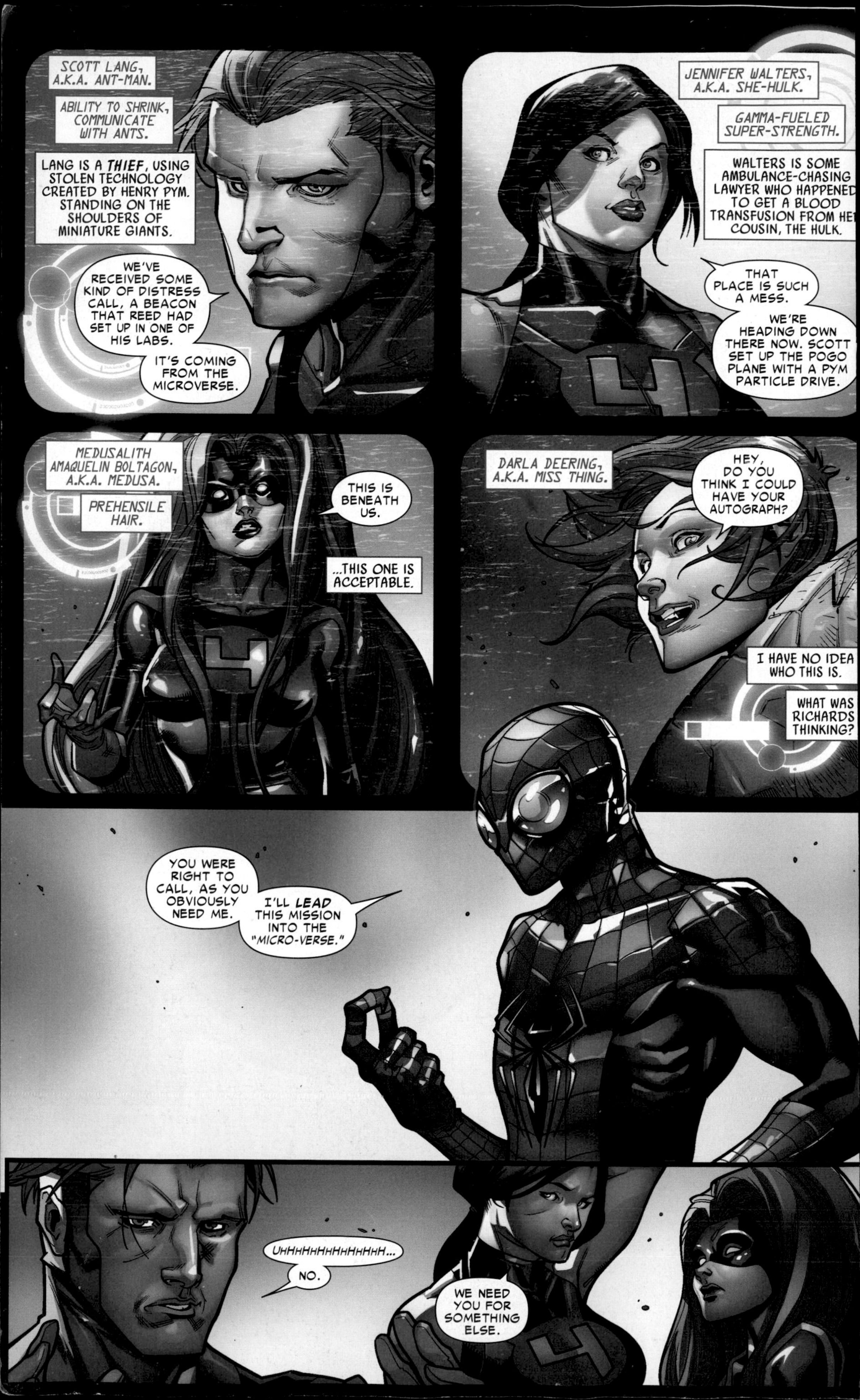
SCOTT LANG, A.K.A. ANT-MAN.
ABILITY TO SHRINK, COMMUNICATE WITH ANTS.
LANG IS A THIEF, USING STOLEN TECHNOLOGY CREATED BY HENRY PYM. STANDING ON THE SHOULDERS OF MINIATURE GIANTS.
WE'VE RECEIVED SOME KIND OF DISTRESS CALL, A BEACON THAT REED HAD SET UP IN ONE OF HIS LABS.
IT'S COMING FROM THE MICROVERSE.
JENNIFER WALTERS, A.K.A. SHE-HULK.
GAMMA-FUELED SUPER-STRENGTH.
WALTERS IS SOME AMBULANCE-CHASING LAWYER WHO HAPPENED TO GET A BLOOD TRANSFUSION FROM HER COUSIN, THE HULK.
THAT PLACE IS SUCH A MESS.
WE'RE HEADING DOWN THERE NOW. SCOTT SET UP THE POGO PLANE WITH A PYM PARTICLE DRIVE.
MEDUSALITH AMAQUELIN BOLTAGON, A.K.A. MEDUSA.
PREHENSILE HAIR.
THIS IS BENEATH US.
...THIS ONE IS ACCEPTABLE.
DARLA DEERING, A.K.A. MISS THING.
HEY, DO YOU THINK I COULD HAVE YOUR AUTOGRAPH?
I HAVE NO IDEA WHO THIS IS.
WHAT WAS RICHARDS THINKING?
YOU WERE RIGHT TO CALL, AS YOU OBVIOUSLY NEED ME.
I'LL LEAD THIS MISSION INTO THE "MICRO-VERSE."
UHHHHHHHHHHHHHH...
NO.
WE NEED YOU FOR SOMETHING ELSE.

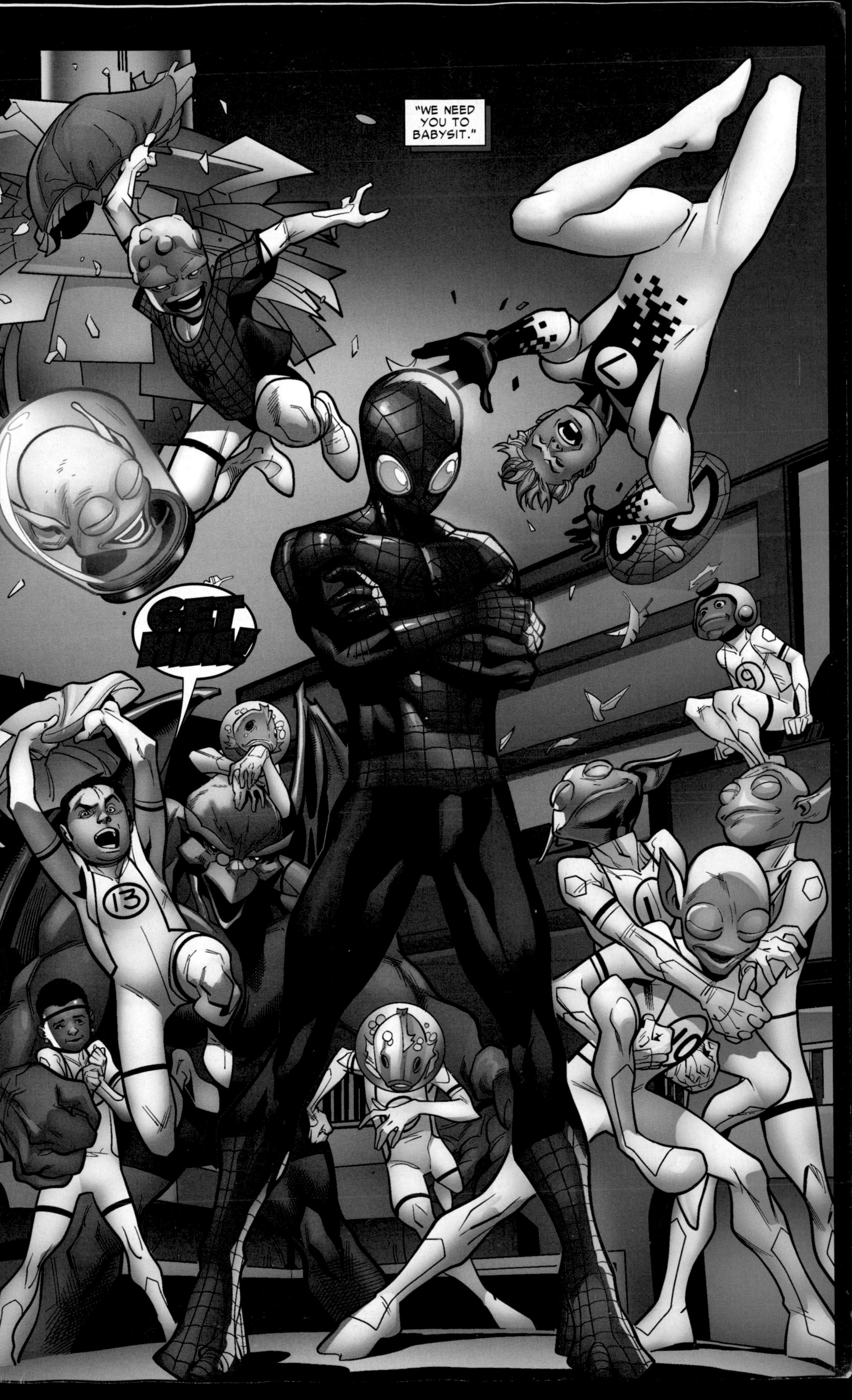
"WE NEED YOU TO BABYSIT."
GET HIM!

OTTO OCTAVIUS, the villain known as DOCTOR OCTOPUS, was dying. In order to cheat death, he used his skills as a mad scientist to swap minds with his greatest enemy, PETER PARKER, the spectacular SPIDER-MAN.
However, the transfer gave Octavius MORE than just SPIDER-MAN'S great powers, it gave him PARKER'S experiences as well… including the lesson of great responsibility! Now Otto Octavius is beginning a NEW life as a hero—possibly the greatest hero of all.  He is--

The world's most brilliant young minds were handpicked by Reed Richards regardless of race, creed, color, gender, species or super villain DNA to be crafted into the leaders of tomorrow. They are

# THE FUTURE FOUNDATION

|  |  |  |  |  |  |
|---|---|---|---|---|---|
| **ALEX POWER** | **ONOME** | **LEECH** | **ARTIE MADDICKS** | **BENTLEY-23** | **DRAGON MAN** |

|  | |  | |  |  |
|---|---|---|---|---|---|
| **VIL** | **WU** | **MIK** | **KORR** | **TURG** | **TONG** |

# AVENGING
# SPIDER-MAN

## PREVIOUSLY...

Spider-Man's mind died in Doctor Octopus's body.  Doctor Octopus's mind lives on in Spider-Man's body as the Superior Spider-Man.  The Fantastic Four are lost in space and time and have chosen new heroes to take their place.

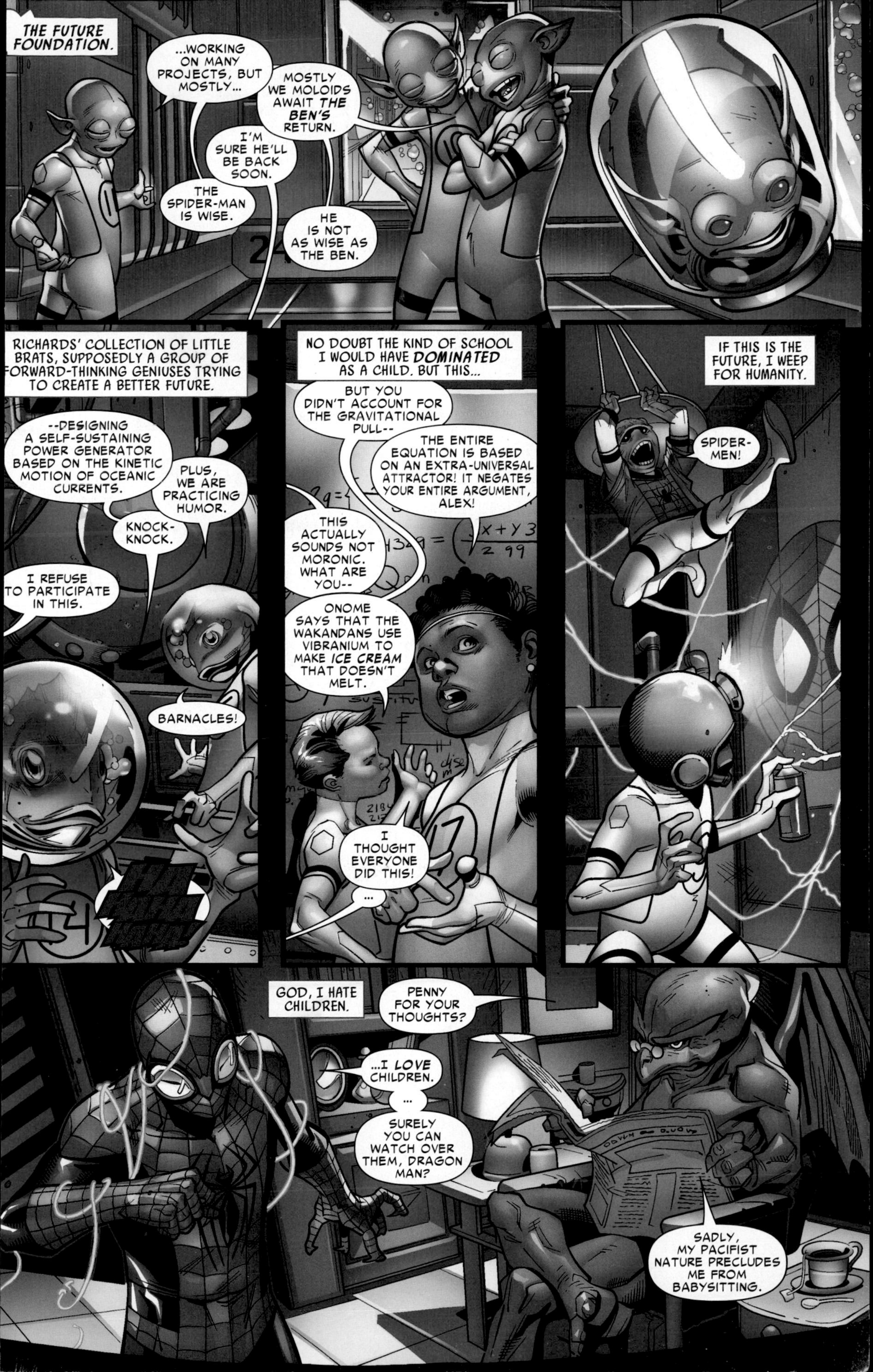
THE FUTURE FOUNDATION.
...WORKING ON MANY PROJECTS, BUT MOSTLY...
MOSTLY WE MOLOIDS AWAIT THE BEN'S RETURN.
I'M SURE HE'LL BE BACK SOON.
THE SPIDER-MAN IS WISE.
HE IS NOT AS WISE AS THE BEN.
RICHARDS' COLLECTION OF LITTLE BRATS, SUPPOSEDLY A GROUP OF FORWARD-THINKING GENIUSES TRYING TO CREATE A BETTER FUTURE.
--DESIGNING A SELF-SUSTAINING POWER GENERATOR BASED ON THE KINETIC MOTION OF OCEANIC CURRENTS.
PLUS, WE ARE PRACTICING HUMOR.
KNOCK-KNOCK.
I REFUSE TO PARTICIPATE IN THIS.
BARNACLES!
NO DOUBT THE KIND OF SCHOOL I WOULD HAVE DOMINATED AS A CHILD. BUT THIS...
BUT YOU DIDN'T ACCOUNT FOR THE GRAVITATIONAL PULL--
THE ENTIRE EQUATION IS BASED ON AN EXTRA-UNIVERSAL ATTRACTOR! IT NEGATES YOUR ENTIRE ARGUMENT, ALEX!
THIS ACTUALLY SOUNDS NOT MORONIC. WHAT ARE YOU--
ONOME SAYS THAT THE WAKANDANS USE VIBRANIUM TO MAKE ICE CREAM THAT DOESN'T MELT.
I THOUGHT EVERYONE DID THIS!
...
IF THIS IS THE FUTURE, I WEEP FOR HUMANITY.
SPIDER-MEN!
GOD, I HATE CHILDREN.
PENNY FOR YOUR THOUGHTS?
...I LOVE CHILDREN.
...
SURELY YOU CAN WATCH OVER THEM, DRAGON MAN?
SADLY, MY PACIFIST NATURE PRECLUDES ME FROM BABYSITTING.

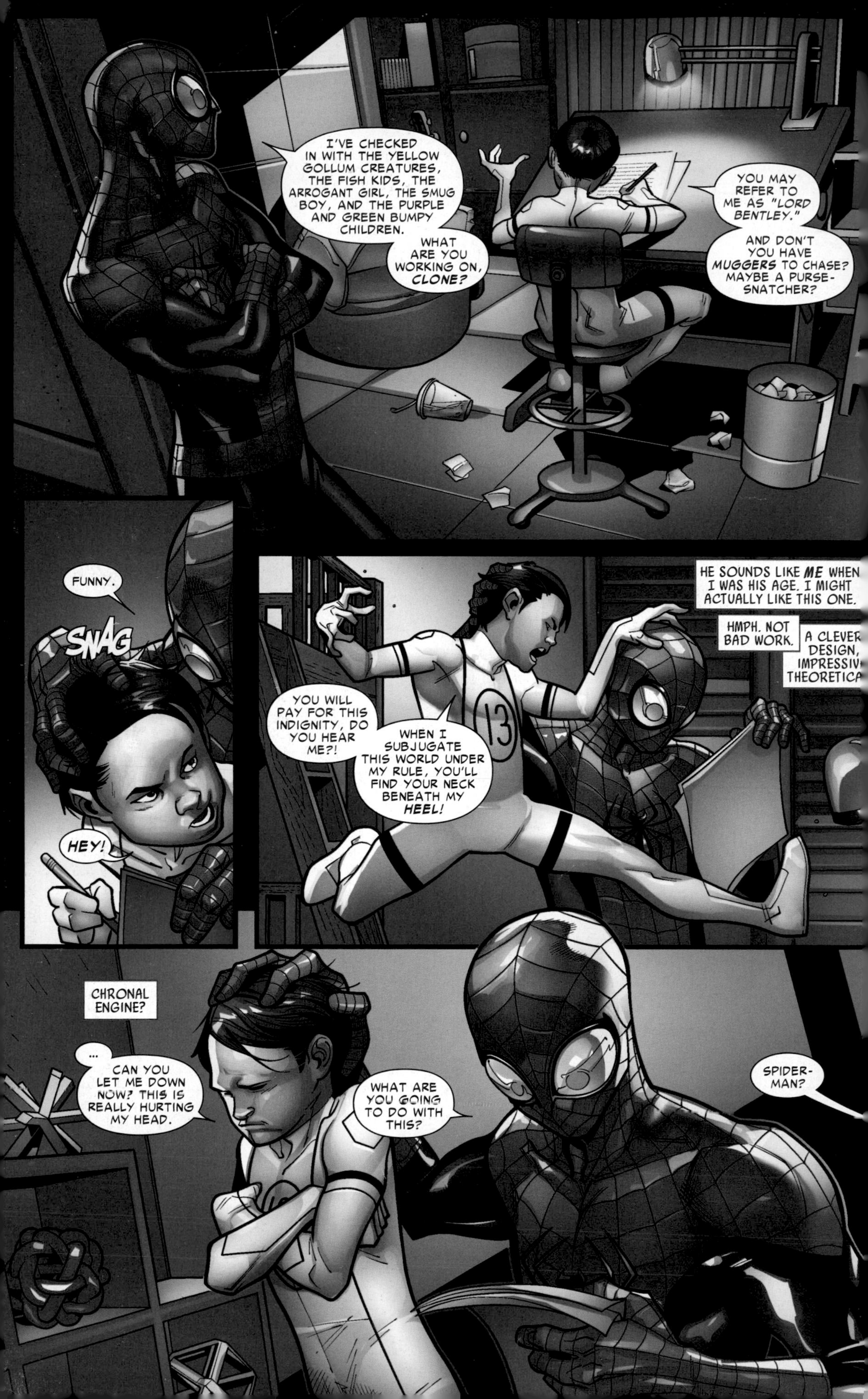

I'VE CHECKED IN WITH THE YELLOW GOLLUM CREATURES, THE FISH KIDS, THE ARROGANT GIRL, THE SMUG BOY, AND THE PURPLE AND GREEN BUMPY CHILDREN.
WHAT ARE YOU WORKING ON, CLONE?
YOU MAY REFER TO ME AS "LORD BENTLEY."
AND DON'T YOU HAVE MUGGERS TO CHASE? MAYBE A PURSE-SNATCHER?
FUNNY.
SNAG
HEY!
HE SOUNDS LIKE ME WHEN I WAS HIS AGE. I MIGHT ACTUALLY LIKE THIS ONE.
HMPH. NOT BAD WORK.
A CLEVER DESIGN, IMPRESSIV THEORETICA
YOU WILL PAY FOR THIS INDIGNITY, DO YOU HEAR ME?!
WHEN I SUBJUGATE THIS WORLD UNDER MY RULE, YOU'LL FIND YOUR NECK BENEATH MY HEEL!
CHRONAL ENGINE?
... CAN YOU LET ME DOWN NOW? THIS IS REALLY HURTING MY HEAD.
WHAT ARE YOU GOING TO DO WITH THIS?
SPIDER-MAN?

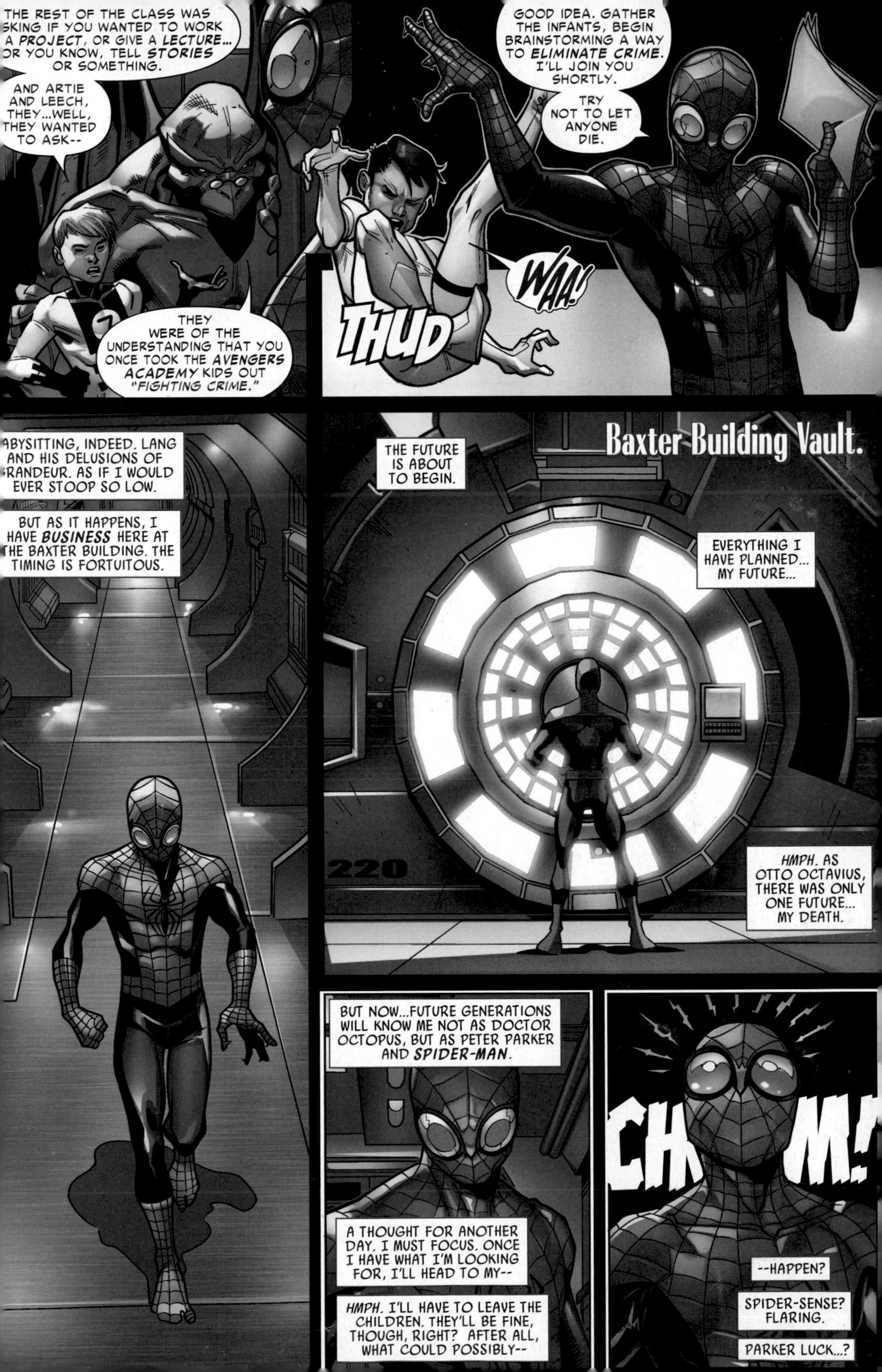
THE REST OF THE CLASS WAS ASKING IF YOU WANTED TO WORK ON A PROJECT, OR GIVE A LECTURE... OR YOU KNOW, TELL STORIES OR SOMETHING.
AND ARTIE AND LEECH, THEY...WELL, THEY WANTED TO ASK--
THEY WERE OF THE UNDERSTANDING THAT YOU ONCE TOOK THE AVENGERS ACADEMY KIDS OUT "FIGHTING CRIME."
GOOD IDEA. GATHER THE INFANTS, BEGIN BRAINSTORMING A WAY TO ELIMINATE CRIME. I'LL JOIN YOU SHORTLY.
TRY NOT TO LET ANYONE DIE.
WAA!
THUD
BABYSITTING, INDEED. LANG AND HIS DELUSIONS OF GRANDEUR. AS IF I WOULD EVER STOOP SO LOW.
BUT AS IT HAPPENS, I HAVE BUSINESS HERE AT THE BAXTER BUILDING. THE TIMING IS FORTUITOUS.
Baxter Building Vault.
THE FUTURE IS ABOUT TO BEGIN.
EVERYTHING I HAVE PLANNED... MY FUTURE...
220
HMPH. AS OTTO OCTAVIUS, THERE WAS ONLY ONE FUTURE... MY DEATH.
BUT NOW...FUTURE GENERATIONS WILL KNOW ME NOT AS DOCTOR OCTOPUS, BUT AS PETER PARKER AND SPIDER-MAN.
A THOUGHT FOR ANOTHER DAY. I MUST FOCUS. ONCE I HAVE WHAT I'M LOOKING FOR, I'LL HEAD TO MY--
HMPH. I'LL HAVE TO LEAVE THE CHILDREN. THEY'LL BE FINE, THOUGH, RIGHT? AFTER ALL, WHAT COULD POSSIBLY--
--HAPPEN?
SPIDER-SENSE? FLARING.
PARKER LUCK...?

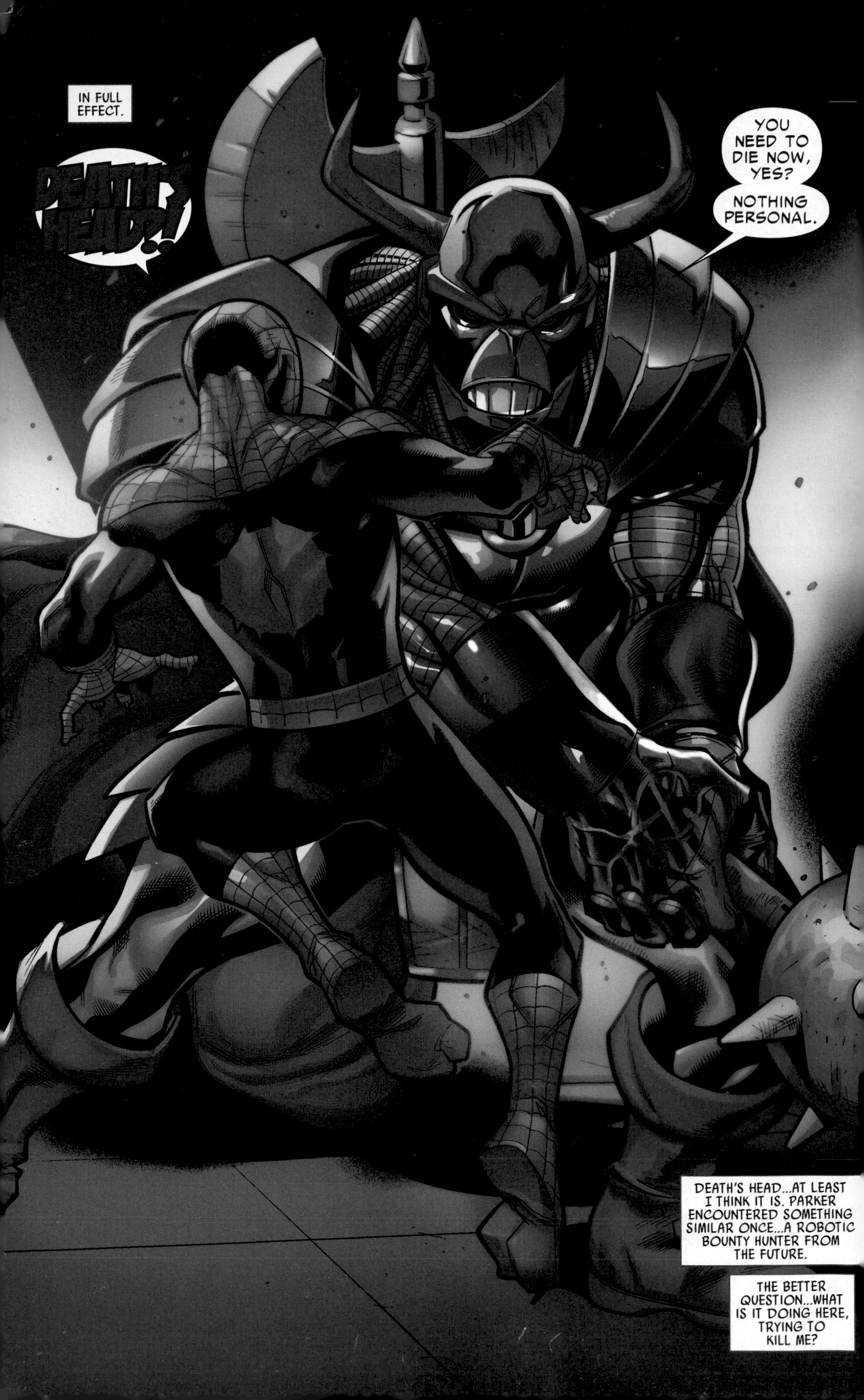
IN FULL EFFECT.
DEATH'S HEAD?!
YOU NEED TO DIE NOW, YES?
NOTHING PERSONAL.
DEATH'S HEAD...AT LEAST I THINK IT IS. PARKER ENCOUNTERED SOMETHING SIMILAR ONCE...A ROBOTIC BOUNTY HUNTER FROM THE FUTURE.
THE BETTER QUESTION...WHAT IS IT DOING HERE, TRYING TO KILL ME?

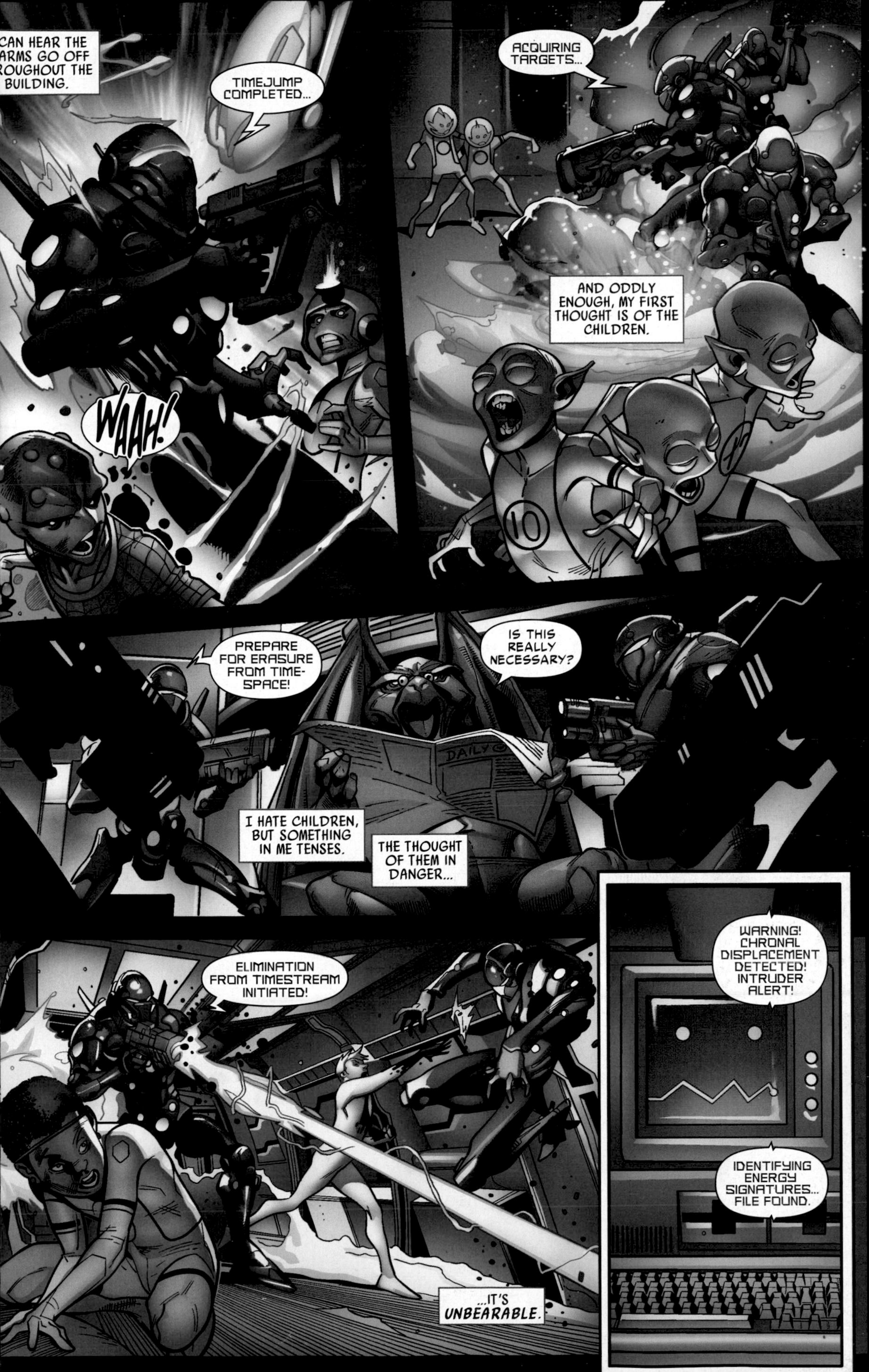
CAN HEAR THE
ARMS GO OFF
ROUGHOUT THE
BUILDING.
TIMEJUMP COMPLETED...
WAAH!
ACQUIRING TARGETS...
AND ODDLY ENOUGH, MY FIRST THOUGHT IS OF THE CHILDREN.
PREPARE FOR ERASURE FROM TIME-SPACE!
IS THIS REALLY NECESSARY?
DAILY
I HATE CHILDREN, BUT SOMETHING IN ME TENSES.
THE THOUGHT OF THEM IN DANGER...
ELIMINATION FROM TIMESTREAM INITIATED!
...IT'S UNBEARABLE.
WARNING! CHRONAL DISPLACEMENT DETECTED! INTRUDER ALERT!
IDENTIFYING ENERGY SIGNATURES... FILE FOUND.

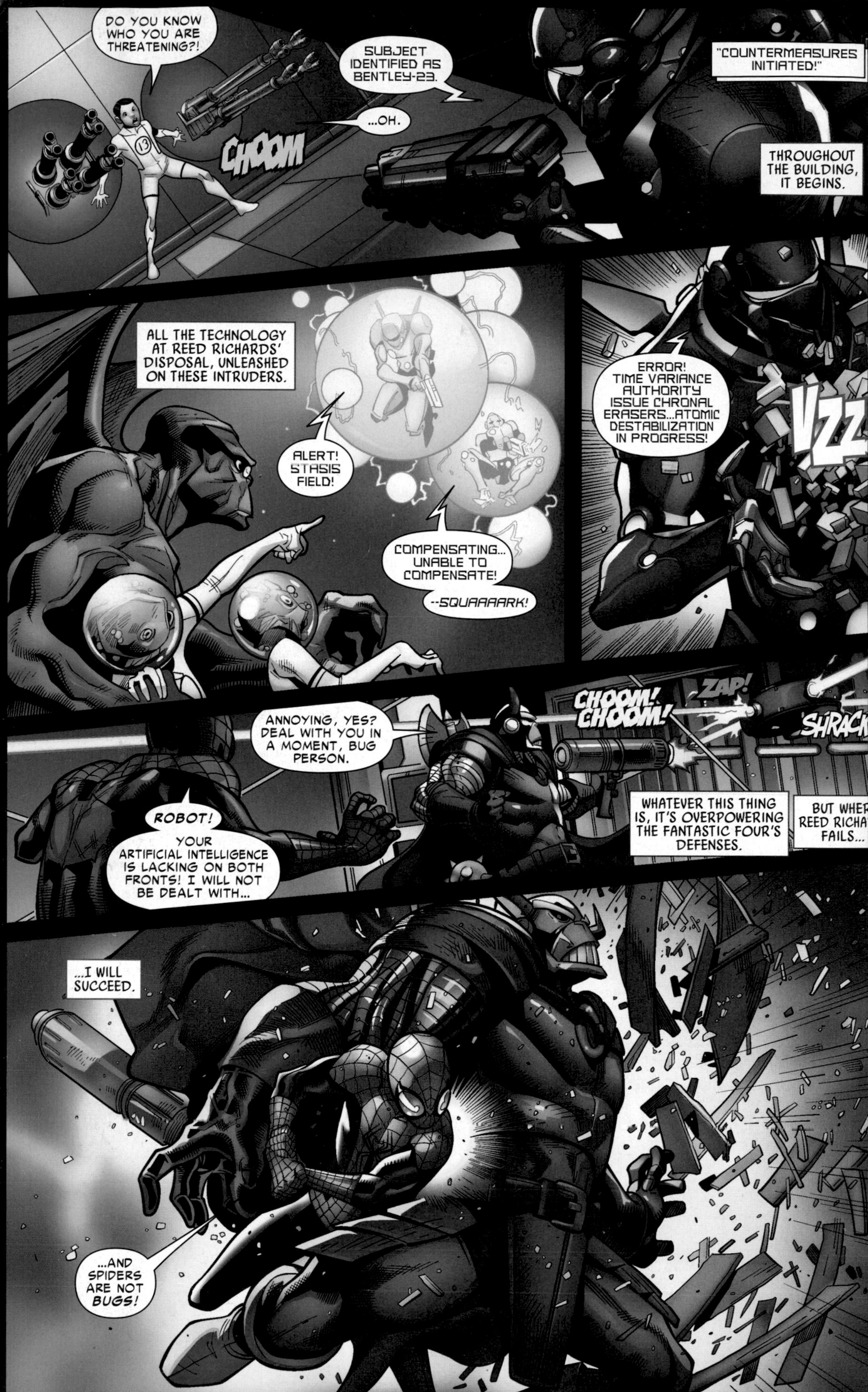

DO YOU KNOW WHO YOU ARE THREATENING?!
SUBJECT IDENTIFIED AS BENTLEY-23.
...OH.
CHOOM
"COUNTERMEASURES INITIATED!"
THROUGHOUT THE BUILDING, IT BEGINS.
ALL THE TECHNOLOGY AT REED RICHARDS' DISPOSAL, UNLEASHED ON THESE INTRUDERS.
ALERT! STASIS FIELD!
COMPENSATING... UNABLE TO COMPENSATE!
--SQUAAAARK!
ERROR! TIME VARIANCE AUTHORITY ISSUE CHRONAL ERASERS...ATOMIC DESTABILIZATION IN PROGRESS!
VZZ
CHOOM! CHOOM!
ZAP!
SHRACK
ANNOYING, YES? DEAL WITH YOU IN A MOMENT, BUG PERSON.
ROBOT! YOUR ARTIFICIAL INTELLIGENCE IS LACKING ON BOTH FRONTS! I WILL NOT BE DEALT WITH...
WHATEVER THIS THING IS, IT'S OVERPOWERING THE FANTASTIC FOUR'S DEFENSES.
BUT WHER REED RICHA FAILS...
...I WILL SUCCEED.
...AND SPIDERS ARE NOT BUGS!

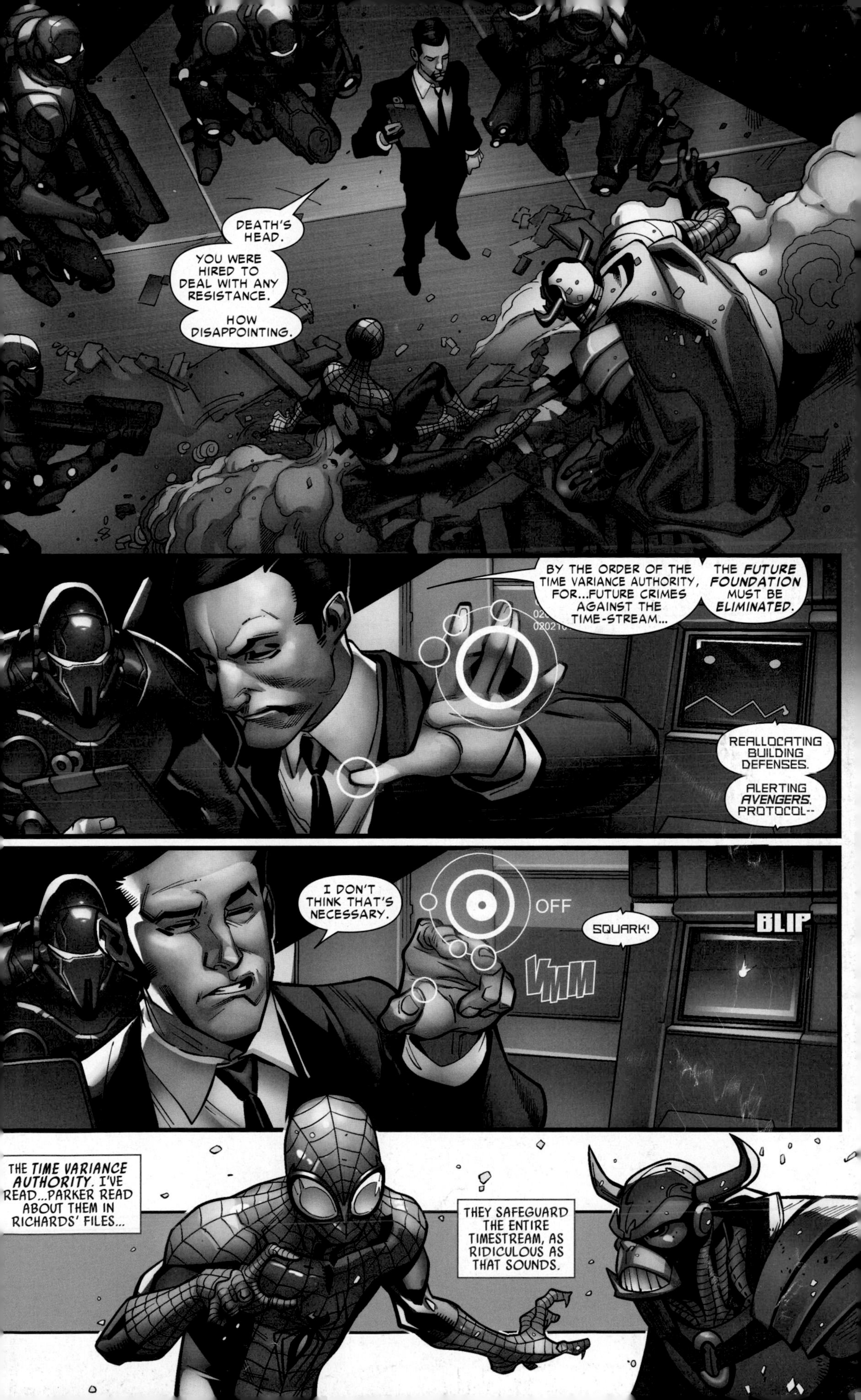
DEATH'S HEAD.
YOU WERE HIRED TO DEAL WITH ANY RESISTANCE.
HOW DISAPPOINTING.
BY THE ORDER OF THE TIME VARIANCE AUTHORITY, FOR...FUTURE CRIMES AGAINST THE TIME-STREAM...
THE *FUTURE FOUNDATION* MUST BE *ELIMINATED*.
REALLOCATING BUILDING DEFENSES.
ALERTING *AVENGERS*. PROTOCOL--
I DON'T THINK THAT'S NECESSARY.
OFF
VMM
SQUARK!
BLIP
THE *TIME VARIANCE AUTHORITY*. I'VE READ...PARKER READ ABOUT THEM IN RICHARDS' FILES...
THEY SAFEGUARD THE ENTIRE TIMESTREAM, AS RIDICULOUS AS THAT SOUNDS.

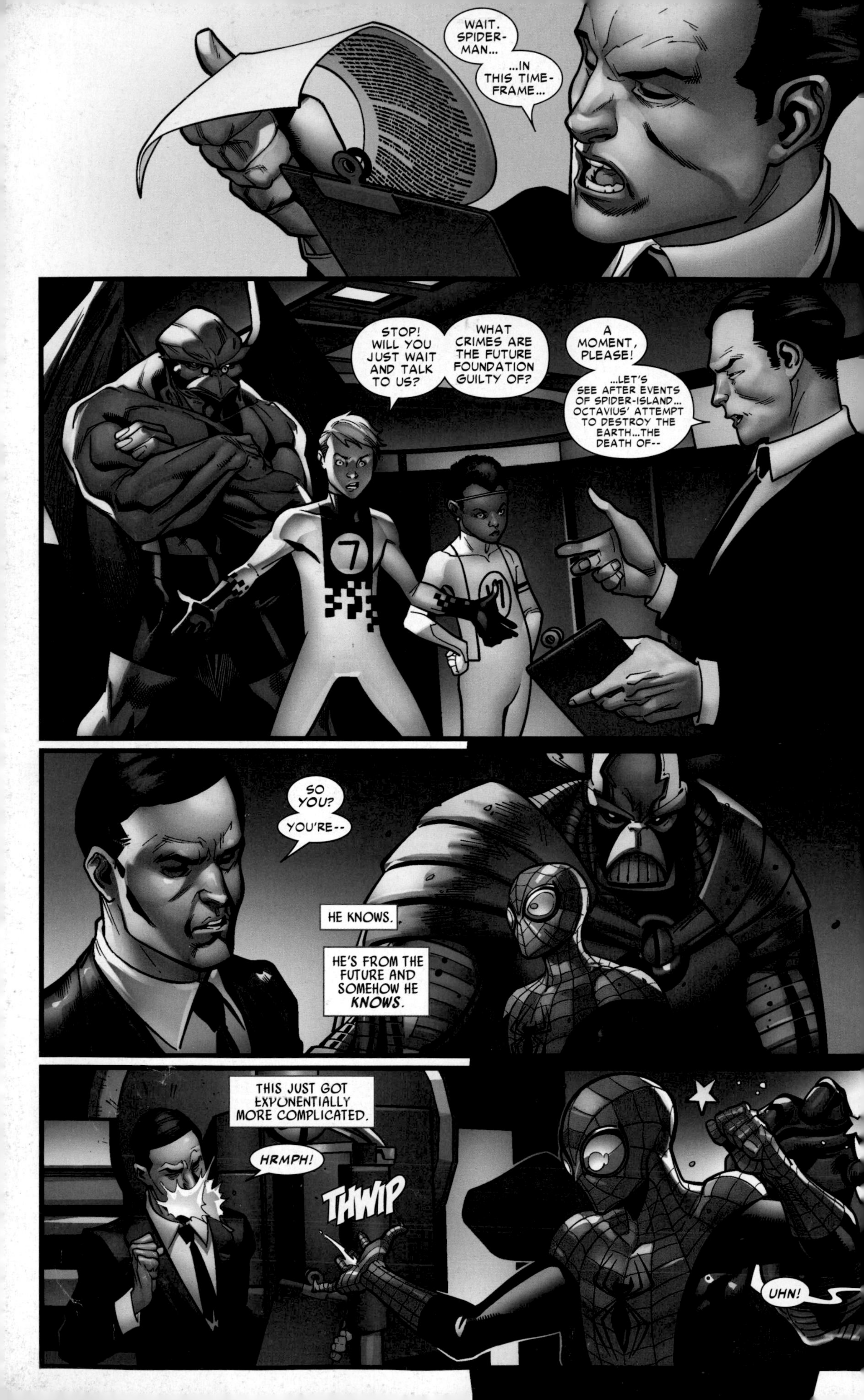
WAIT. SPIDER-MAN...
...IN THIS TIME-FRAME...
STOP! WILL YOU JUST WAIT AND TALK TO US?
WHAT CRIMES ARE THE FUTURE FOUNDATION GUILTY OF?
A MOMENT, PLEASE!
...LET'S SEE AFTER EVENTS OF SPIDER-ISLAND... OCTAVIUS' ATTEMPT TO DESTROY THE EARTH...THE DEATH OF--
SO YOU?
YOU'RE--
HE KNOWS.
HE'S FROM THE FUTURE AND SOMEHOW HE KNOWS.
THIS JUST GOT EXPONENTIALLY MORE COMPLICATED.
HRMPH!
THWIP
UHN!

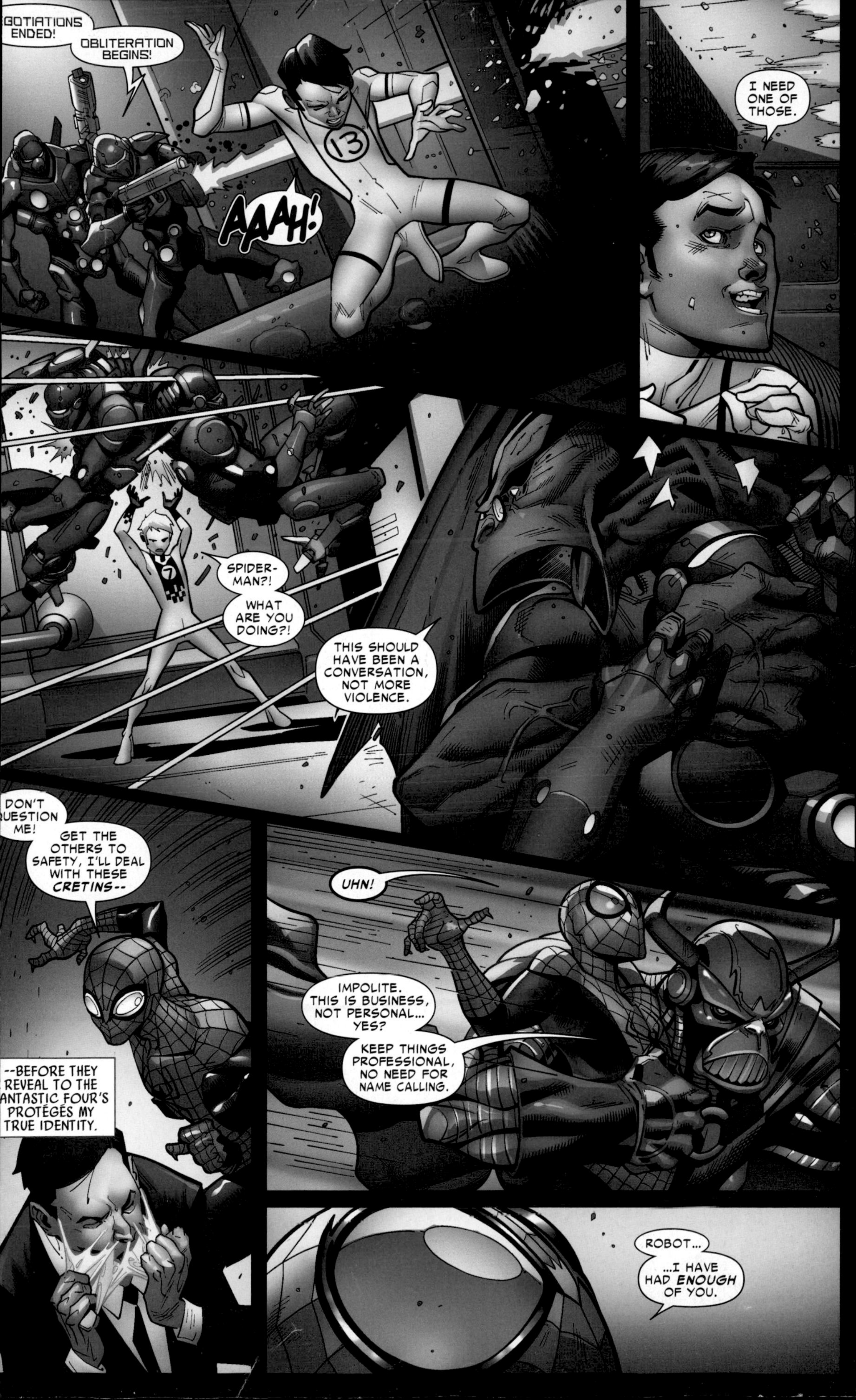
GOTIATIONS ENDED!
OBLITERATION BEGINS!
AAAH!
I NEED ONE OF THOSE.
SPIDER-MAN?!
WHAT ARE YOU DOING?!
THIS SHOULD HAVE BEEN A CONVERSATION, NOT MORE VIOLENCE.
DON'T UESTION ME!
GET THE OTHERS TO SAFETY, I'LL DEAL WITH THESE *CRETINS*--
--BEFORE THEY REVEAL TO THE ANTASTIC FOUR'S PROTÉGÉS MY TRUE IDENTITY.
UHN!
IMPOLITE. THIS IS BUSINESS, NOT PERSONAL... YES?
KEEP THINGS PROFESSIONAL, NO NEED FOR NAME CALLING.
ROBOT...
...I HAVE HAD *ENOUGH* OF YOU.

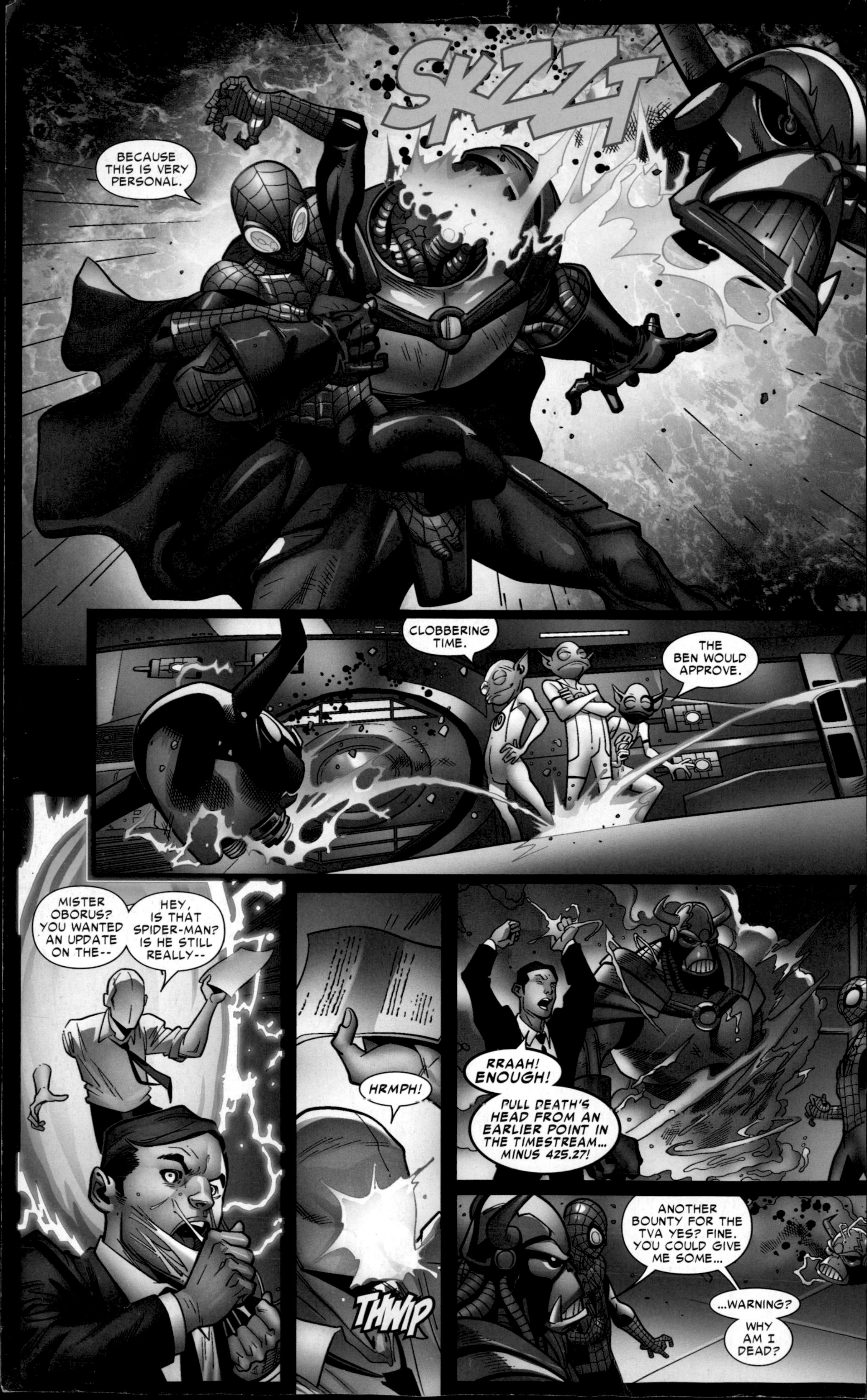
SKZZT
BECAUSE THIS IS VERY PERSONAL.
CLOBBERING TIME.
THE BEN WOULD APPROVE.
MISTER OBORUS? YOU WANTED AN UPDATE ON THE--
HEY, IS THAT SPIDER-MAN? IS HE STILL REALLY--
HRMPH!
THWIP
RRAAH! ENOUGH!
PULL DEATH'S HEAD FROM AN EARLIER POINT IN THE TIMESTREAM... MINUS 425.27!
ANOTHER BOUNTY FOR THE TVA YES? FINE. YOU COULD GIVE ME SOME...
...WARNING?
WHY AM I DEAD?

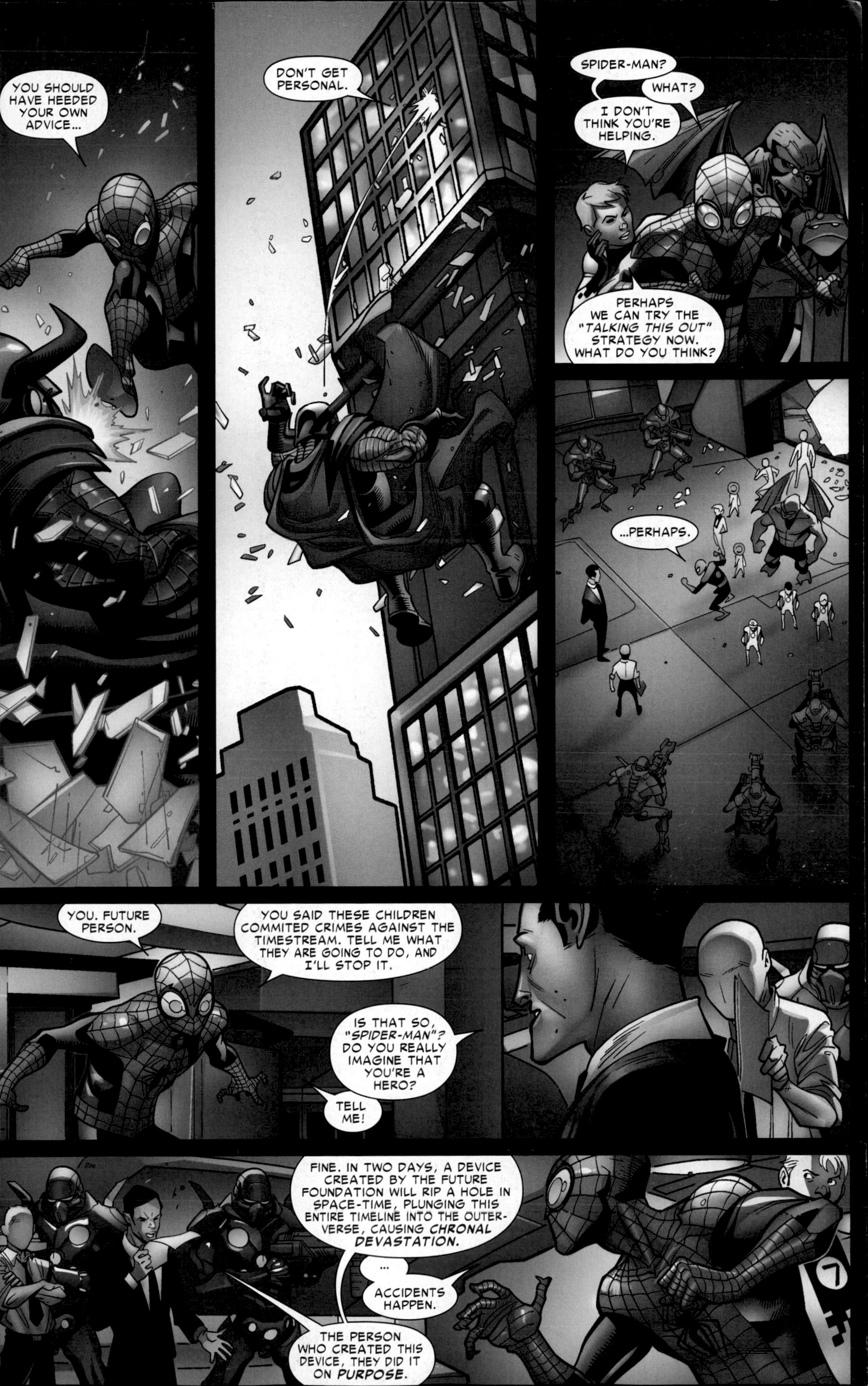
YOU SHOULD HAVE HEEDED YOUR OWN ADVICE...
DON'T GET PERSONAL.
SPIDER-MAN?
WHAT?
I DON'T THINK YOU'RE HELPING.
PERHAPS WE CAN TRY THE "TALKING THIS OUT" STRATEGY NOW. WHAT DO YOU THINK?
...PERHAPS.
YOU. FUTURE PERSON.
YOU SAID THESE CHILDREN COMMITED CRIMES AGAINST THE TIMESTREAM. TELL ME WHAT THEY ARE GOING TO DO, AND I'LL STOP IT.
IS THAT SO, "SPIDER-MAN"? DO YOU REALLY IMAGINE THAT YOU'RE A HERO?
TELL ME!
FINE. IN TWO DAYS, A DEVICE CREATED BY THE FUTURE FOUNDATION WILL RIP A HOLE IN SPACE-TIME, PLUNGING THIS ENTIRE TIMELINE INTO THE OUTER-VERSE, CAUSING CHRONAL DEVASTATION.
...
ACCIDENTS HAPPEN.
THE PERSON WHO CREATED THIS DEVICE, THEY DID IT ON PURPOSE.

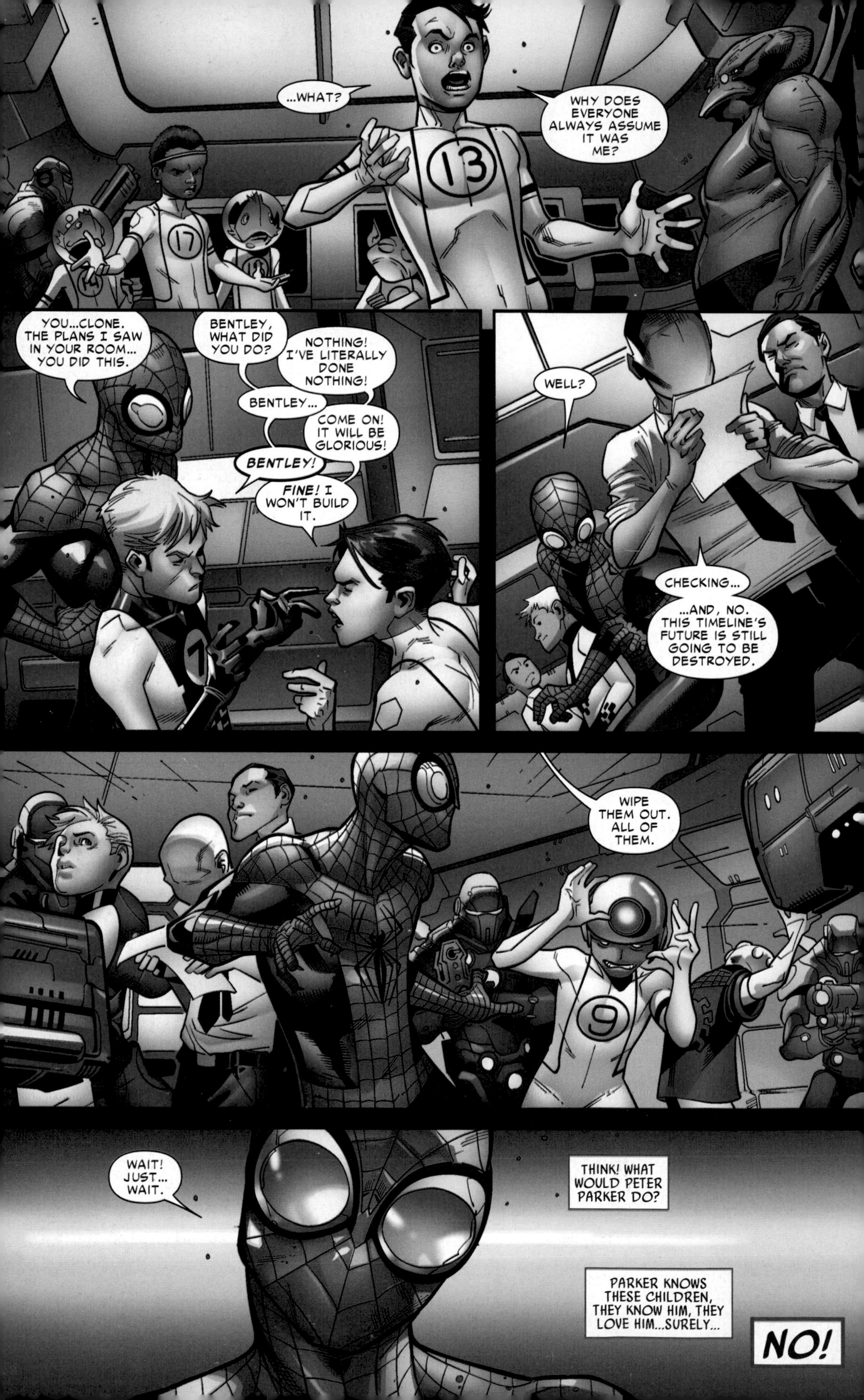
...WHAT?
WHY DOES EVERYONE ALWAYS ASSUME IT WAS ME?
YOU...CLONE. THE PLANS I SAW IN YOUR ROOM... YOU DID THIS.
BENTLEY, WHAT DID YOU DO?
NOTHING! I'VE LITERALLY DONE NOTHING!
BENTLEY...
COME ON! IT WILL BE GLORIOUS!
BENTLEY!
FINE! I WON'T BUILD IT.
WELL?
CHECKING...
...AND, NO. THIS TIMELINE'S FUTURE IS STILL GOING TO BE DESTROYED.
WIPE THEM OUT. ALL OF THEM.
WAIT! JUST... WAIT.
THINK! WHAT WOULD PETER PARKER DO?
PARKER KNOWS THESE CHILDREN, THEY KNOW HIM, THEY LOVE HIM...SURELY...
NO!

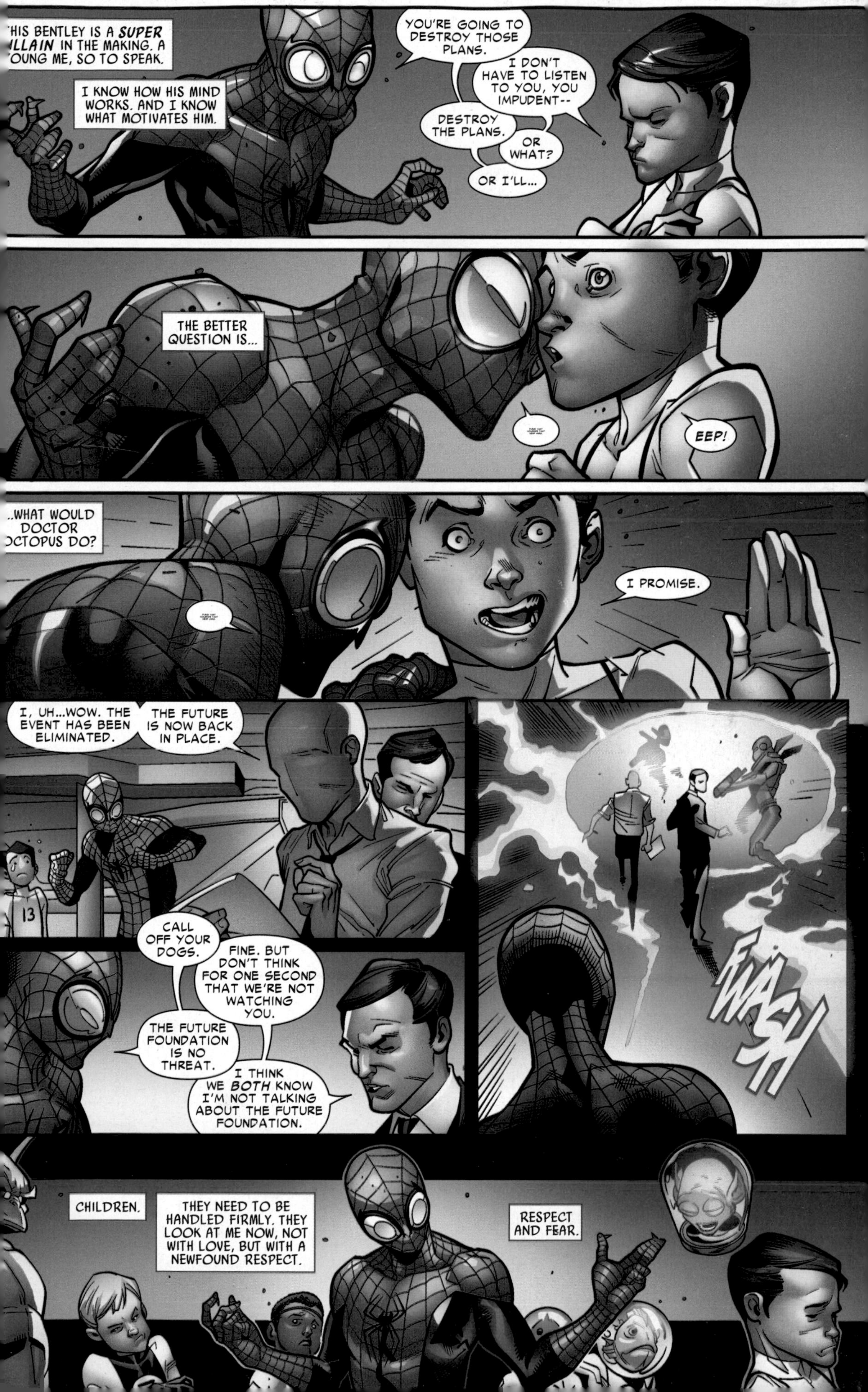

HIS BENTLEY IS A *SUPER* *ILLAIN* IN THE MAKING. A OUNG ME, SO TO SPEAK.
I KNOW HOW HIS MIND WORKS. AND I KNOW WHAT MOTIVATES HIM.
YOU'RE GOING TO DESTROY THOSE PLANS.
I DON'T HAVE TO LISTEN TO YOU, YOU IMPUDENT--
DESTROY THE PLANS.
OR WHAT?
OR I'LL...
THE BETTER QUESTION IS...
*EEP!*
..WHAT WOULD DOCTOR OCTOPUS DO?
I PROMISE.
I, UH...WOW. THE EVENT HAS BEEN ELIMINATED.
THE FUTURE IS NOW BACK IN PLACE.
13
CALL OFF YOUR DOGS.
FINE. BUT DON'T THINK FOR ONE SECOND THAT WE'RE NOT WATCHING YOU.
THE FUTURE FOUNDATION IS NO THREAT.
I THINK WE *BOTH* KNOW I'M NOT TALKING ABOUT THE FUTURE FOUNDATION.
FWASH
CHILDREN.
THEY NEED TO BE HANDLED FIRMLY. THEY LOOK AT ME NOW, NOT WITH LOVE, BUT WITH A NEWFOUND RESPECT.
RESPECT AND FEAR.

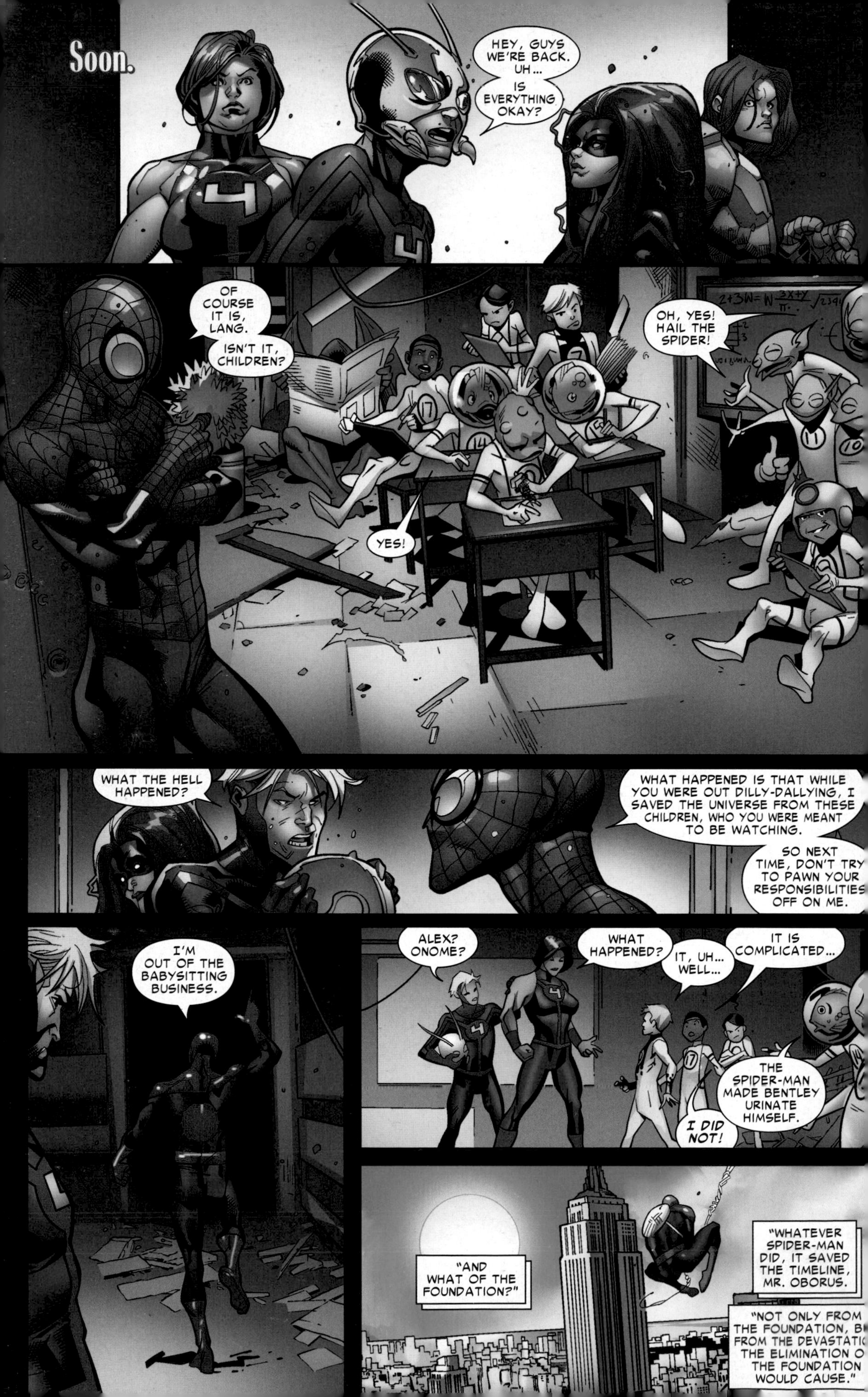
Soon.
HEY, GUYS WE'RE BACK. UH... IS EVERYTHING OKAY?
OF COURSE IT IS, LANG.
ISN'T IT, CHILDREN?
OH, YES! HAIL THE SPIDER!
YES!
WHAT THE HELL HAPPENED?
WHAT HAPPENED IS THAT WHILE YOU WERE OUT DILLY-DALLYING, I SAVED THE UNIVERSE FROM THESE CHILDREN, WHO YOU WERE MEANT TO BE WATCHING.
SO NEXT TIME, DON'T TRY TO PAWN YOUR RESPONSIBILITIES OFF ON ME.
I'M OUT OF THE BABYSITTING BUSINESS.
ALEX? ONOME?
WHAT HAPPENED?
IT, UH... WELL...
IT IS COMPLICATED...
THE SPIDER-MAN MADE BENTLEY URINATE HIMSELF.
I DID NOT!
"AND WHAT OF THE FOUNDATION?"
"WHATEVER SPIDER-MAN DID, IT SAVED THE TIMELINE, MR. OBORUS.
"NOT ONLY FROM THE FOUNDATION, B FROM THE DEVASTATI THE ELIMINATION O THE FOUNDATION WOULD CAUSE."

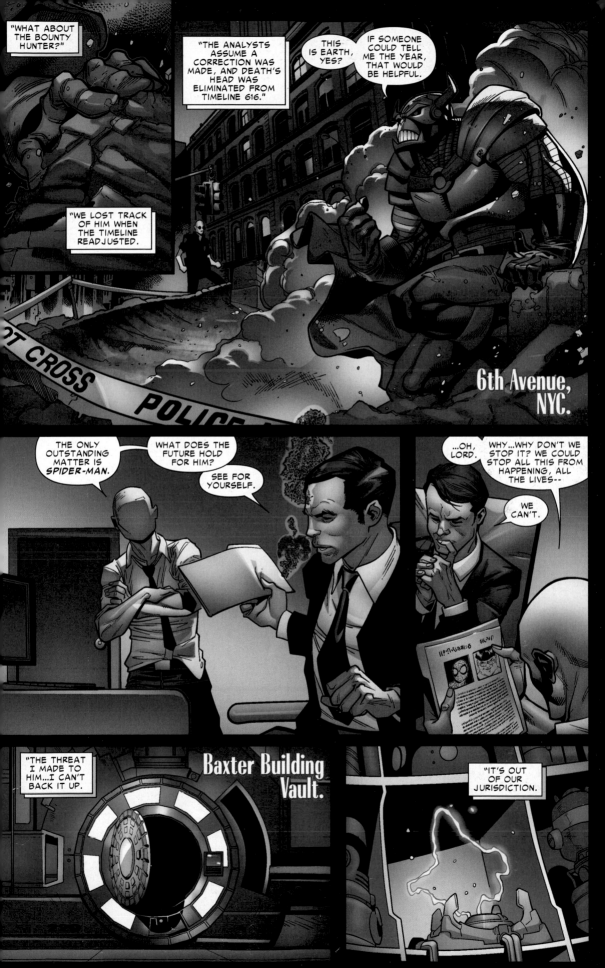

"WHAT ABOUT THE BOUNTY HUNTER?"

"THE ANALYSTS ASSUME A CORRECTION WAS MADE, AND DEATH'S HEAD WAS ELIMINATED FROM TIMELINE 616."

THIS IS EARTH, YES?

IF SOMEONE COULD TELL ME THE YEAR, THAT WOULD BE HELPFUL.

"WE LOST TRACK OF HIM WHEN THE TIMELINE READJUSTED."

6th Avenue, NYC.

THE ONLY OUTSTANDING MATTER IS SPIDER-MAN.

WHAT DOES THE FUTURE HOLD FOR HIM?

SEE FOR YOURSELF.

...OH, LORD.

WHY...WHY DON'T WE STOP IT? WE COULD STOP ALL THIS FROM HAPPENING, ALL THE LIVES--

WE CAN'T.

"THE THREAT I MADE TO HIM...I CAN'T BACK IT UP.

Baxter Building Vault.

"IT'S OUT OF OUR JURISDICTION.

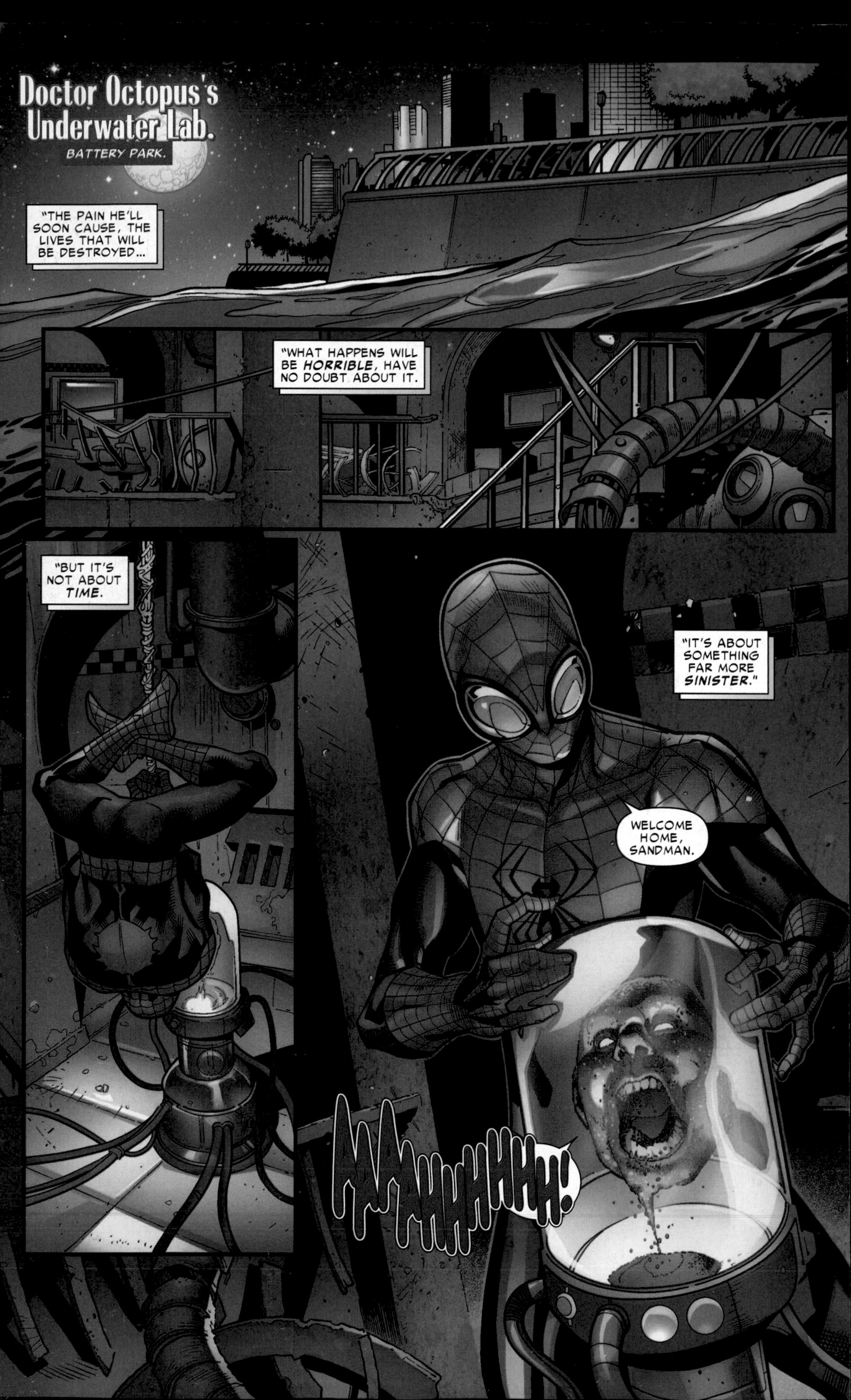

Doctor Octopus's Underwater Lab.
BATTERY PARK.
"THE PAIN HE'LL SOON CAUSE, THE LIVES THAT WILL BE DESTROYED...
"WHAT HAPPENS WILL BE HORRIBLE, HAVE NO DOUBT ABOUT IT.
"BUT IT'S NOT ABOUT TIME.
"IT'S ABOUT SOMETHING FAR MORE SINISTER."
WELCOME HOME, SANDMAN.
AAAHHHHHHH!

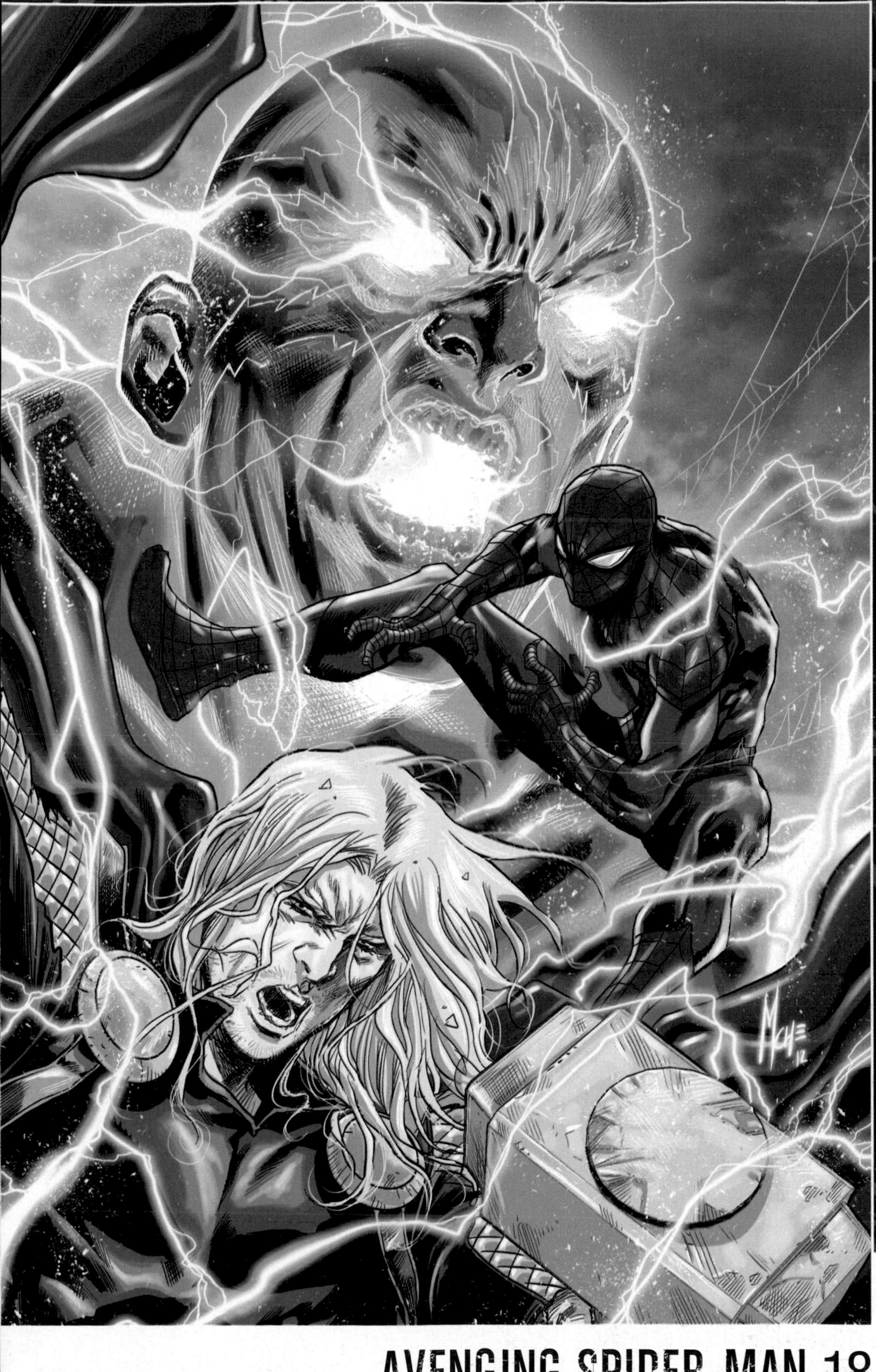

AVENGING SPIDER-MAN 18

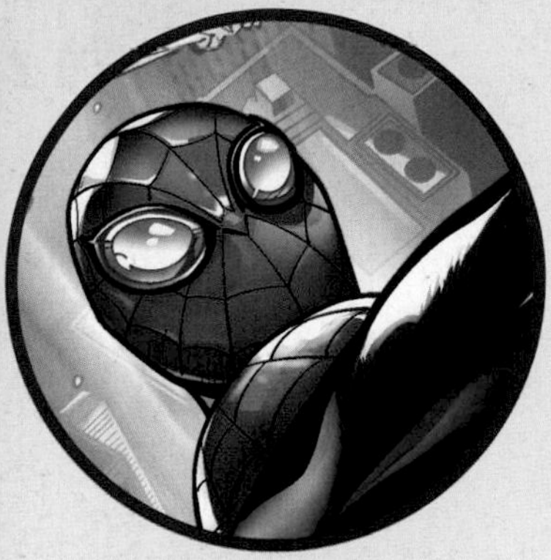

OTTO OCTAVIUS, the villain known as DOCTOR OCTOPUS, was dying. In order to cheat death, he used his skills as a mad scientist to swap minds with his greatest enemy, PETER PARK the spectacular SPIDER-MAN.

However, the transfer gave Octavius MORE than just SPIDER-MAN'S great powers, it gave him PARKER'S experiences as well… including the lesson of great responsibility! Now Otto Octavius beginning a NEW life as a hero—possibly the greatest hero of all. He is the--

# THE SUPERIOR SPIDER-MAN

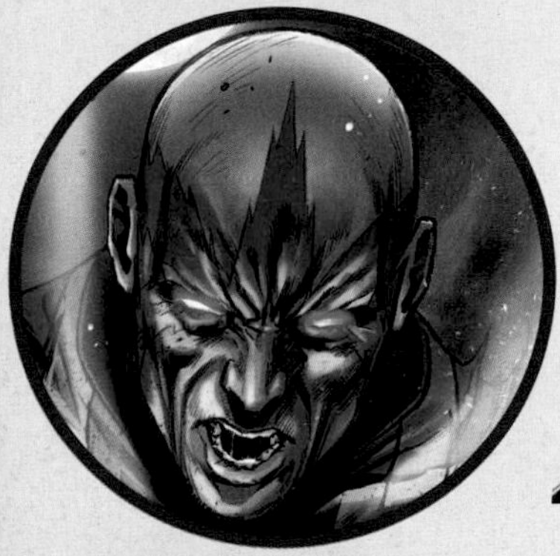

MAX DILLON was an engineer who was electrocuted while repairing a power line. The shock cause a mutation within his body that turned him into a human electrical capacitor. He turned to a life crime, calling himself…

# ELECTRO

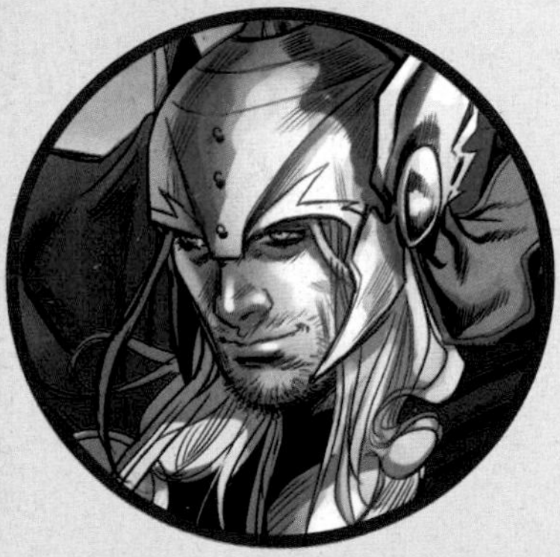

There is only one God of Thunder and he is known as…

# THE MIGHTY THOR

## *PREVIOUSLY…*

Several months ago, The Avengers fought the Sinister Six. When Electro took the form of pure electricity, Thor used his hammer to absorb the villain like lightning and shoot him into space. It brok Aroldis Chapman's record for the world's fastest pitch. Electro has not been seen since.

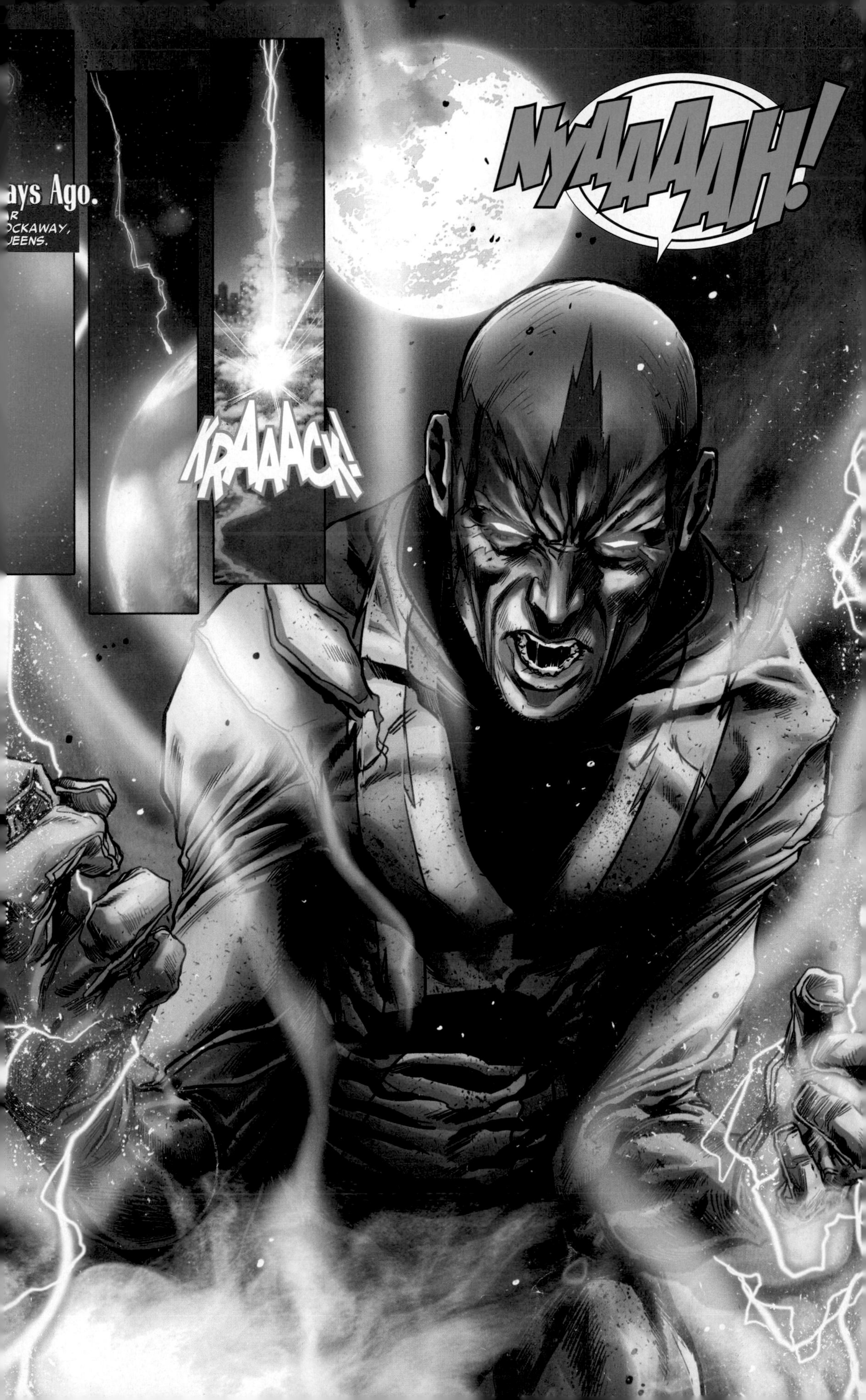

ays Ago.
R
OCKAWAY,
UEENS.
KRAAACK!
NYAAAAAH!

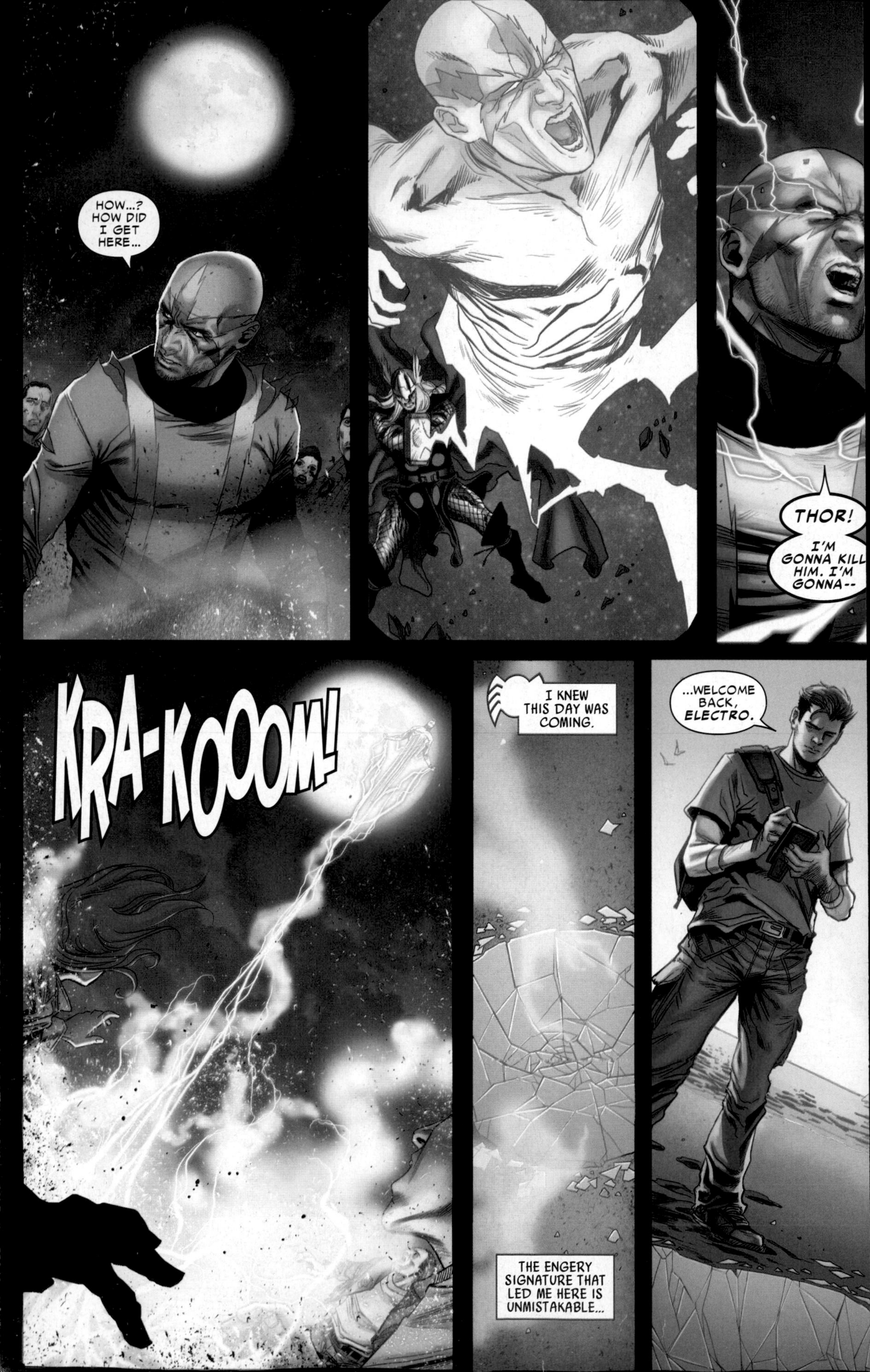
HOW...? HOW DID I GET HERE...
THOR!
I'M GONNA KILL HIM. I'M GONNA--
KRA-KOOOM!
I KNEW THIS DAY WAS COMING.
THE ENGERY SIGNATURE THAT LED ME HERE IS UNMISTAKABLE...
...WELCOME BACK, ELECTRO.

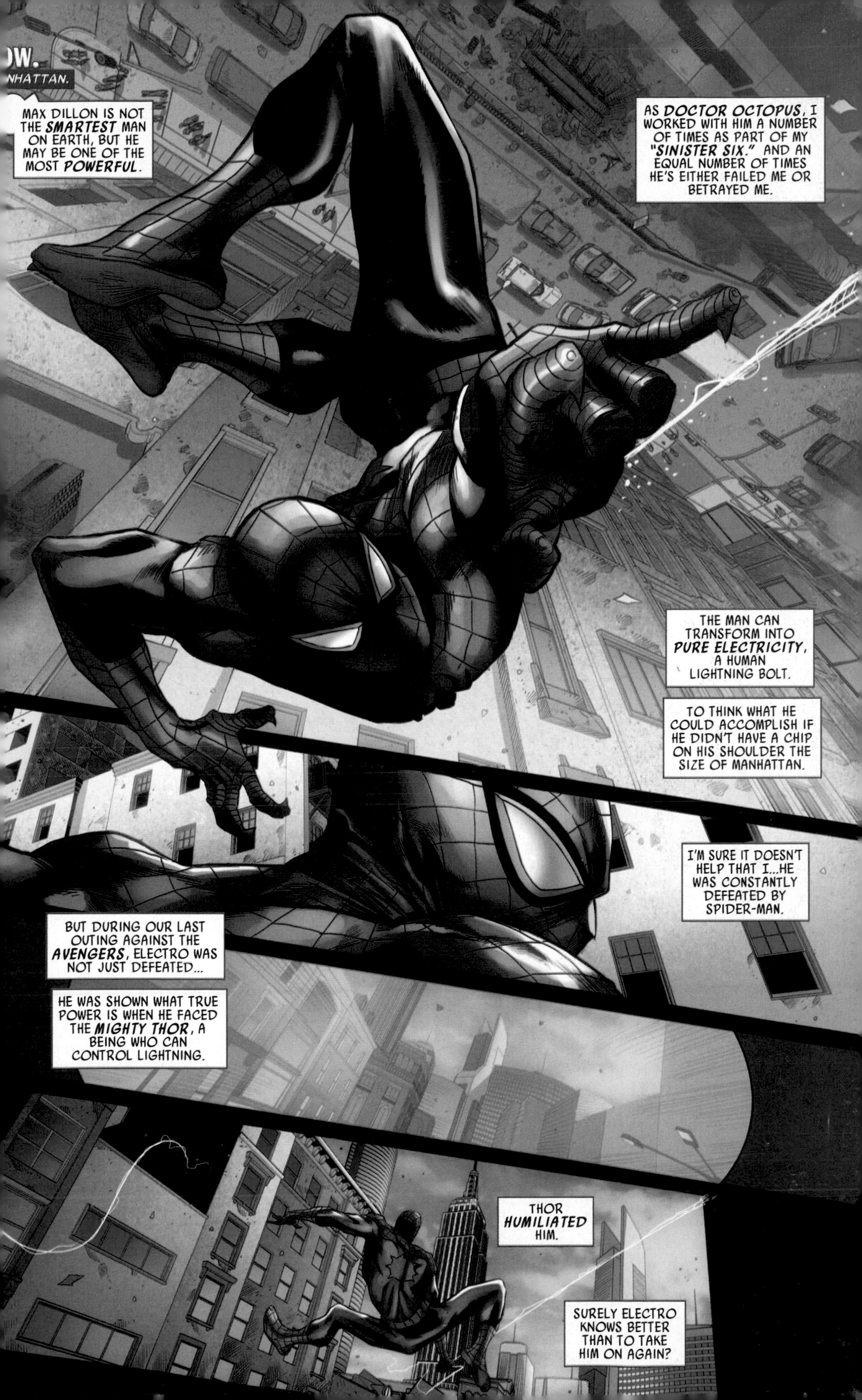

MAX DILLON IS NOT THE SMARTEST MAN ON EARTH, BUT HE MAY BE ONE OF THE MOST POWERFUL.
AS DOCTOR OCTOPUS, I WORKED WITH HIM A NUMBER OF TIMES AS PART OF MY "SINISTER SIX." AND AN EQUAL NUMBER OF TIMES HE'S EITHER FAILED ME OR BETRAYED ME.
THE MAN CAN TRANSFORM INTO PURE ELECTRICITY, A HUMAN LIGHTNING BOLT.
TO THINK WHAT HE COULD ACCOMPLISH IF HE DIDN'T HAVE A CHIP ON HIS SHOULDER THE SIZE OF MANHATTAN.
I'M SURE IT DOESN'T HELP THAT I...HE WAS CONSTANTLY DEFEATED BY SPIDER-MAN.
BUT DURING OUR LAST OUTING AGAINST THE AVENGERS, ELECTRO WAS NOT JUST DEFEATED...
HE WAS SHOWN WHAT TRUE POWER IS WHEN HE FACED THE MIGHTY THOR, A BEING WHO CAN CONTROL LIGHTNING.
THOR HUMILIATED HIM.
SURELY ELECTRO KNOWS BETTER THAN TO TAKE HIM ON AGAIN?

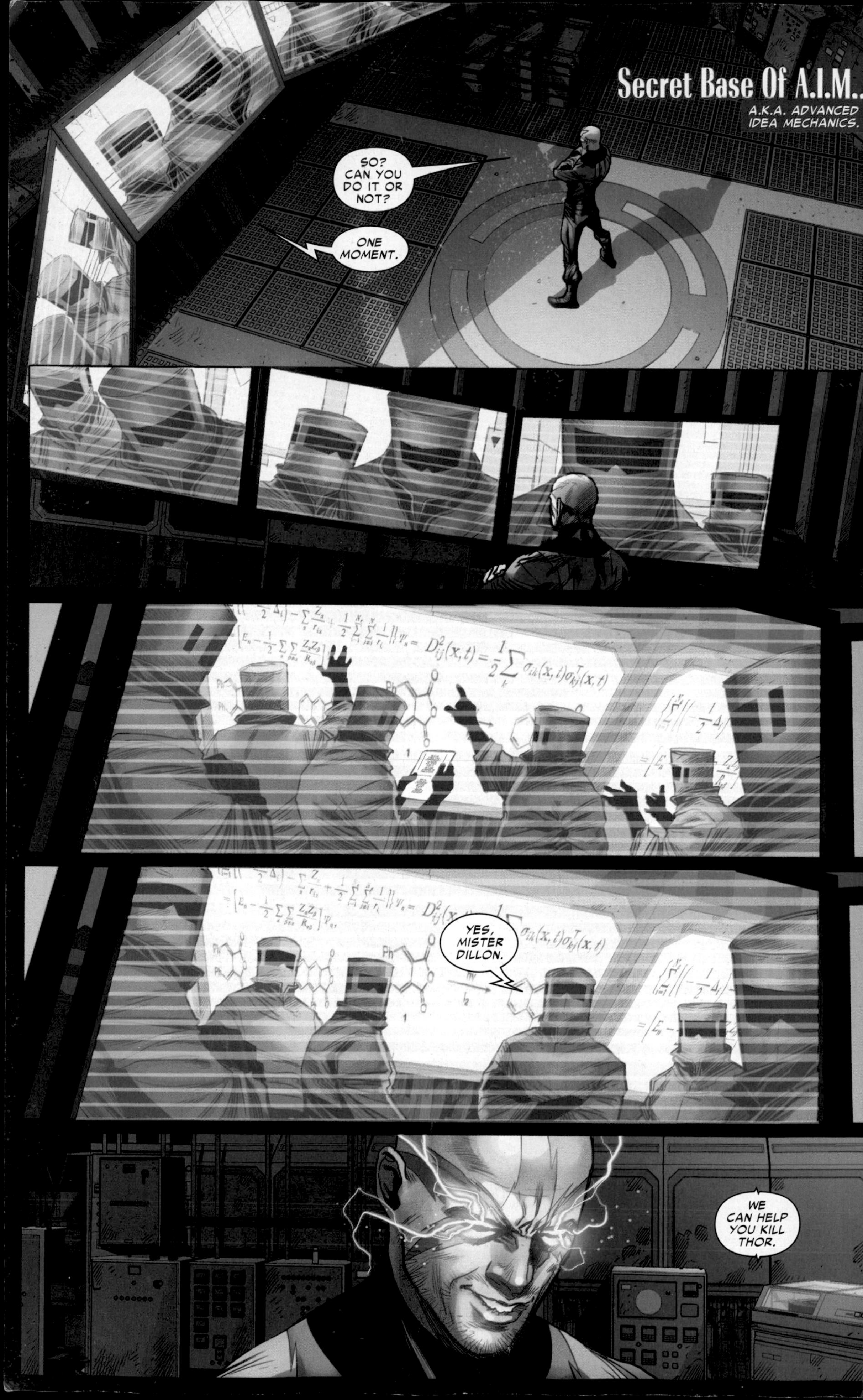
Secret Base Of A.I.M...
A.K.A. ADVANCED IDEA MECHANICS.
SO? CAN YOU DO IT OR NOT?
ONE MOMENT.
YES, MISTER DILLON.
WE CAN HELP YOU KILL THOR.

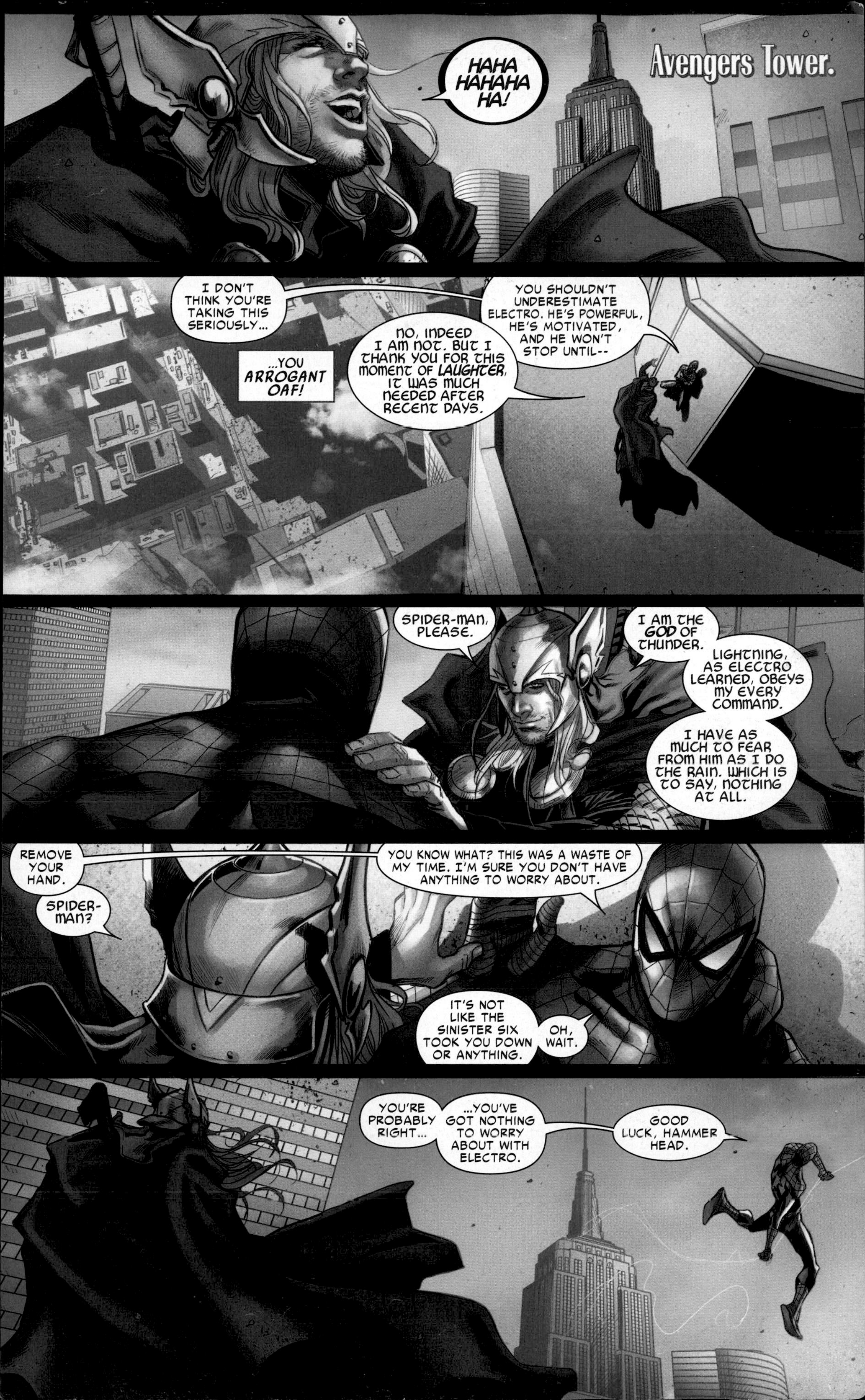
Avengers Tower.
HAHA HAHAHA HA!
I DON'T THINK YOU'RE TAKING THIS SERIOUSLY...
...YOU ARROGANT OAF!
YOU SHOULDN'T UNDERESTIMATE ELECTRO. HE'S POWERFUL, HE'S MOTIVATED, AND HE WON'T STOP UNTIL--
NO, INDEED I AM NOT. BUT I THANK YOU FOR THIS MOMENT OF LAUGHTER, IT WAS MUCH NEEDED AFTER RECENT DAYS.
SPIDER-MAN, PLEASE.
I AM THE GOD OF THUNDER.
LIGHTNING, AS ELECTRO LEARNED, OBEYS MY EVERY COMMAND.
I HAVE AS MUCH TO FEAR FROM HIM AS I DO THE RAIN. WHICH IS TO SAY, NOTHING AT ALL.
REMOVE YOUR HAND.
YOU KNOW WHAT? THIS WAS A WASTE OF MY TIME. I'M SURE YOU DON'T HAVE ANYTHING TO WORRY ABOUT.
SPIDER-MAN?
IT'S NOT LIKE THE SINISTER SIX TOOK YOU DOWN OR ANYTHING.
OH, WAIT.
YOU'RE PROBABLY RIGHT...
...YOU'VE GOT NOTHING TO WORRY ABOUT WITH ELECTRO.
GOOD LUCK, HAMMER HEAD.

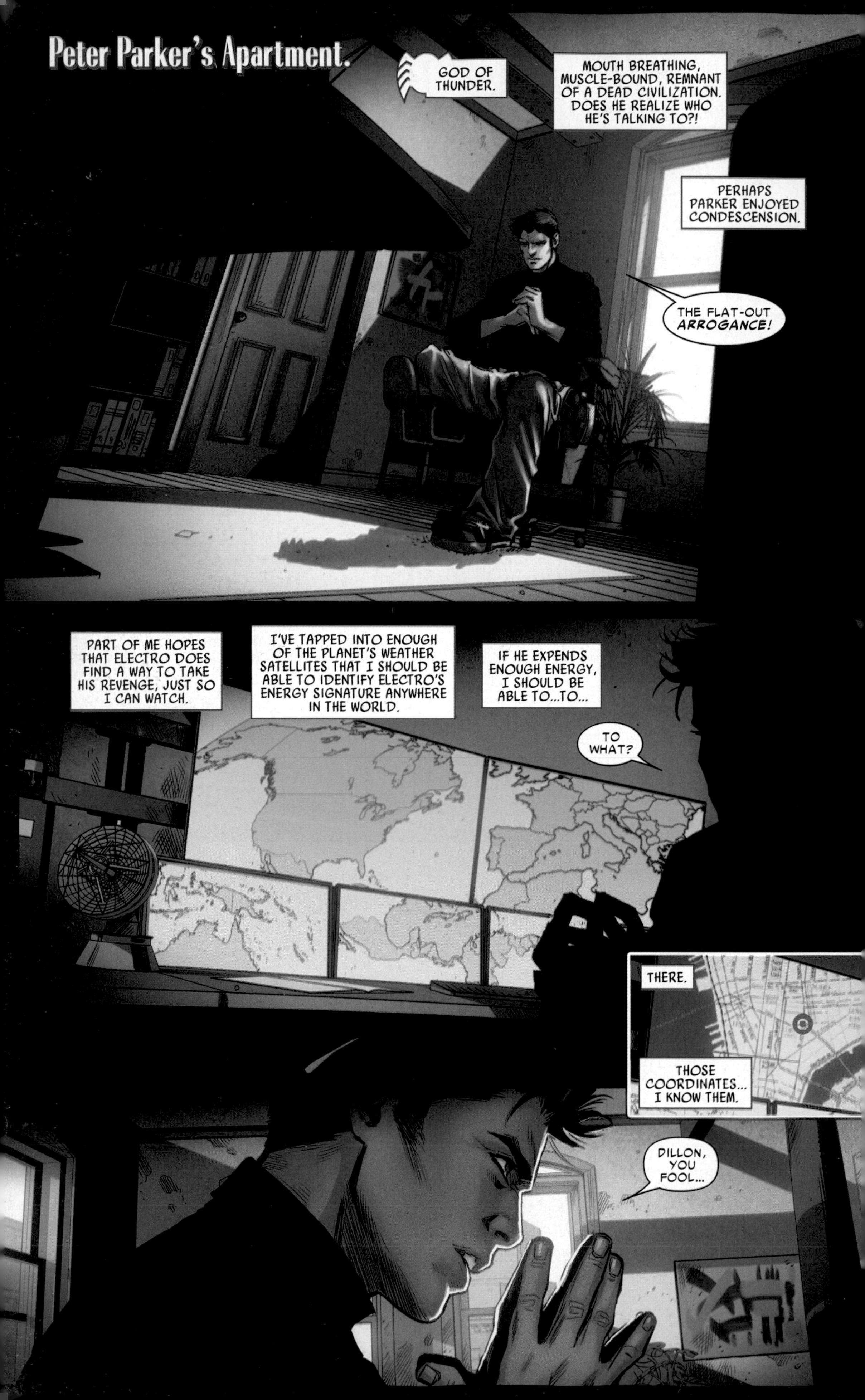
Peter Parker's Apartment.
GOD OF THUNDER.
MOUTH BREATHING, MUSCLE-BOUND, REMNANT OF A DEAD CIVILIZATION. DOES HE REALIZE WHO HE'S TALKING TO?!
PERHAPS PARKER ENJOYED CONDESCENSION.
THE FLAT-OUT ARROGANCE!
PART OF ME HOPES THAT ELECTRO DOES FIND A WAY TO TAKE HIS REVENGE, JUST SO I CAN WATCH.
I'VE TAPPED INTO ENOUGH OF THE PLANET'S WEATHER SATELLITES THAT I SHOULD BE ABLE TO IDENTIFY ELECTRO'S ENERGY SIGNATURE ANYWHERE IN THE WORLD.
IF HE EXPENDS ENOUGH ENERGY, I SHOULD BE ABLE TO...TO...
TO WHAT?
THERE.
THOSE COORDINATES... I KNOW THEM.
DILLON, YOU FOOL...

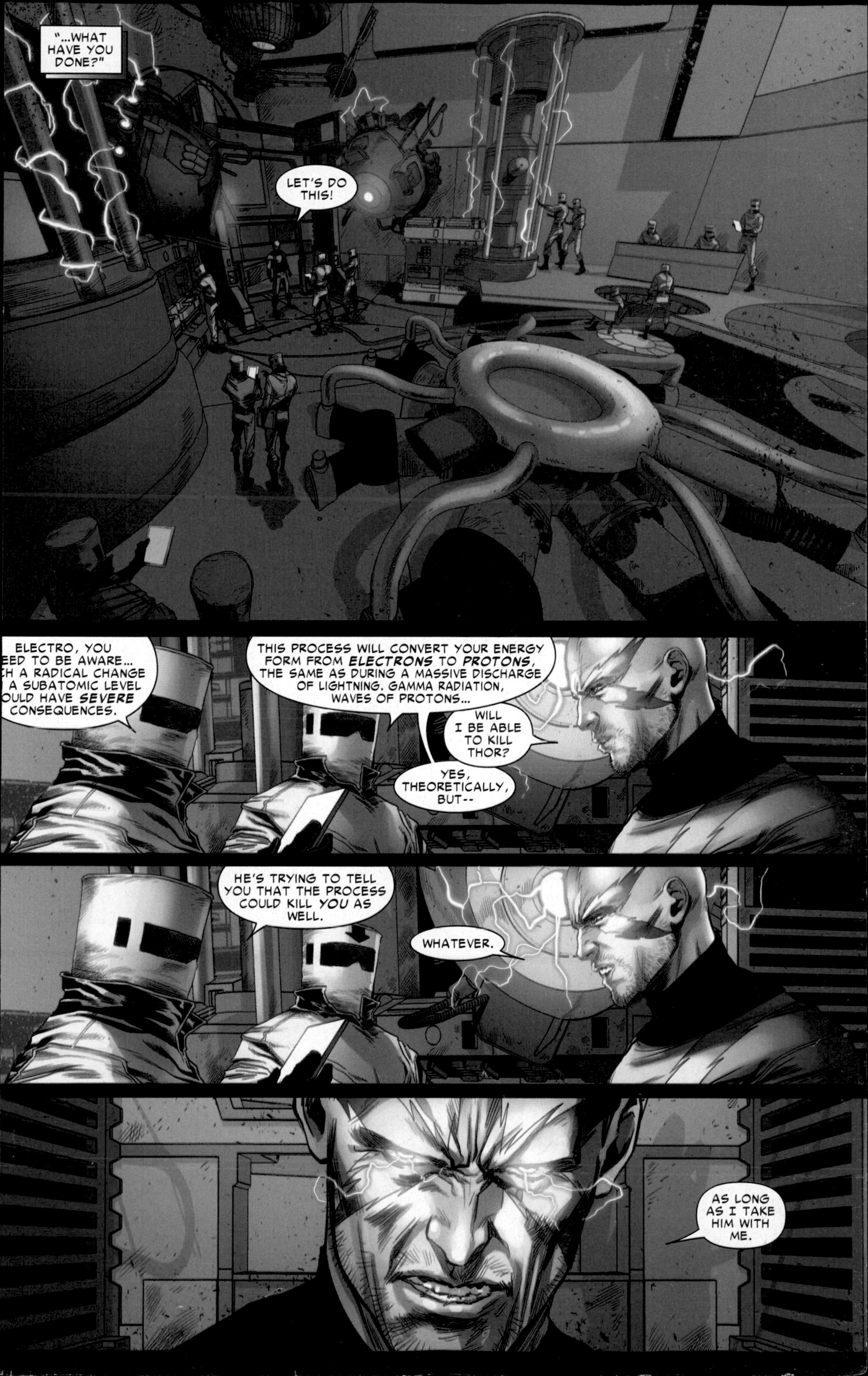
"...WHAT HAVE YOU DONE?"
LET'S DO THIS!
ELECTRO, YOU EED TO BE AWARE... CH A RADICAL CHANGE A SUBATOMIC LEVEL OULD HAVE SEVERE CONSEQUENCES.
THIS PROCESS WILL CONVERT YOUR ENERGY FORM FROM ELECTRONS TO PROTONS, THE SAME AS DURING A MASSIVE DISCHARGE OF LIGHTNING. GAMMA RADIATION, WAVES OF PROTONS...
WILL I BE ABLE TO KILL THOR?
YES, THEORETICALLY, BUT--
HE'S TRYING TO TELL YOU THAT THE PROCESS COULD KILL YOU AS WELL.
WHATEVER.
AS LONG AS I TAKE HIM WITH ME.

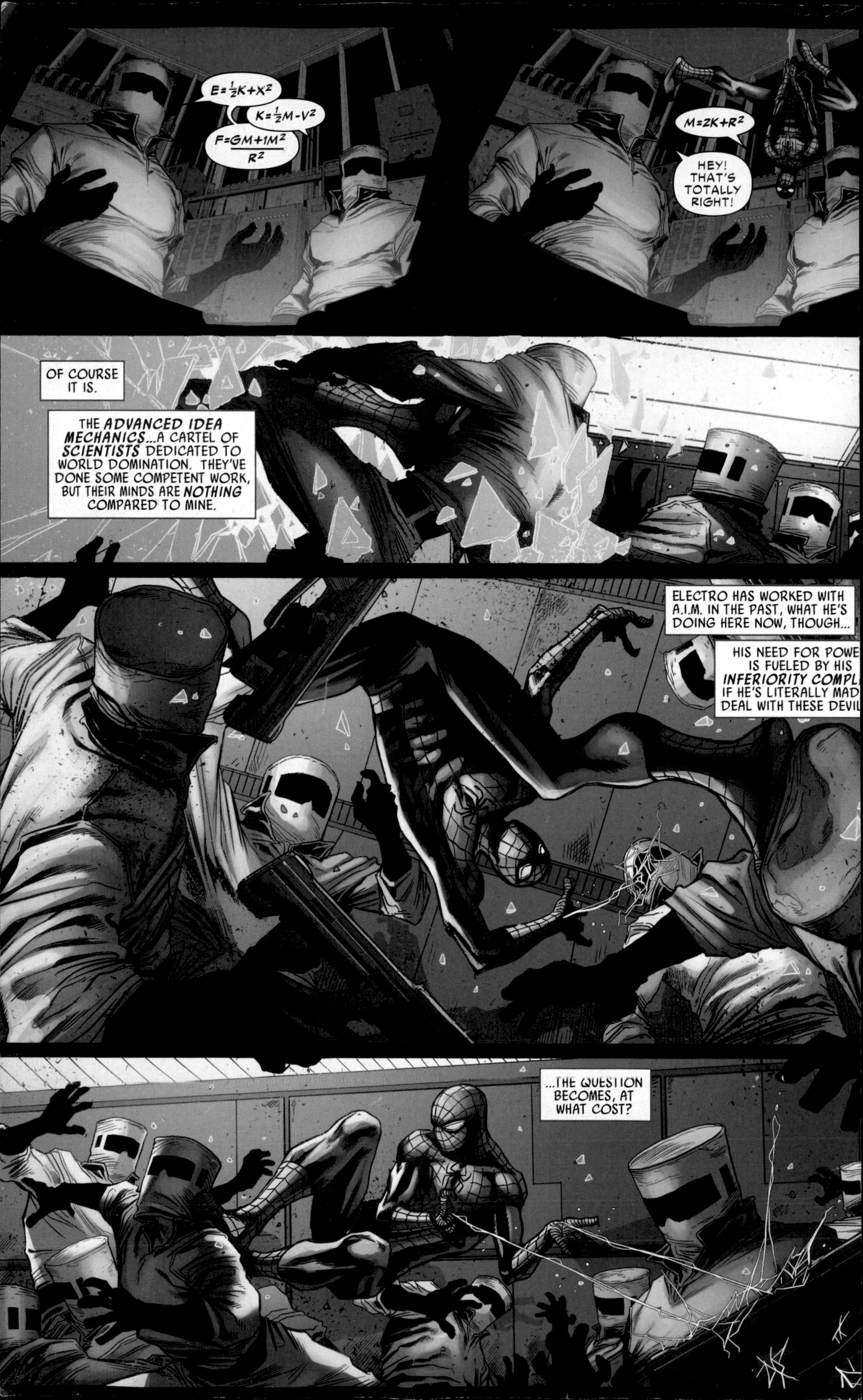

$E=\frac{1}{2}K+X^2$
$K=\frac{1}{2}M-V^2$
$F=\frac{GM+1M^2}{R^2}$
$M=2K+R^2$
HEY! THAT'S TOTALLY RIGHT!
OF COURSE IT IS.
THE ADVANCED IDEA MECHANICS...A CARTEL OF SCIENTISTS DEDICATED TO WORLD DOMINATION. THEY'VE DONE SOME COMPETENT WORK, BUT THEIR MINDS ARE NOTHING COMPARED TO MINE.
ELECTRO HAS WORKED WITH A.I.M. IN THE PAST. WHAT HE'S DOING HERE NOW, THOUGH...
HIS NEED FOR POWE IS FUELED BY HIS INFERIORITY COMPL IF HE'S LITERALLY MAD DEAL WITH THESE DEVIL
...THE QUESTION BECOMES, AT WHAT COST?

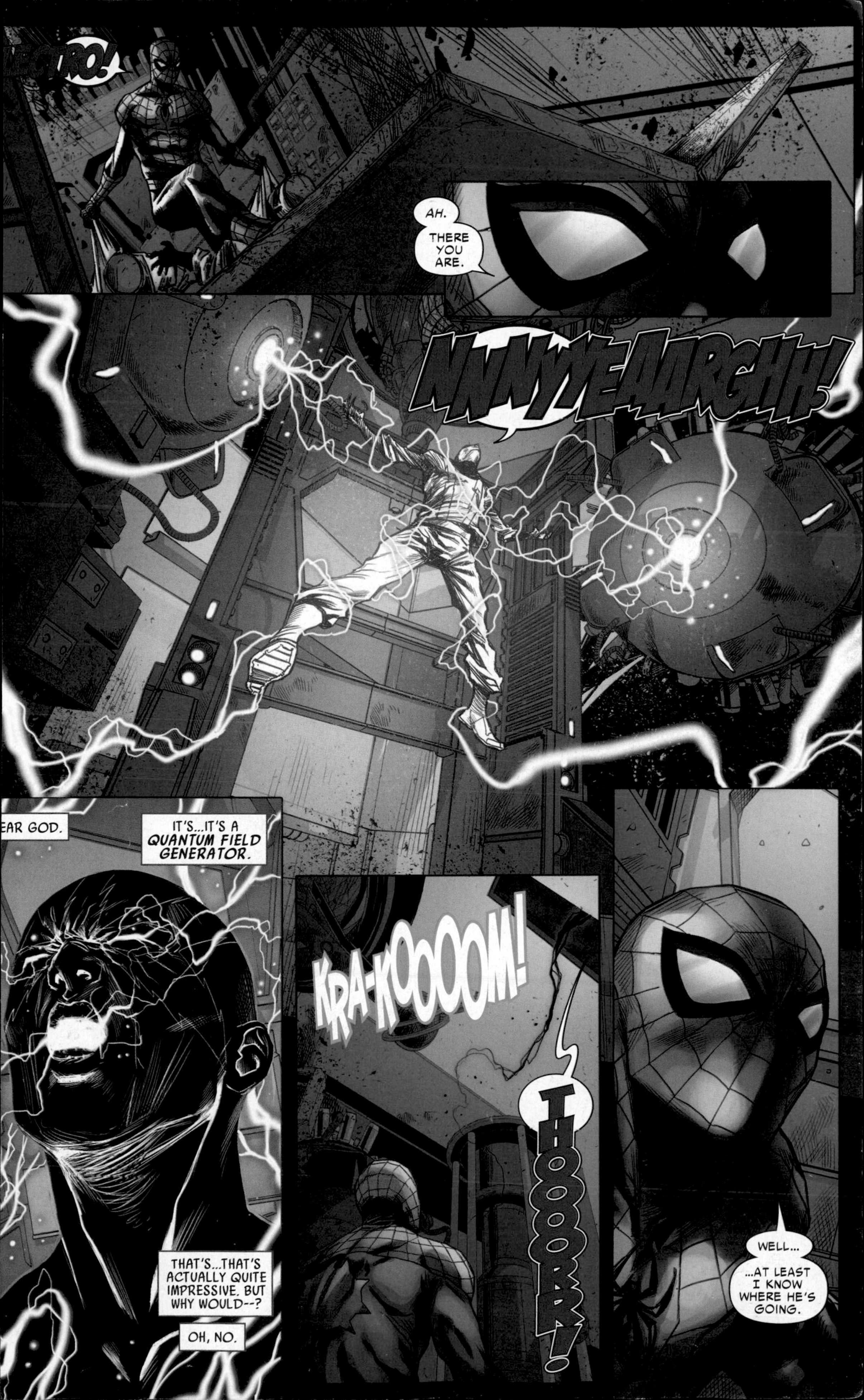

ECTRO!
AH.
THERE YOU ARE.
NNNYYEAARGHH!
EAR GOD.
IT'S...IT'S A *QUANTUM FIELD GENERATOR.*
THAT'S...THAT'S ACTUALLY QUITE IMPRESSIVE. BUT WHY WOULD--?
OH, NO.
KRA-KOOOOM!
THOOOORR!
WELL...
...AT LEAST I KNOW WHERE HE'S GOING.

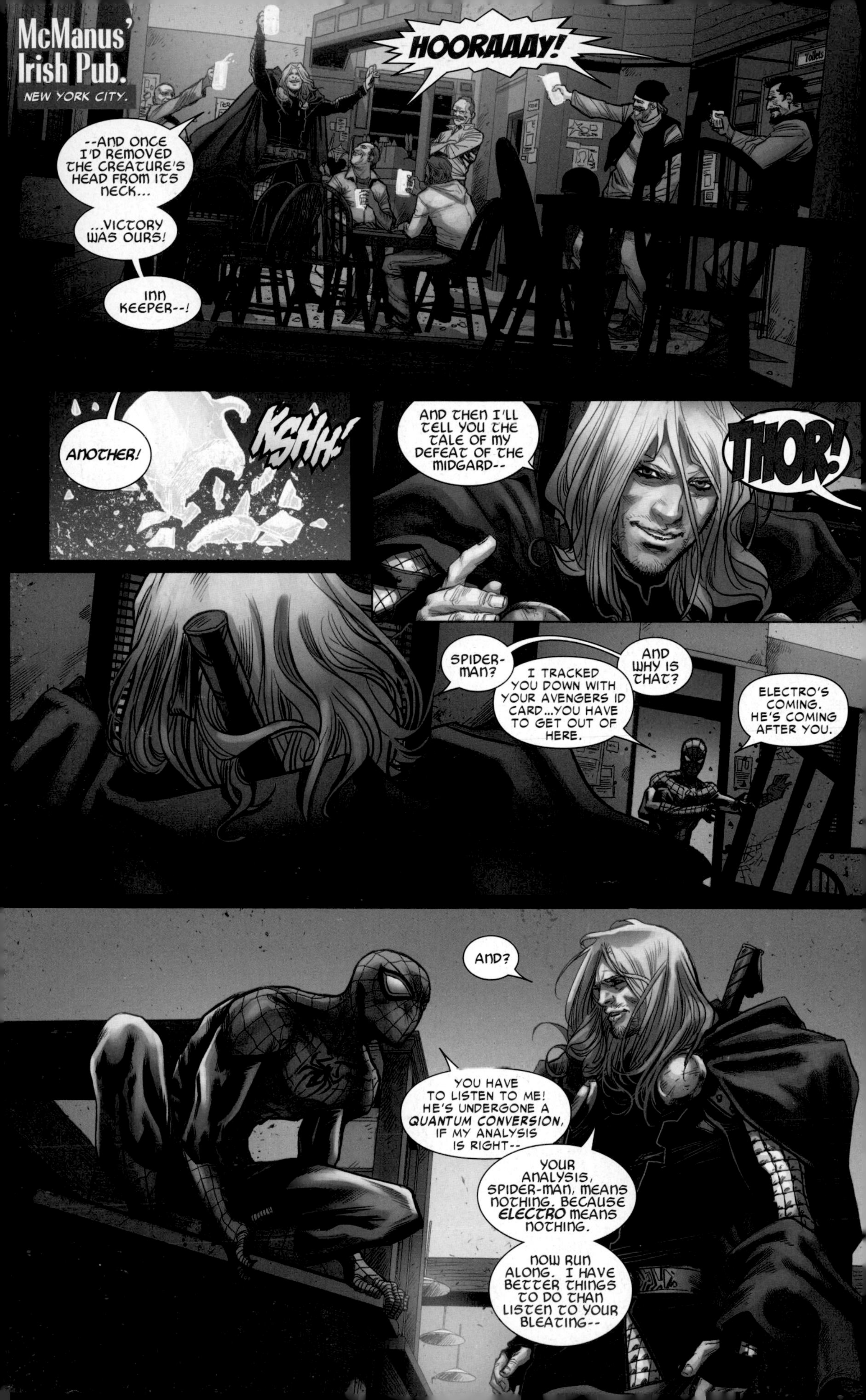

McManus' Irish Pub.
NEW YORK CITY.
HOORAAAY!
--AND ONCE I'D REMOVED THE CREATURE'S HEAD FROM ITS NECK...
...VICTORY WAS OURS!
INN KEEPER--!
ANOTHER!
KSHH!
AND THEN I'LL TELL YOU THE TALE OF MY DEFEAT OF THE MIDGARD--
THOR!
SPIDER-MAN?
AND WHY IS THAT?
I TRACKED YOU DOWN WITH YOUR AVENGERS ID CARD...YOU HAVE TO GET OUT OF HERE.
ELECTRO'S COMING. HE'S COMING AFTER YOU.
AND?
YOU HAVE TO LISTEN TO ME! HE'S UNDERGONE A QUANTUM CONVERSION, IF MY ANALYSIS IS RIGHT--
YOUR ANALYSIS, SPIDER-MAN, MEANS NOTHING. BECAUSE ELECTRO MEANS NOTHING.
NOW RUN ALONG. I HAVE BETTER THINGS TO DO THAN LISTEN TO YOUR BLEATING--

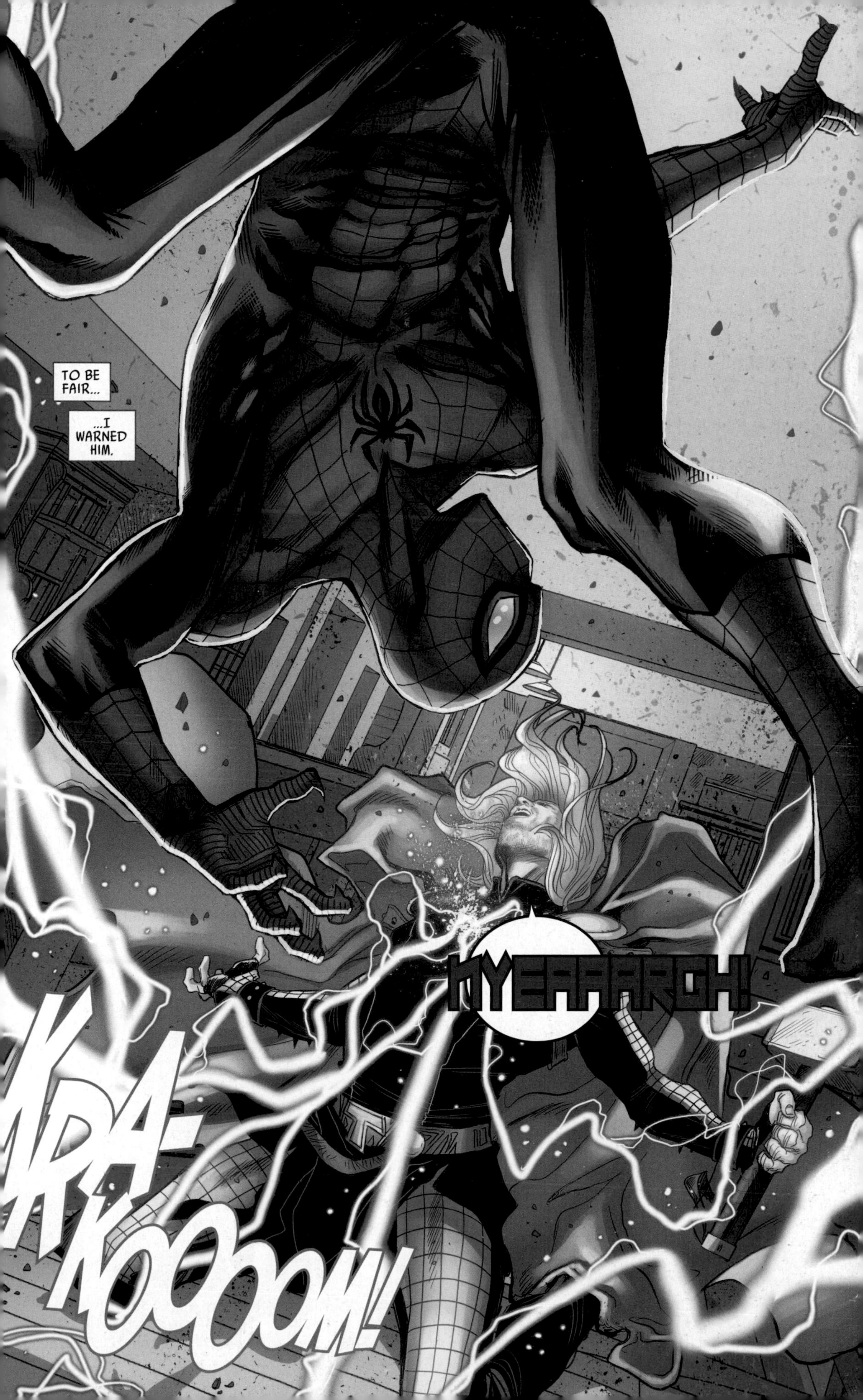
TO BE FAIR...
...I WARNED HIM.
MYEAAARGH!
KRA-KOOOOM!

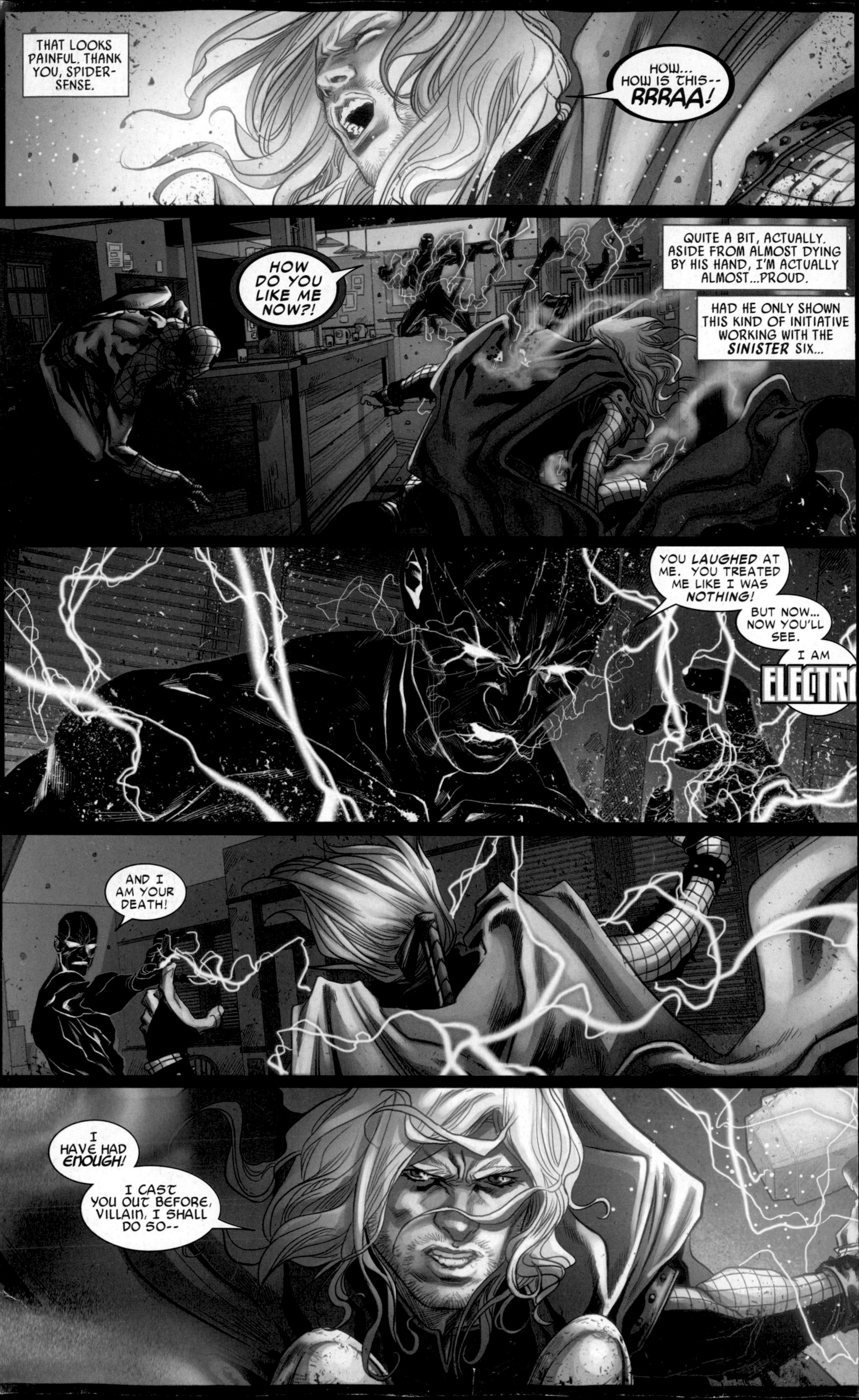
THAT LOOKS PAINFUL. THANK YOU, SPIDER-SENSE.
HOW... HOW IS THIS-- RRRAA!
HOW DO YOU LIKE ME NOW?!
QUITE A BIT, ACTUALLY. ASIDE FROM ALMOST DYING BY HIS HAND, I'M ACTUALLY ALMOST...PROUD.
HAD HE ONLY SHOWN THIS KIND OF INITIATIVE WORKING WITH THE SINISTER SIX...
YOU LAUGHED AT ME. YOU TREATED ME LIKE I WAS NOTHING!
BUT NOW... NOW YOU'LL SEE.
I AM
AND I AM YOUR DEATH!
I HAVE HAD ENOUGH!
I CAST YOU OUT BEFORE, VILLAIN, I SHALL DO SO--

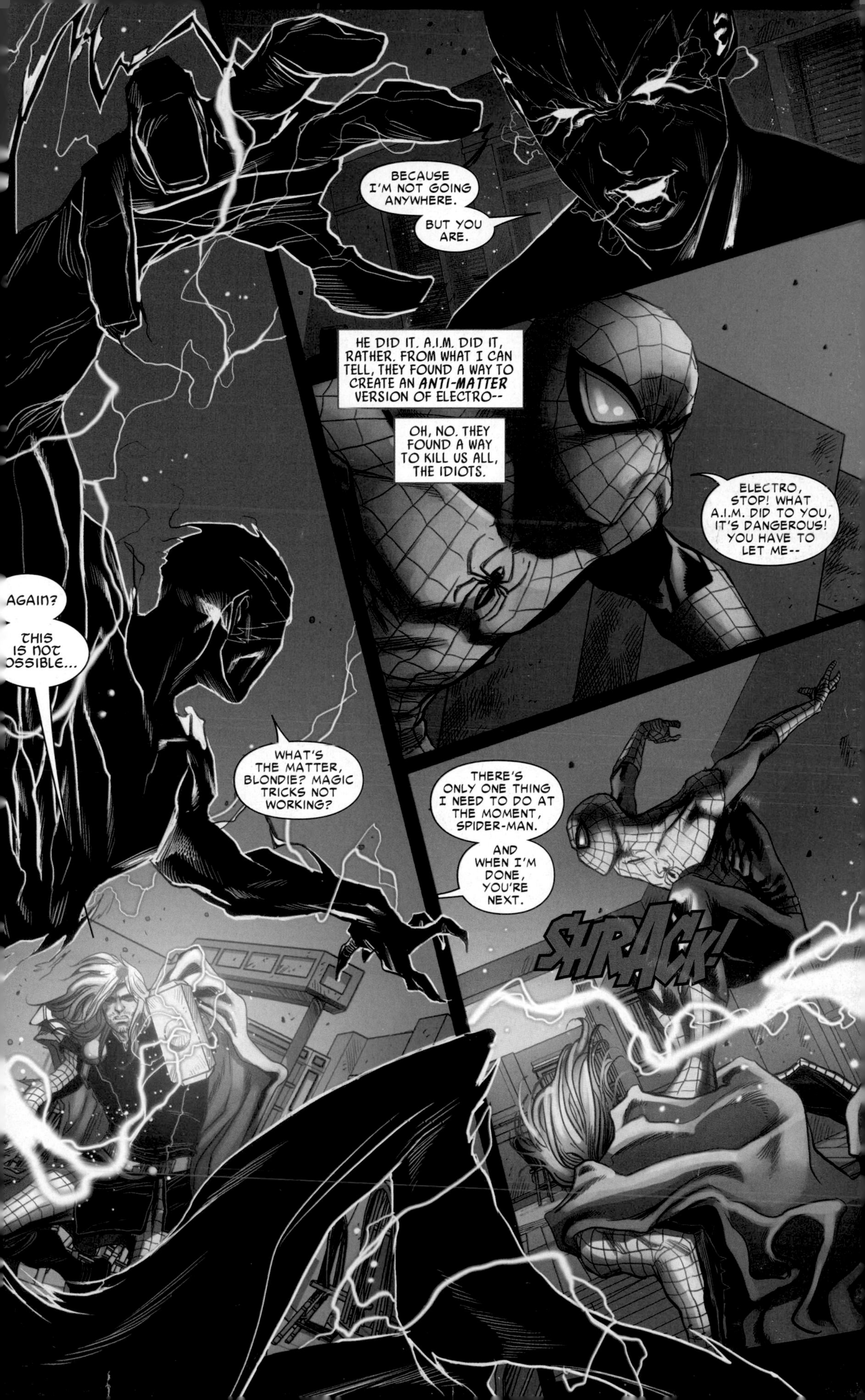
BECAUSE I'M NOT GOING ANYWHERE.
BUT YOU ARE.
HE DID IT. A.I.M. DID IT, RATHER. FROM WHAT I CAN TELL, THEY FOUND A WAY TO CREATE AN ANTI-MATTER VERSION OF ELECTRO--
OH, NO. THEY FOUND A WAY TO KILL US ALL, THE IDIOTS.
ELECTRO, STOP! WHAT A.I.M. DID TO YOU, IT'S DANGEROUS! YOU HAVE TO LET ME--
AGAIN?
THIS IS NOT OSSIBLE...
WHAT'S THE MATTER, BLONDIE? MAGIC TRICKS NOT WORKING?
THERE'S ONLY ONE THING I NEED TO DO AT THE MOMENT, SPIDER-MAN.
AND WHEN I'M DONE, YOU'RE NEXT.
SHRACK!

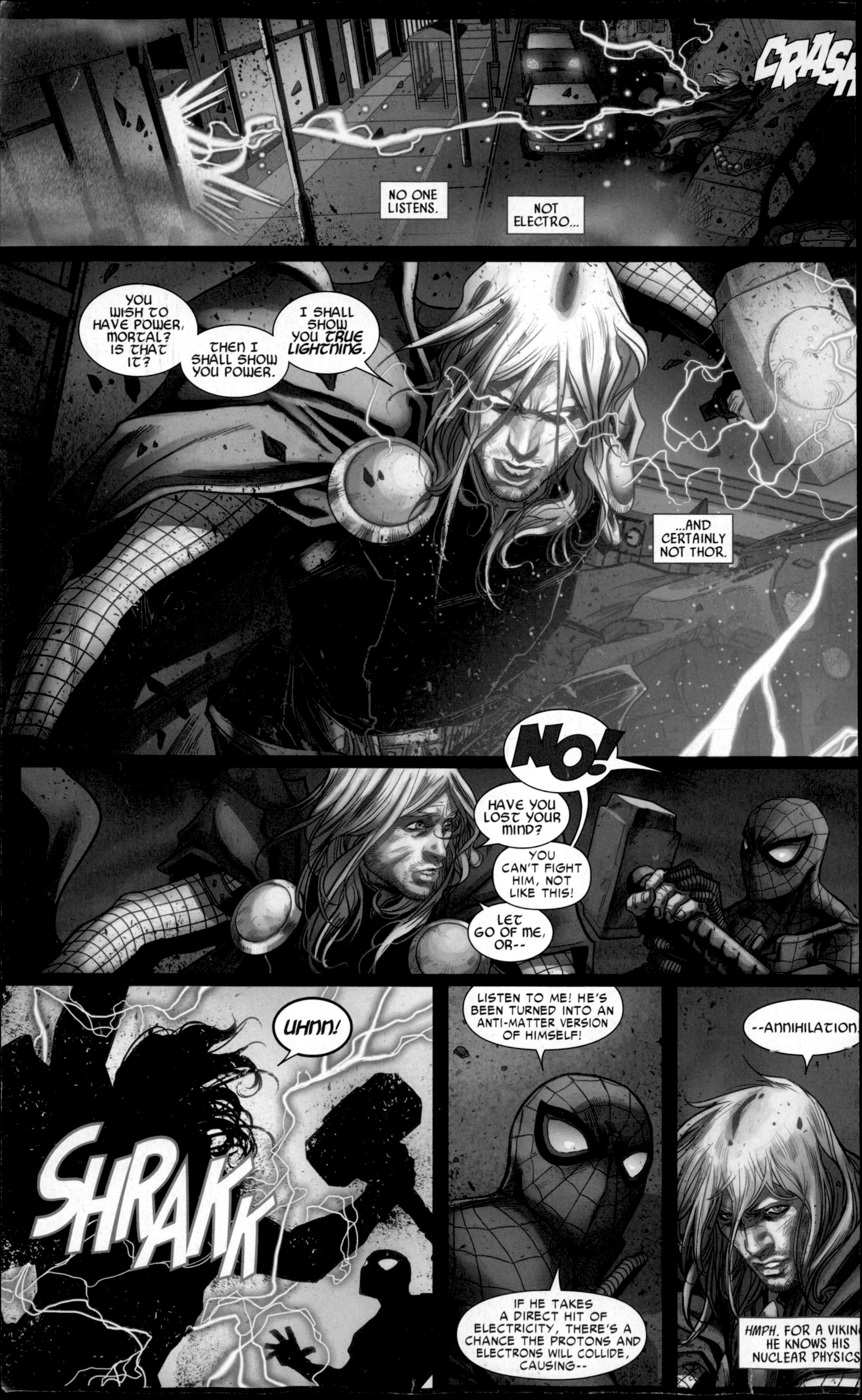
CRASH
NO ONE LISTENS.
NOT ELECTRO...
YOU WISH TO HAVE POWER, MORTAL? IS THAT IT?
THEN I SHALL SHOW YOU POWER.
I SHALL SHOW YOU TRUE LIGHTNING.
...AND CERTAINLY NOT THOR.
NO!
HAVE YOU LOST YOUR MIND?
YOU CAN'T FIGHT HIM, NOT LIKE THIS!
LET GO OF ME, OR--
UHNN!
SHRAKK
LISTEN TO ME! HE'S BEEN TURNED INTO AN ANTI-MATTER VERSION OF HIMSELF!
IF HE TAKES A DIRECT HIT OF ELECTRICITY, THERE'S A CHANCE THE PROTONS AND ELECTRONS WILL COLLIDE, CAUSING--
--ANNIHILATION.
HMPH. FOR A VIKING HE KNOWS HIS NUCLEAR PHYSICS.

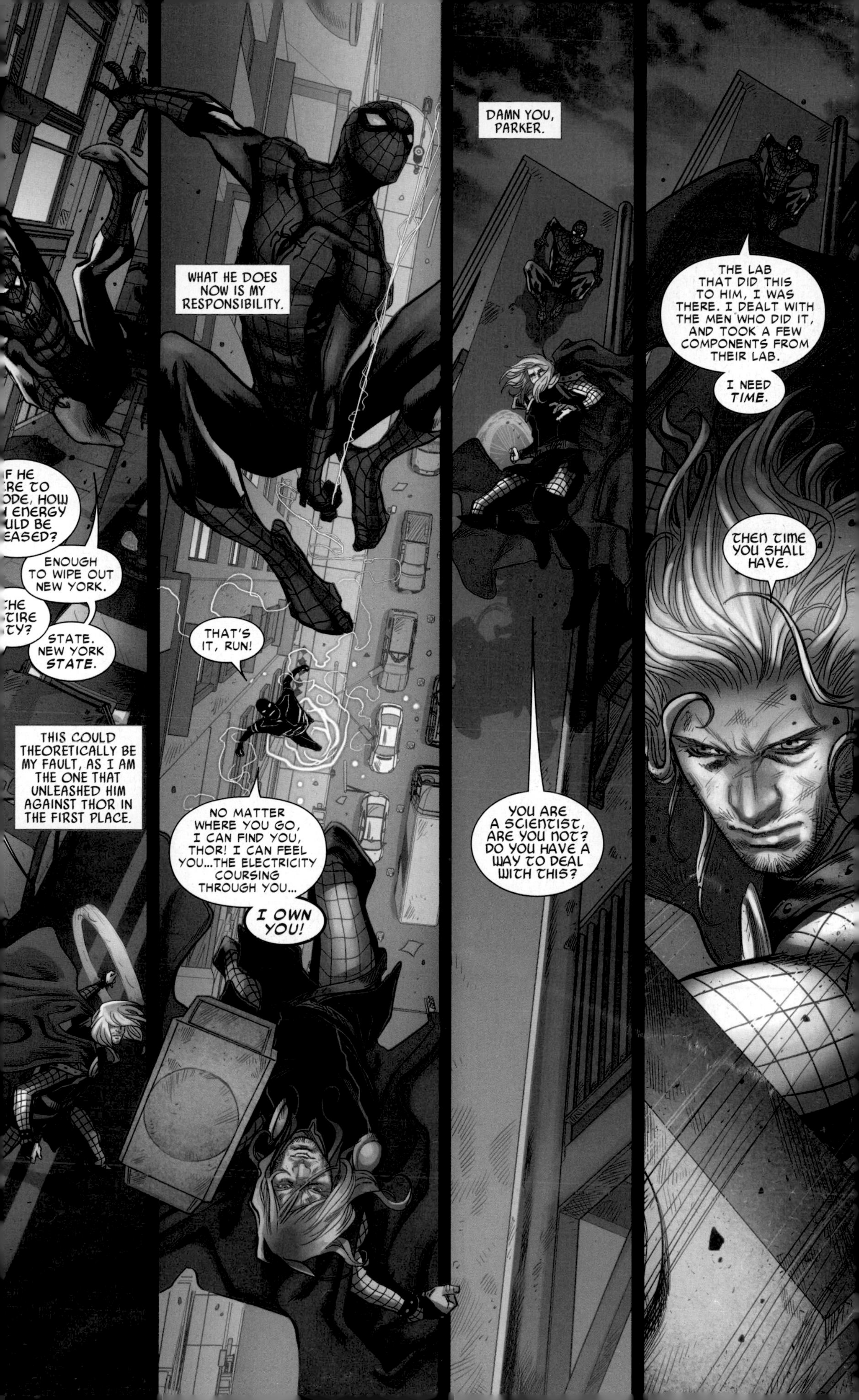

F HE RE TO ODE, HOW ENERGY ULD BE EASED?
ENOUGH TO WIPE OUT NEW YORK.
HE TIRE TY?
STATE. NEW YORK STATE.
THIS COULD THEORETICALLY BE MY FAULT, AS I AM THE ONE THAT UNLEASHED HIM AGAINST THOR IN THE FIRST PLACE.
WHAT HE DOES NOW IS MY RESPONSIBILITY.
THAT'S IT, RUN!
NO MATTER WHERE YOU GO, I CAN FIND YOU, THOR! I CAN FEEL YOU...THE ELECTRICITY COURSING THROUGH YOU...
I OWN YOU!
DAMN YOU, PARKER.
YOU ARE A SCIENTIST, ARE YOU NOT? DO YOU HAVE A WAY TO DEAL WITH THIS?
THE LAB THAT DID THIS TO HIM, I WAS THERE. I DEALT WITH THE MEN WHO DID IT, AND TOOK A FEW COMPONENTS FROM THEIR LAB.
I NEED TIME.
THEN TIME YOU SHALL HAVE.

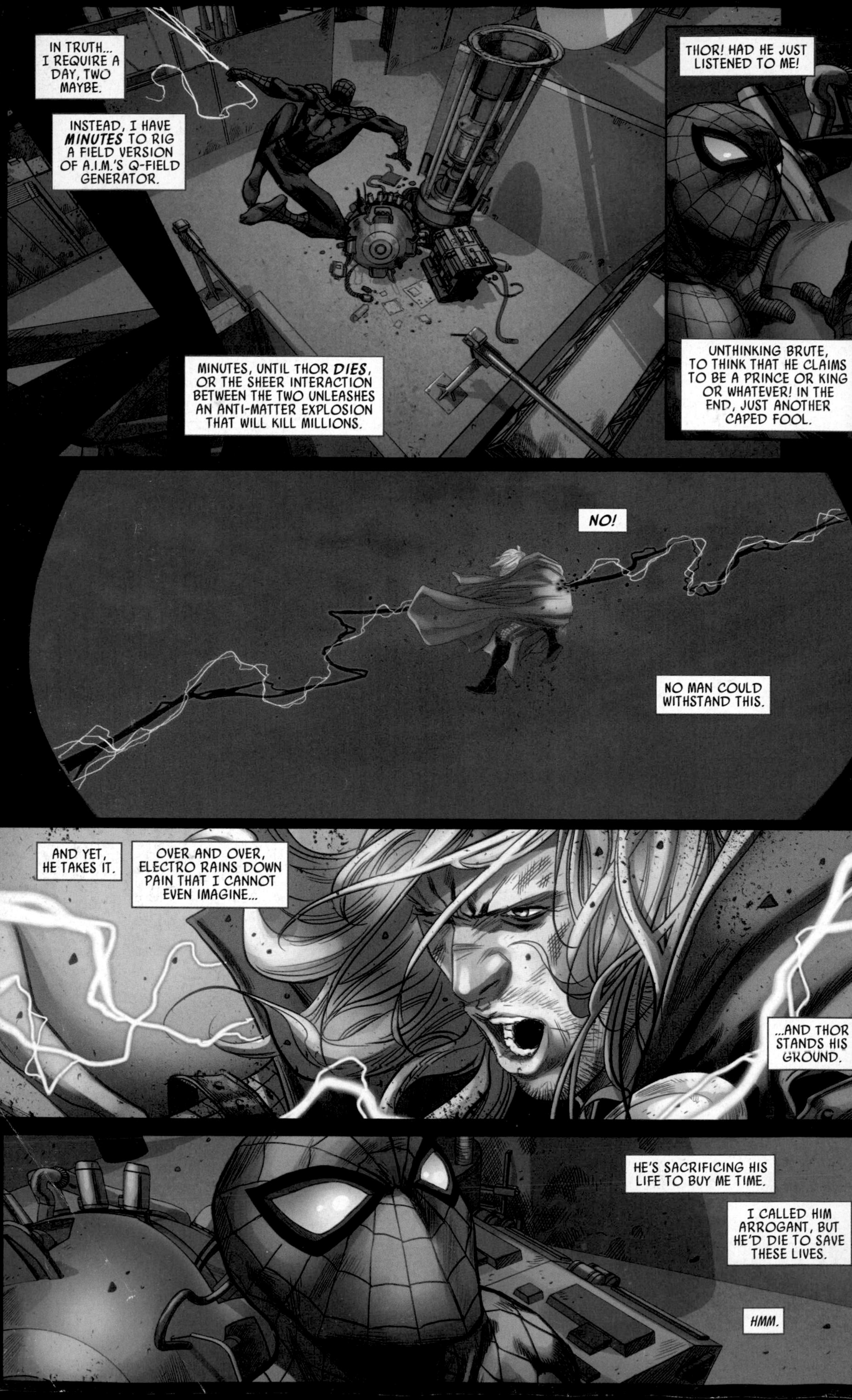
IN TRUTH... I REQUIRE A DAY, TWO MAYBE.
INSTEAD, I HAVE MINUTES TO RIG A FIELD VERSION OF A.I.M.'S Q-FIELD GENERATOR.
MINUTES, UNTIL THOR DIES, OR THE SHEER INTERACTION BETWEEN THE TWO UNLEASHES AN ANTI-MATTER EXPLOSION THAT WILL KILL MILLIONS.
THOR! HAD HE JUST LISTENED TO ME!
UNTHINKING BRUTE, TO THINK THAT HE CLAIMS TO BE A PRINCE OR KING OR WHATEVER! IN THE END, JUST ANOTHER CAPED FOOL.
NO!
NO MAN COULD WITHSTAND THIS.
AND YET, HE TAKES IT.
OVER AND OVER, ELECTRO RAINS DOWN PAIN THAT I CANNOT EVEN IMAGINE...
...AND THOR STANDS HIS GROUND.
HE'S SACRIFICING HIS LIFE TO BUY ME TIME.
I CALLED HIM ARROGANT, BUT HE'D DIE TO SAVE THESE LIVES.
HMM.

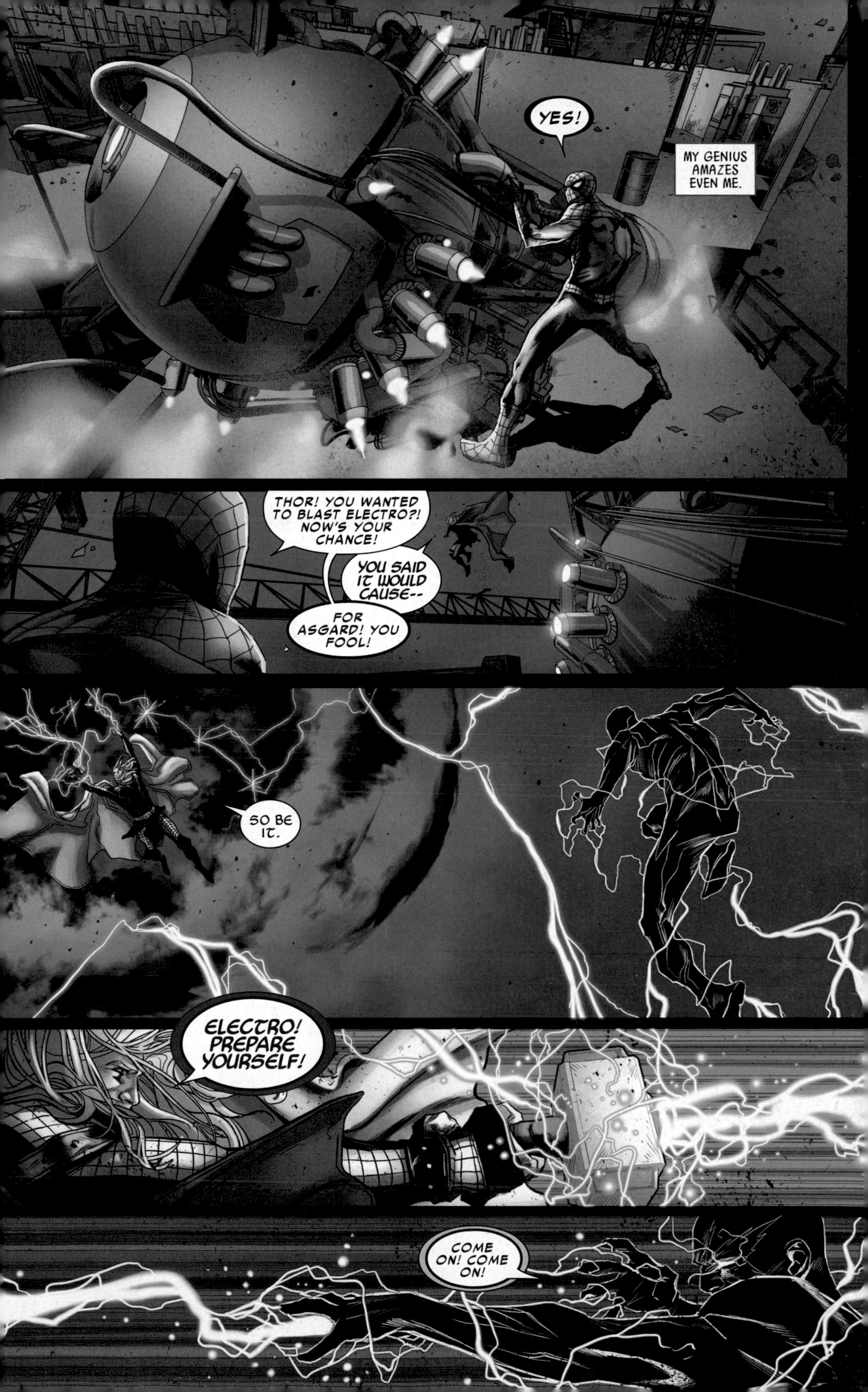
YES!
MY GENIUS AMAZES EVEN ME.
THOR! YOU WANTED TO BLAST ELECTRO?! NOW'S YOUR CHANCE!
YOU SAID IT WOULD CAUSE--
FOR ASGARD! YOU FOOL!
SO BE IT.
ELECTRO! PREPARE YOURSELF!
COME ON! COME ON!

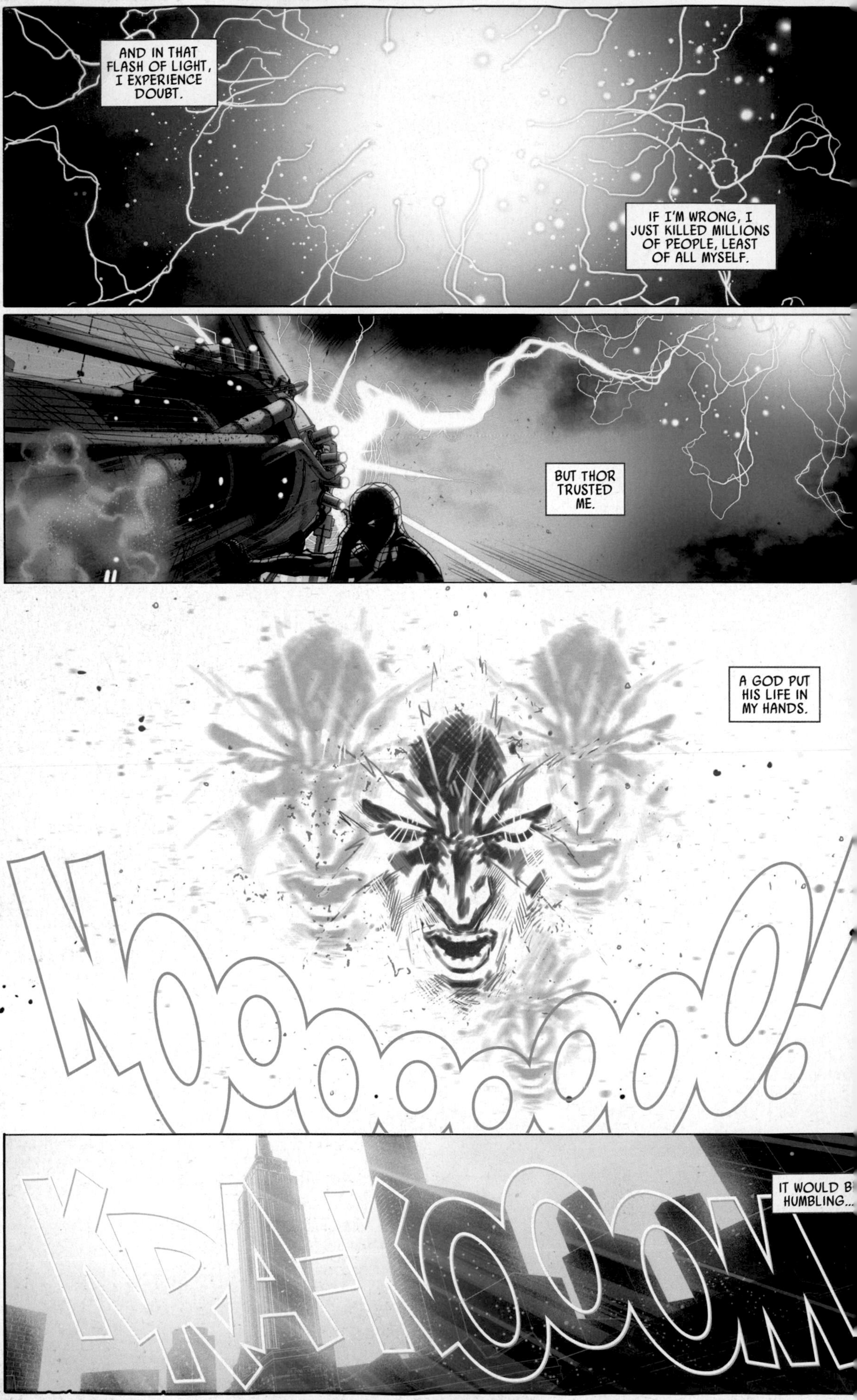
AND IN THAT FLASH OF LIGHT, I EXPERIENCE DOUBT.
IF I'M WRONG, I JUST KILLED MILLIONS OF PEOPLE, LEAST OF ALL MYSELF.
BUT THOR TRUSTED ME.
A GOD PUT HIS LIFE IN MY HANDS.
NOOOOOOOO!
KRA-KOOOOM
IT WOULD B
HUMBLING...

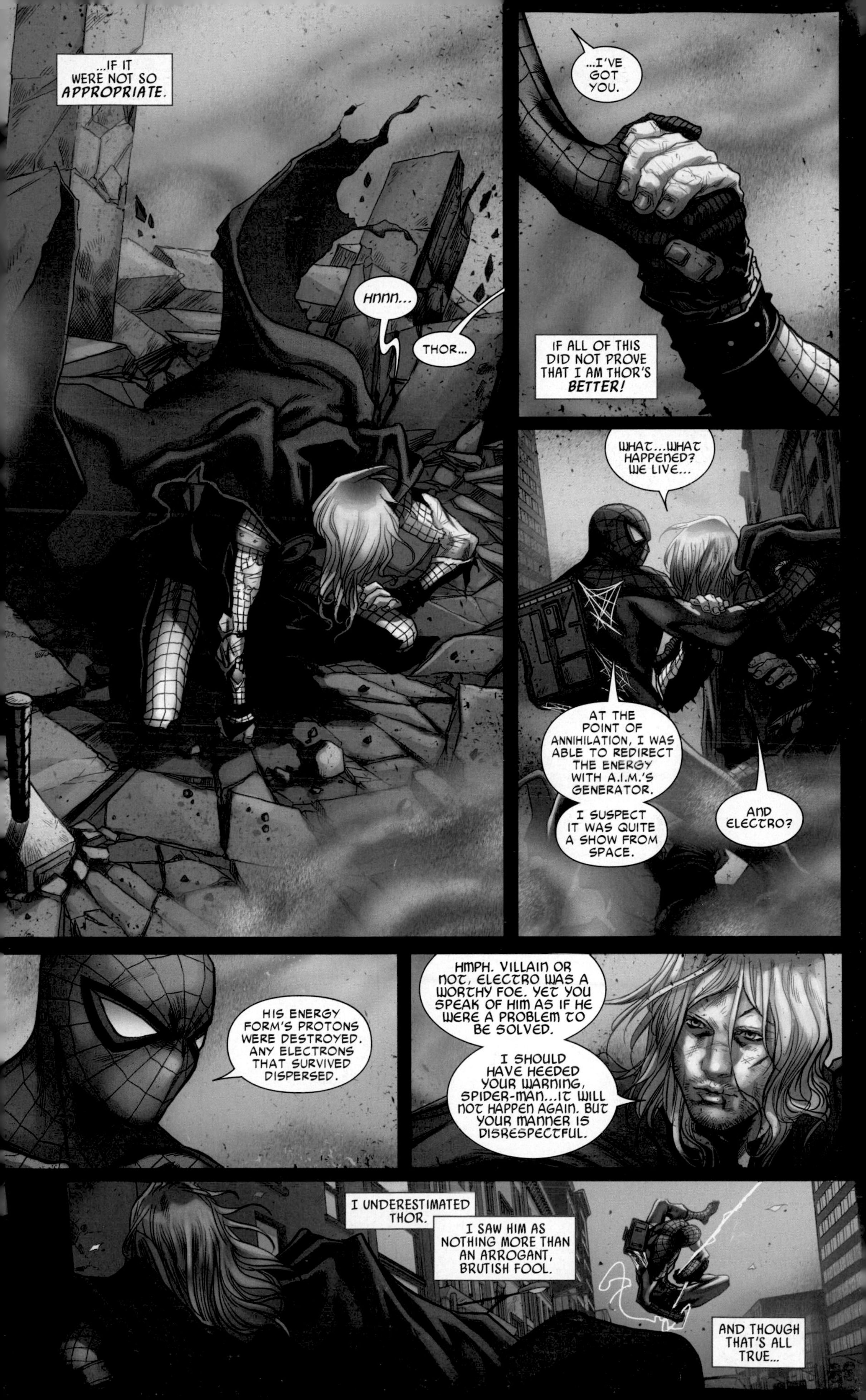
...IF IT WERE NOT SO APPROPRIATE.
HNNN...
THOR...
...I'VE GOT YOU.
IF ALL OF THIS DID NOT PROVE THAT I AM THOR'S BETTER!
WHAT...WHAT HAPPENED? WE LIVE...
AT THE POINT OF ANNIHILATION, I WAS ABLE TO REDIRECT THE ENERGY WITH A.I.M.'S GENERATOR.
I SUSPECT IT WAS QUITE A SHOW FROM SPACE.
AND ELECTRO?
HIS ENERGY FORM'S PROTONS WERE DESTROYED. ANY ELECTRONS THAT SURVIVED DISPERSED.
HMPH. VILLAIN OR NOT, ELECTRO WAS A WORTHY FOE. YET YOU SPEAK OF HIM AS IF HE WERE A PROBLEM TO BE SOLVED.
I SHOULD HAVE HEEDED YOUR WARNING, SPIDER-MAN...IT WILL NOT HAPPEN AGAIN. BUT YOUR MANNER IS DISRESPECTFUL.
I UNDERESTIMATED THOR.
I SAW HIM AS NOTHING MORE THAN AN ARROGANT, BRUTISH FOOL.
AND THOUGH THAT'S ALL TRUE...

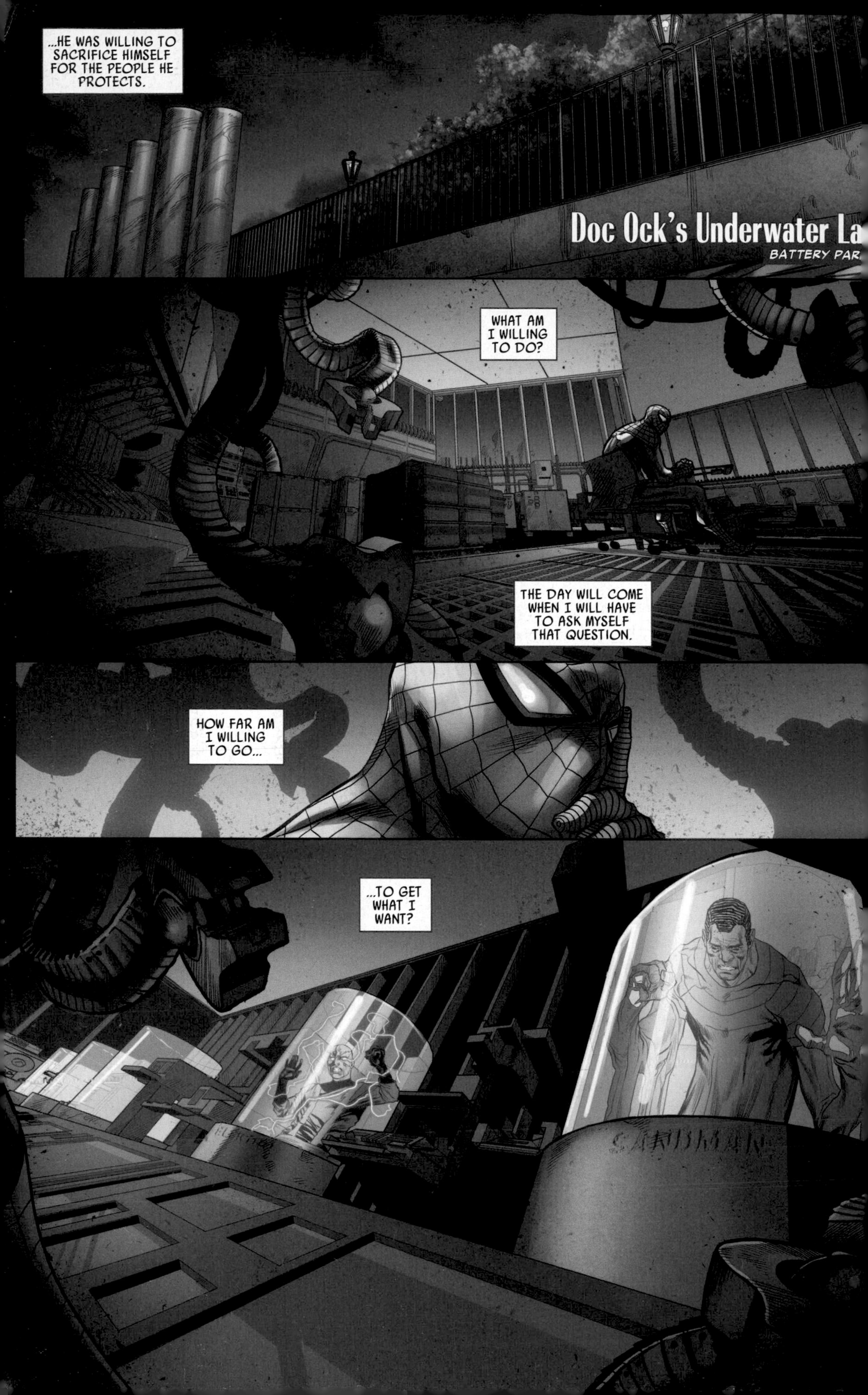
...HE WAS WILLING TO SACRIFICE HIMSELF FOR THE PEOPLE HE PROTECTS.
Doc Ock's Underwater La
BATTERY PAR
WHAT AM I WILLING TO DO?
THE DAY WILL COME WHEN I WILL HAVE TO ASK MYSELF THAT QUESTION.
HOW FAR AM I WILLING TO GO...
...TO GET WHAT I WANT?

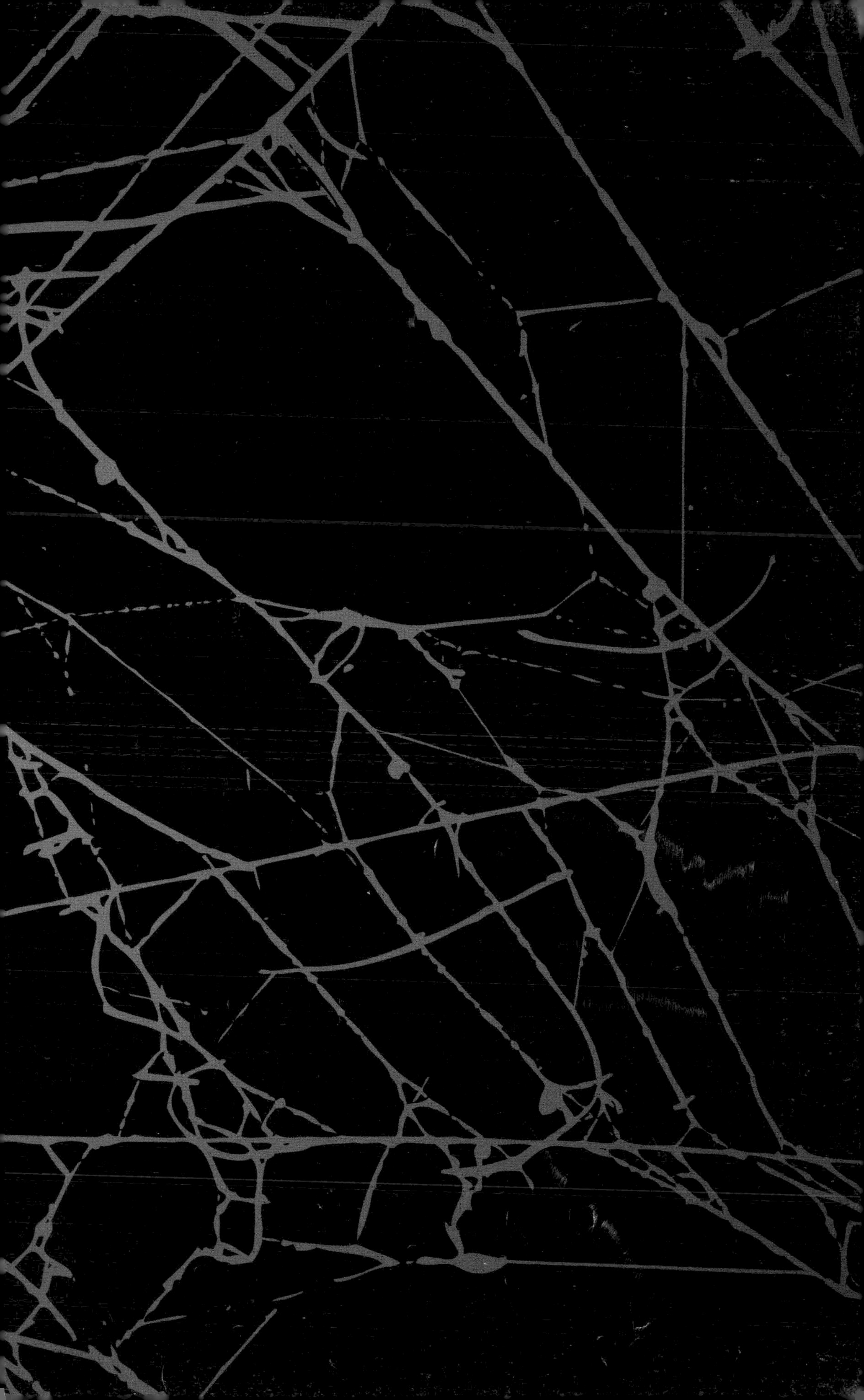

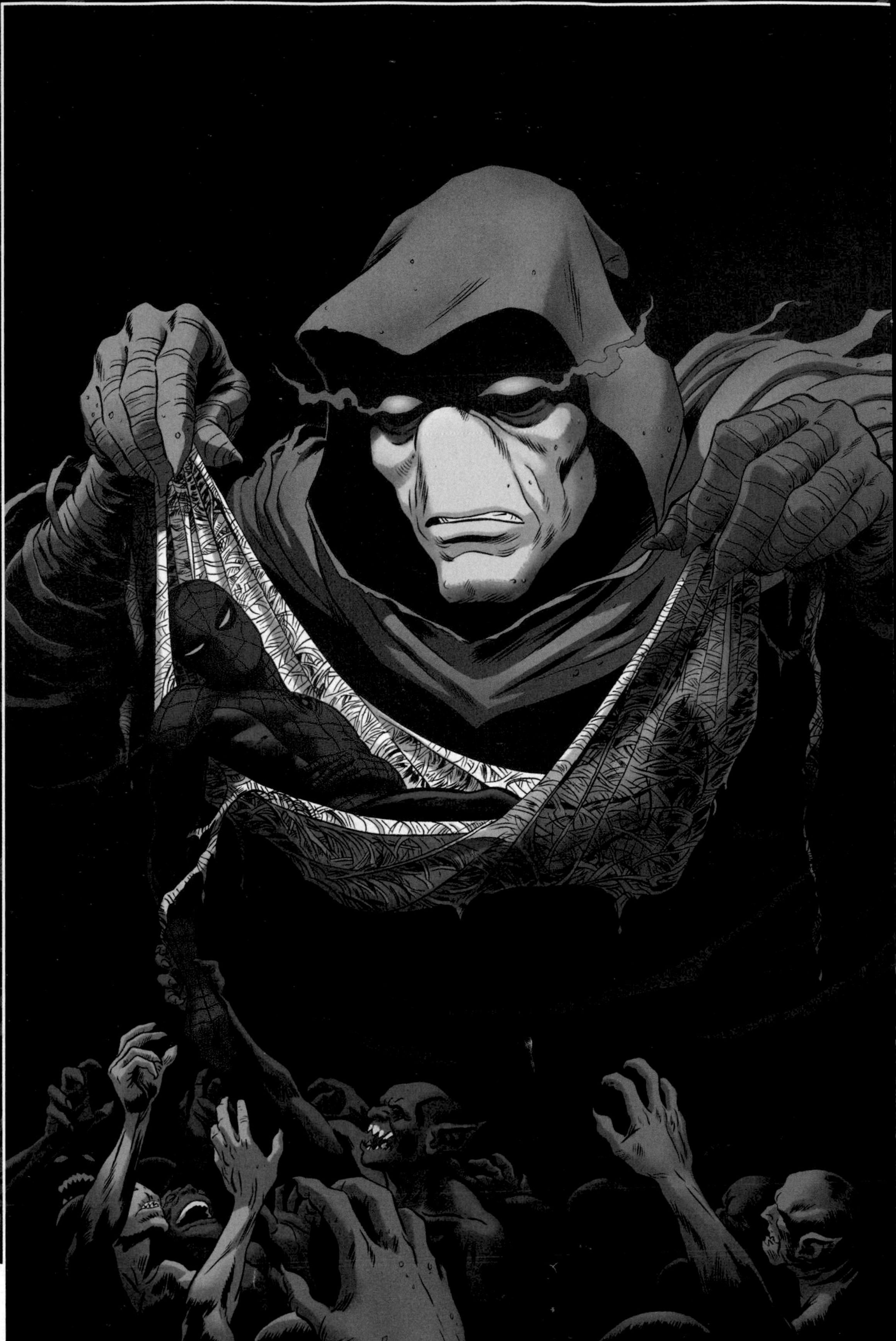

# AVENGING SPIDER-MAN 19

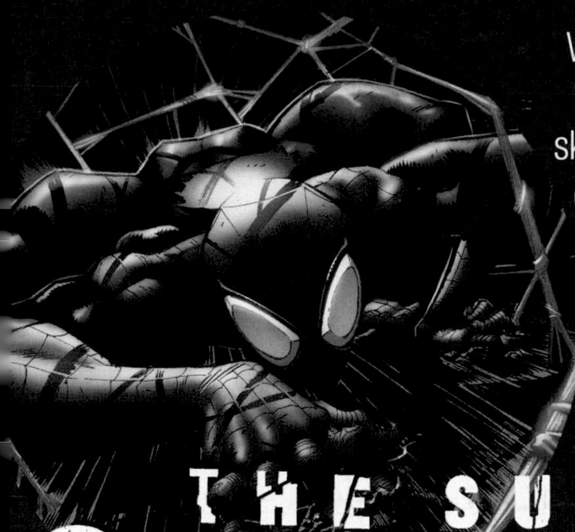

When OTTO OCTAVIUS, the villain known as DOCTOR OCTOPUS, was dying, he used his skills as a mad scientist to swap minds with his greatest enemy, PETER PARKER, the amazing Spider-Man. The transfer gave Otto Parker's powers and his memories--namely the lesson of great responsibility. Now Otto Octavius is beginning a new life as a hero, possibly the greatest hero of all as...

# THE SUPERIOR SPIDER-MAN

## IN

# BAD DREAMS

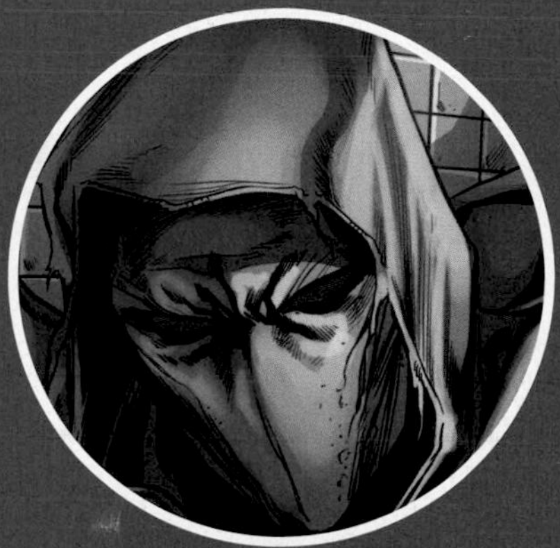

Protecting the minds of all sentient beings from evil creatures infiltrating its borders, Rick Sheridan roams the Mindscape as...

# SLEEPWALKER

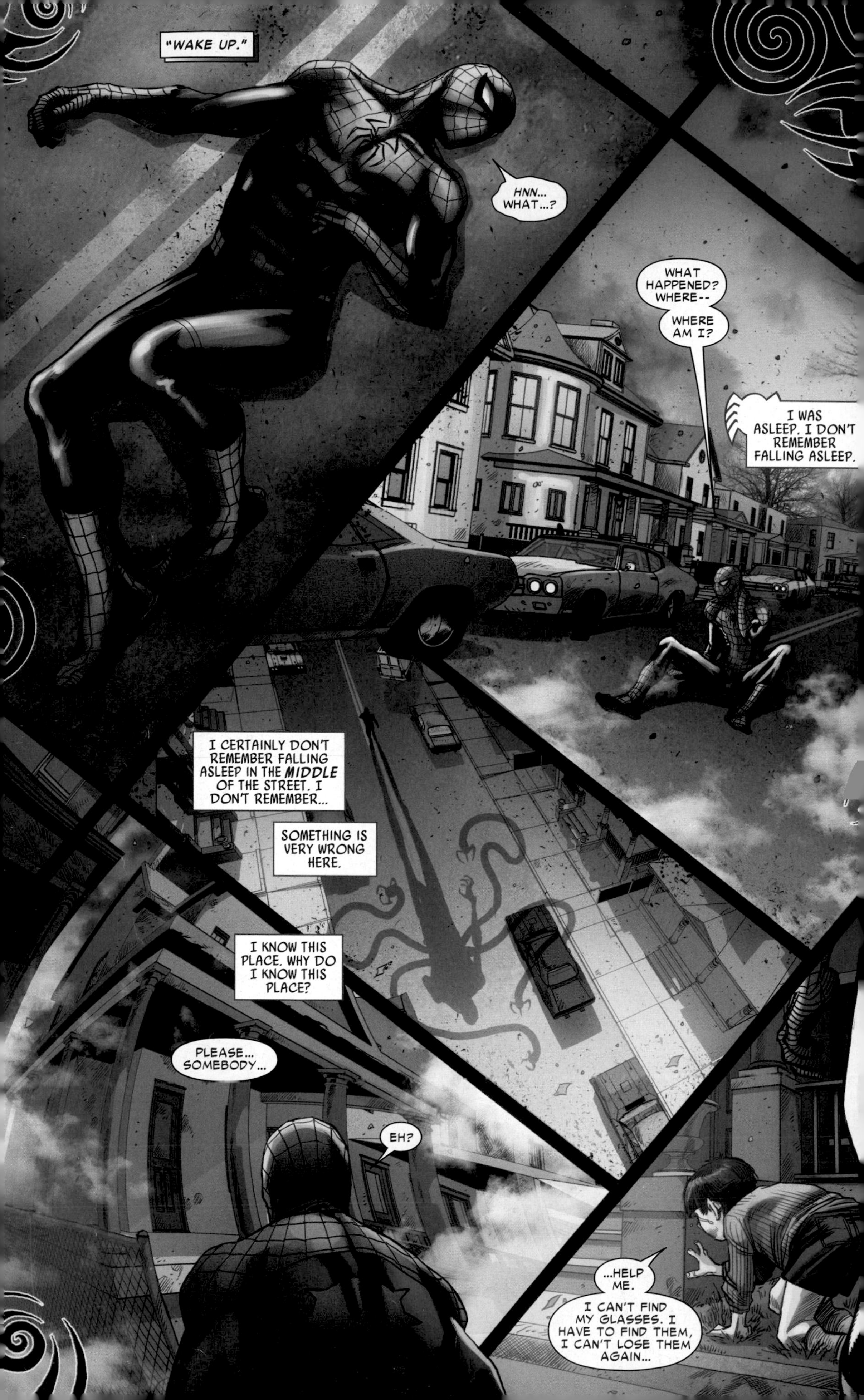
"WAKE UP."
HNN... WHAT...?
WHAT HAPPENED? WHERE--
WHERE AM I?
I WAS ASLEEP. I DON'T REMEMBER FALLING ASLEEP.
I CERTAINLY DON'T REMEMBER FALLING ASLEEP IN THE MIDDLE OF THE STREET. I DON'T REMEMBER...
SOMETHING IS VERY WRONG HERE.
I KNOW THIS PLACE. WHY DO I KNOW THIS PLACE?
PLEASE... SOMEBODY...
EH?
...HELP ME.
I CAN'T FIND MY GLASSES. I HAVE TO FIND THEM, I CAN'T LOSE THEM AGAIN...

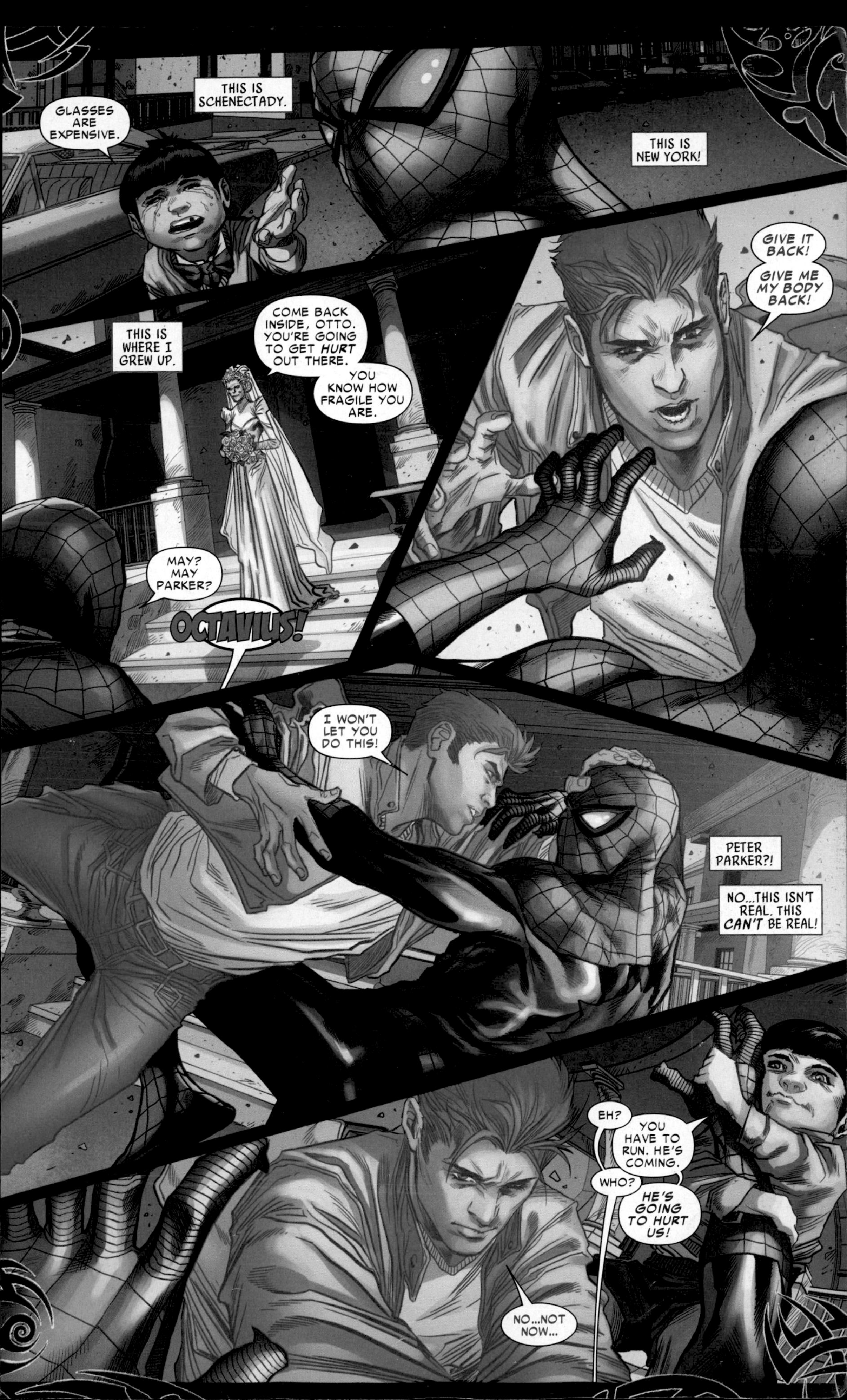
GLASSES ARE EXPENSIVE.
THIS IS SCHENECTADY.
THIS IS NEW YORK!
GIVE IT BACK!
GIVE ME MY BODY BACK!
THIS IS WHERE I GREW UP.
COME BACK INSIDE, OTTO. YOU'RE GOING TO GET HURT OUT THERE.
YOU KNOW HOW FRAGILE YOU ARE.
MAY? MAY PARKER?
OCTAVIUS!
I WON'T LET YOU DO THIS!
PETER PARKER?!
NO...THIS ISN'T REAL. THIS CAN'T BE REAL!
EH?
YOU HAVE TO RUN. HE'S COMING.
WHO?
HE'S GOING TO HURT US!
NO...NOT NOW...

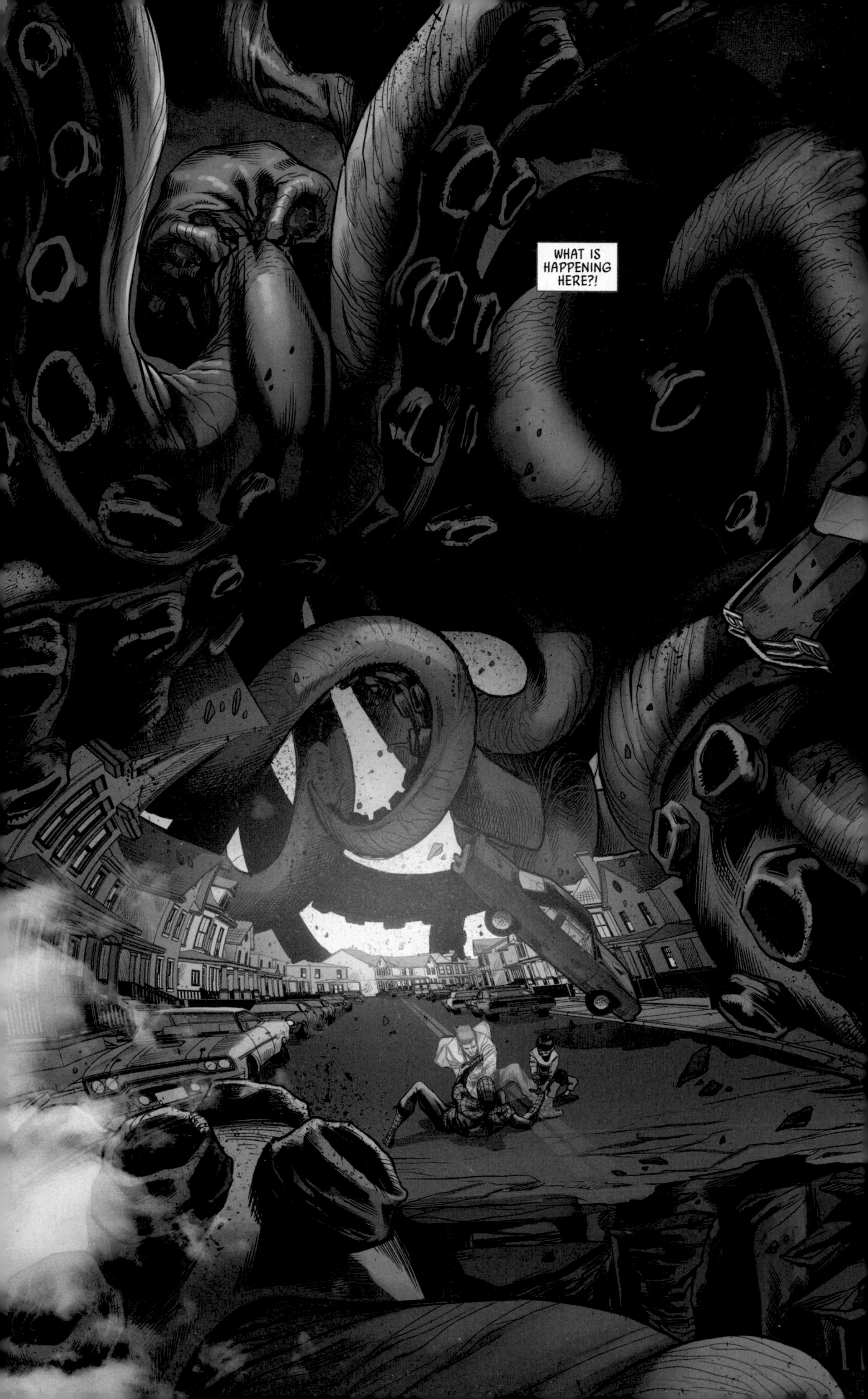
WHAT IS HAPPENING HERE?!

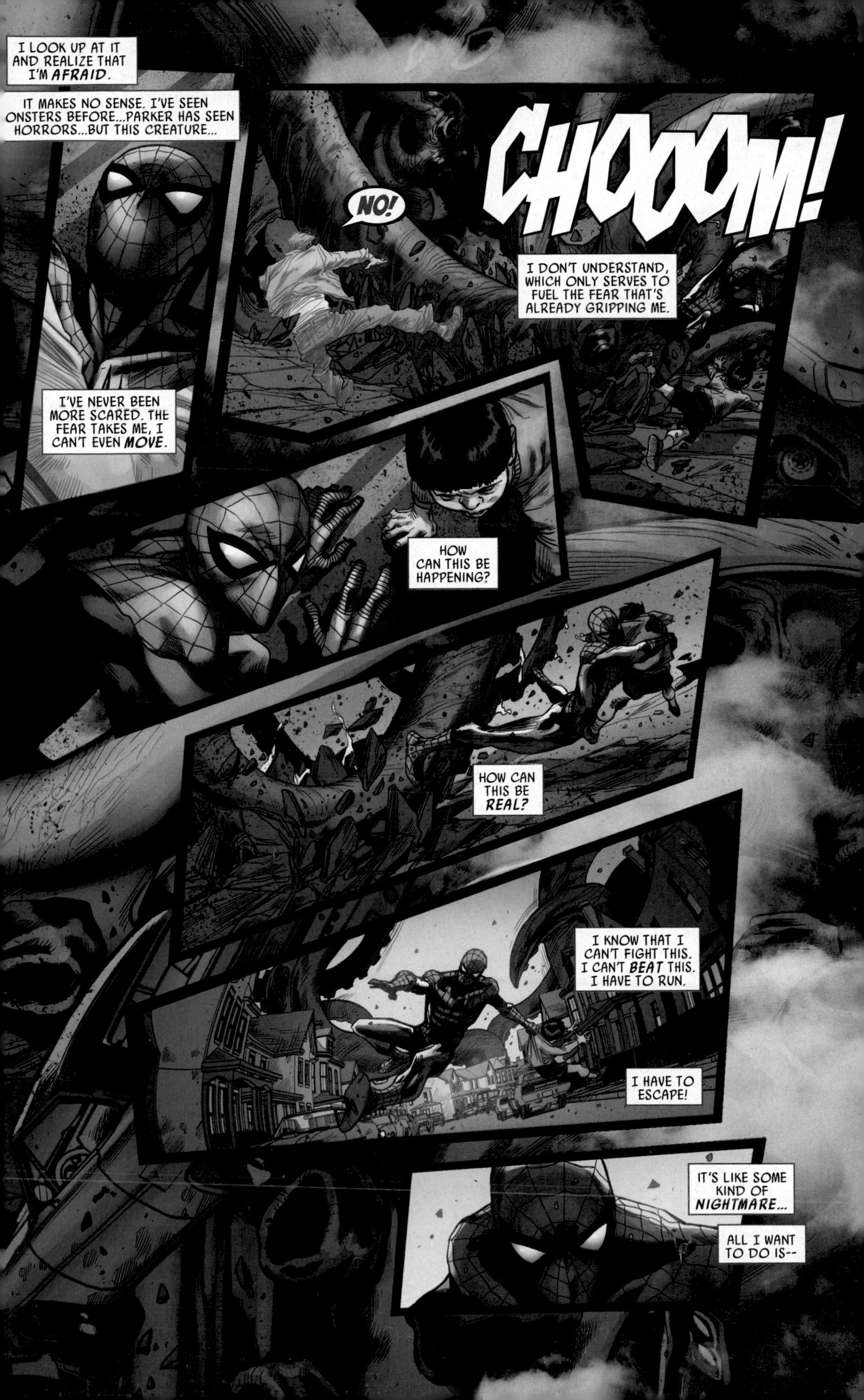
I LOOK UP AT IT AND REALIZE THAT I'M AFRAID.
IT MAKES NO SENSE. I'VE SEEN ONSTERS BEFORE...PARKER HAS SEEN HORRORS...BUT THIS CREATURE...
NO!
CHOOOM!
I DON'T UNDERSTAND, WHICH ONLY SERVES TO FUEL THE FEAR THAT'S ALREADY GRIPPING ME.
I'VE NEVER BEEN MORE SCARED. THE FEAR TAKES ME, I CAN'T EVEN MOVE.
HOW CAN THIS BE HAPPENING?
HOW CAN THIS BE REAL?
I KNOW THAT I CAN'T FIGHT THIS. I CAN'T BEAT THIS. I HAVE TO RUN.
I HAVE TO ESCAPE!
IT'S LIKE SOME KIND OF NIGHTMARE...
ALL I WANT TO DO IS--

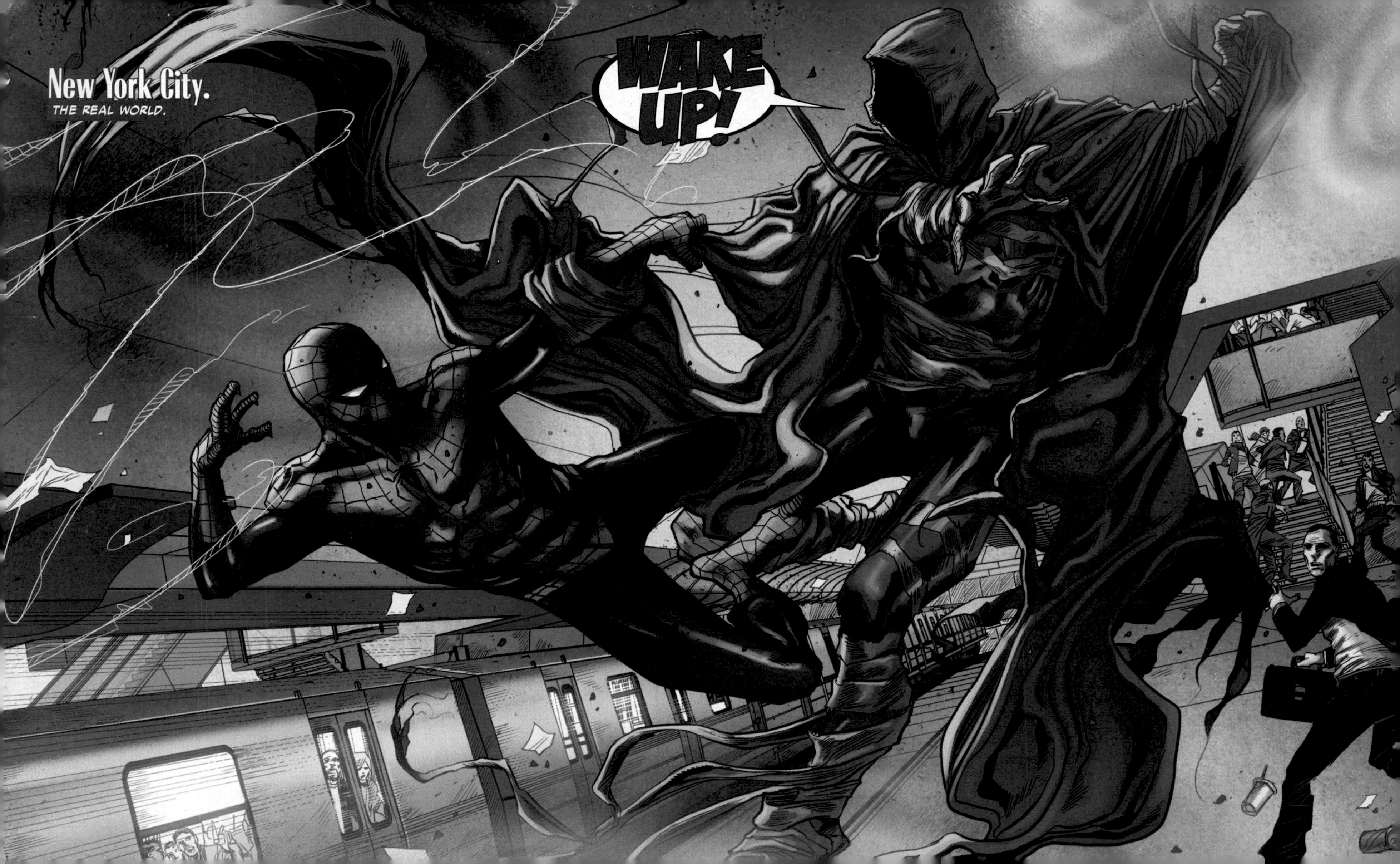
New York City.
THE REAL WORLD.
WAKE UP!

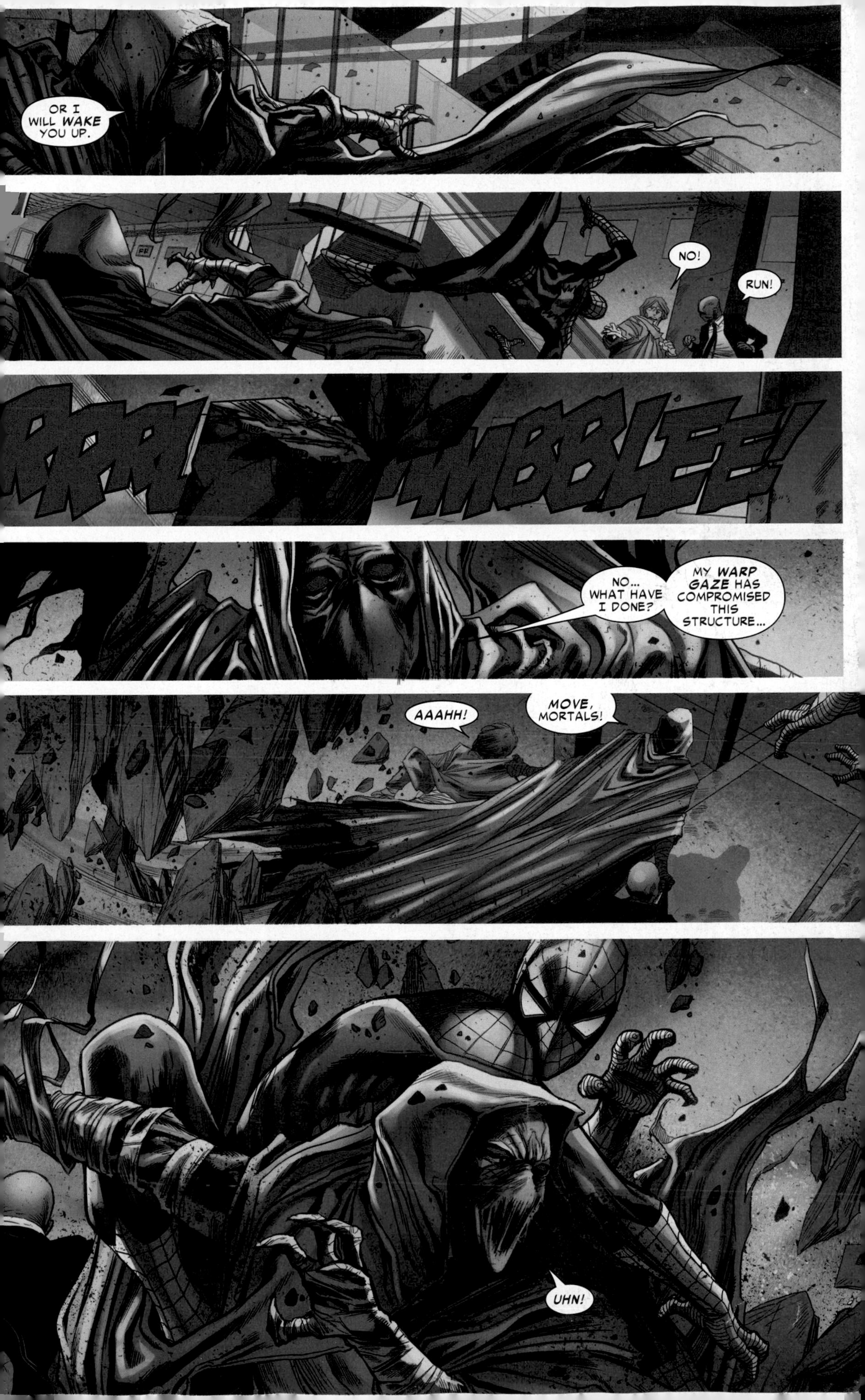
OR I WILL WAKE YOU UP.
NO!
RUN!
NO... WHAT HAVE I DONE?
MY WARP GAZE HAS COMPROMISED THIS STRUCTURE...
AAAHH!
MOVE, MORTALS!
UHN!

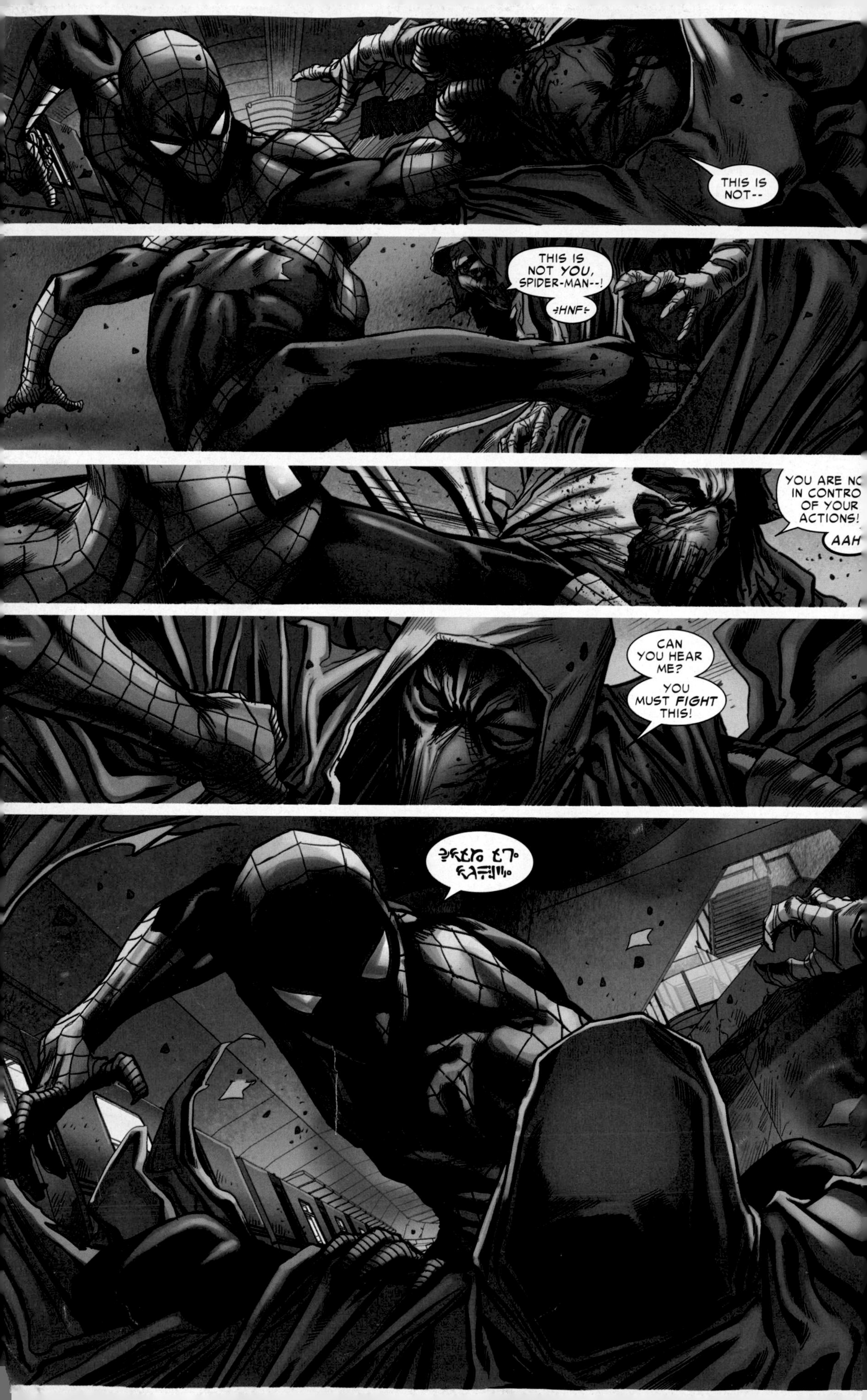
THIS IS NOT--
THIS IS NOT YOU, SPIDER-MAN--!
HNF
YOU ARE NO IN CONTRO OF YOUR ACTIONS!
AAH
CAN YOU HEAR ME?
YOU MUST FIGHT THIS!

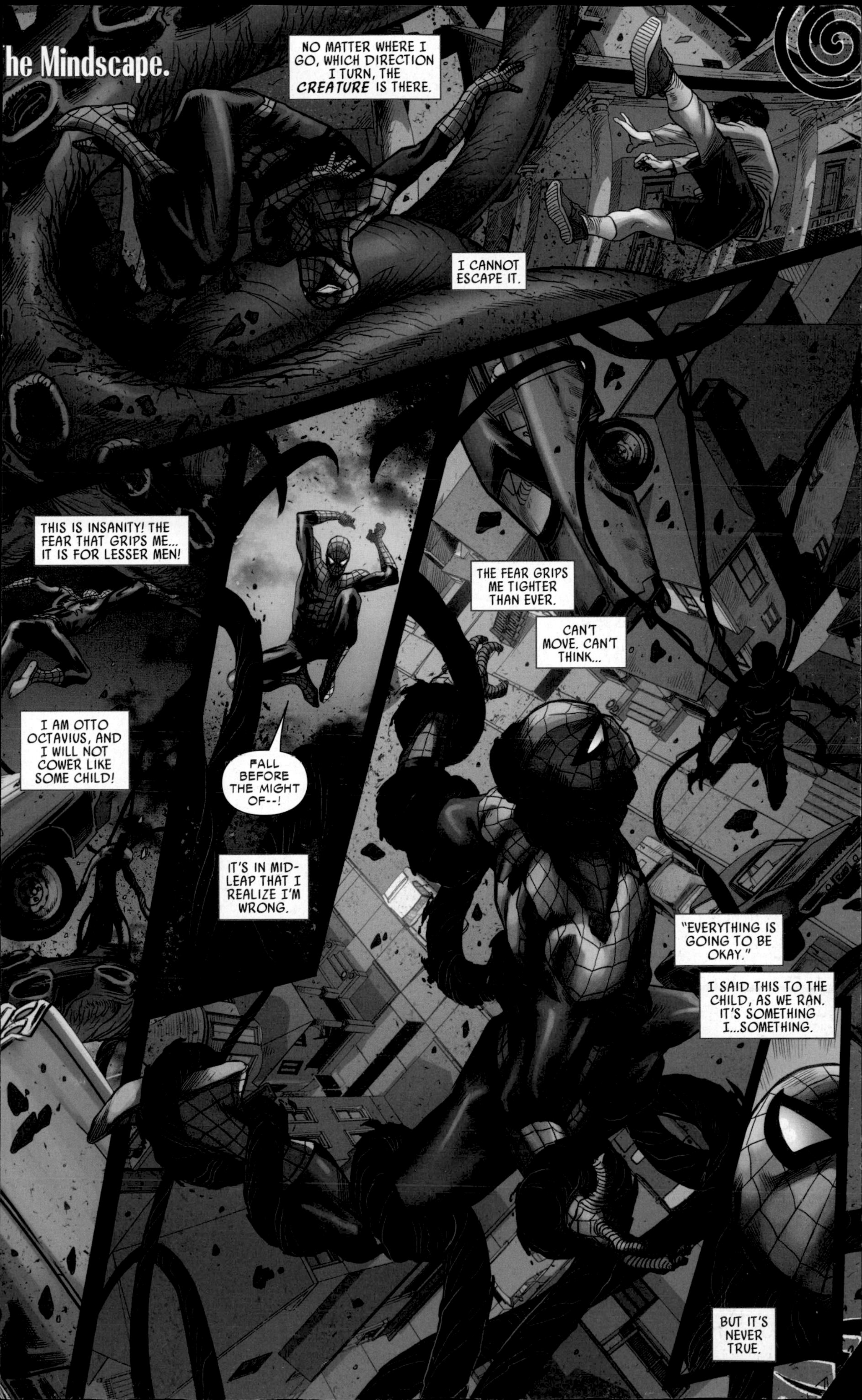
he Mindscape.
NO MATTER WHERE I GO, WHICH DIRECTION I TURN, THE CREATURE IS THERE.
I CANNOT ESCAPE IT.
THIS IS INSANITY! THE FEAR THAT GRIPS ME... IT IS FOR LESSER MEN!
I AM OTTO OCTAVIUS, AND I WILL NOT COWER LIKE SOME CHILD!
FALL BEFORE THE MIGHT OF--!
IT'S IN MID-LEAP THAT I REALIZE I'M WRONG.
THE FEAR GRIPS ME TIGHTER THAN EVER.
CAN'T MOVE. CAN'T THINK...
"EVERYTHING IS GOING TO BE OKAY."
I SAID THIS TO THE CHILD, AS WE RAN. IT'S SOMETHING I...SOMETHING.
BUT IT'S NEVER TRUE.

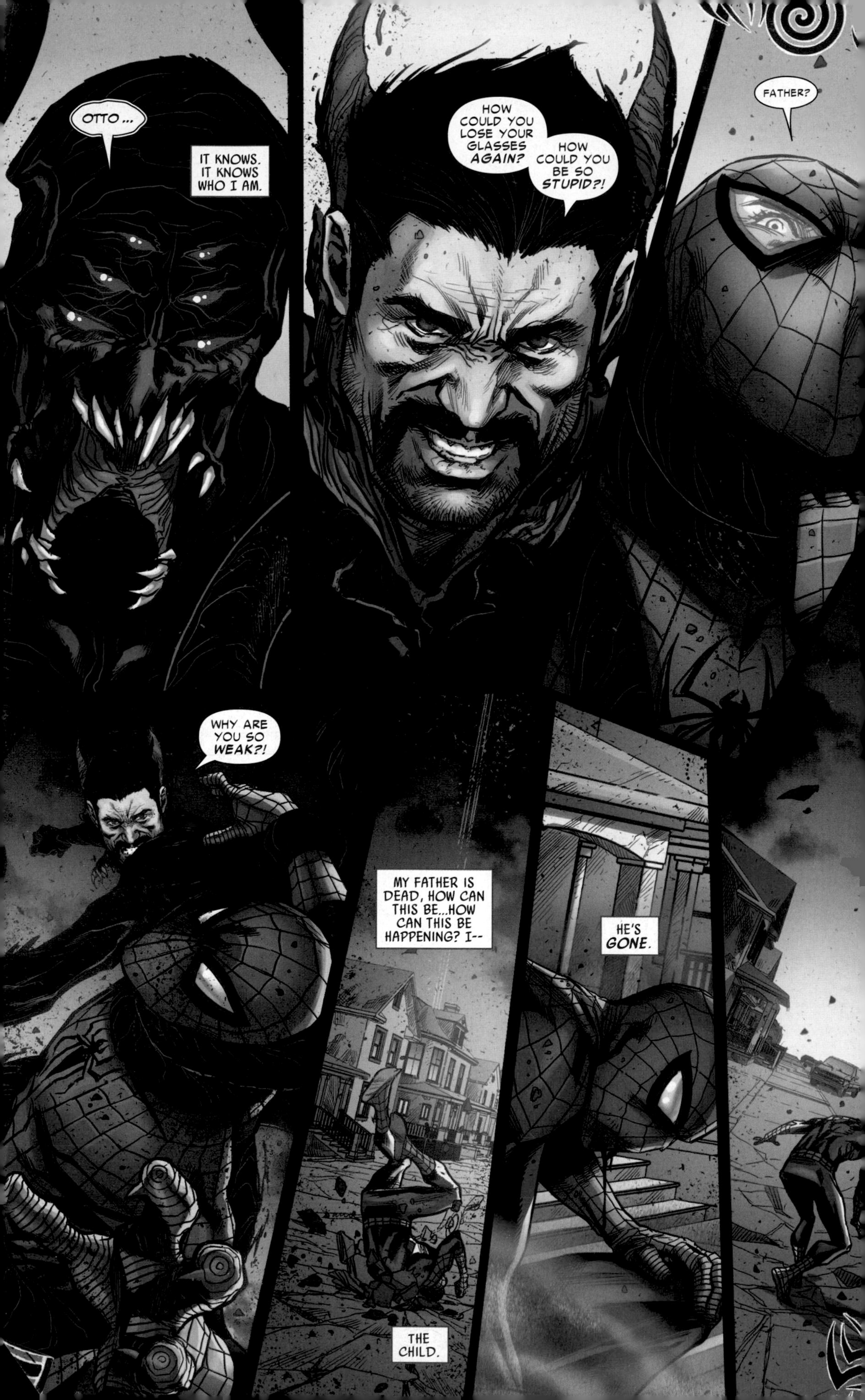
OTTO...
IT KNOWS. IT KNOWS WHO I AM.
HOW COULD YOU LOSE YOUR GLASSES AGAIN?
HOW COULD YOU BE SO STUPID?!
FATHER?
WHY ARE YOU SO WEAK?!
MY FATHER IS DEAD, HOW CAN THIS BE...HOW CAN THIS BE HAPPENING? I--
THE CHILD.
HE'S GONE.

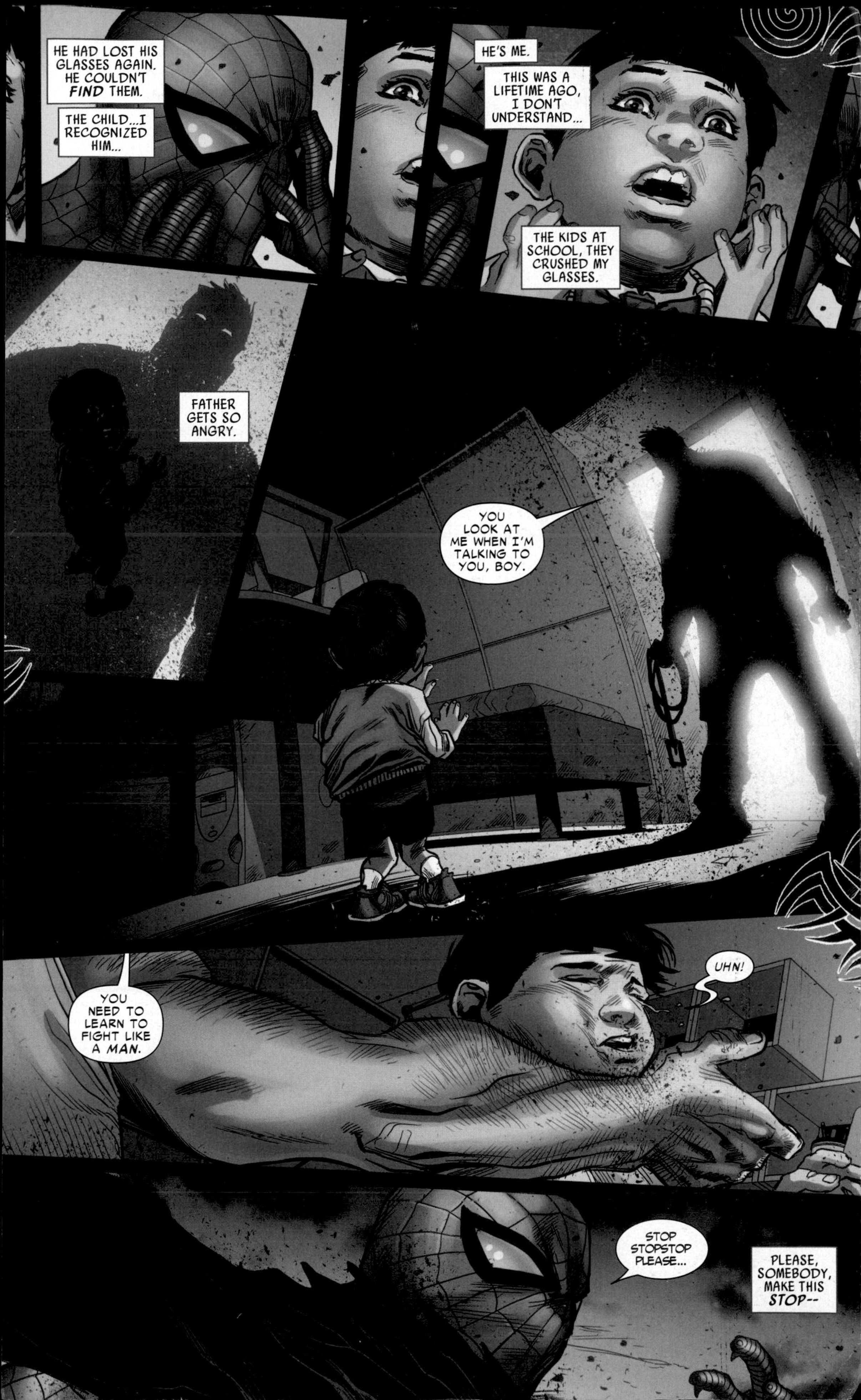
HE HAD LOST HIS GLASSES AGAIN. HE COULDN'T *FIND* THEM.
THE CHILD...I RECOGNIZED HIM...
HE'S ME.
THIS WAS A LIFETIME AGO, I DON'T UNDERSTAND...
THE KIDS AT SCHOOL, THEY CRUSHED MY GLASSES.
FATHER GETS SO ANGRY.
YOU LOOK AT ME WHEN I'M TALKING TO YOU, BOY.
YOU NEED TO LEARN TO FIGHT LIKE A *MAN*.
UHN!
STOP STOPSTOP PLEASE...
PLEASE, SOMEBODY, MAKE THIS *STOP--*

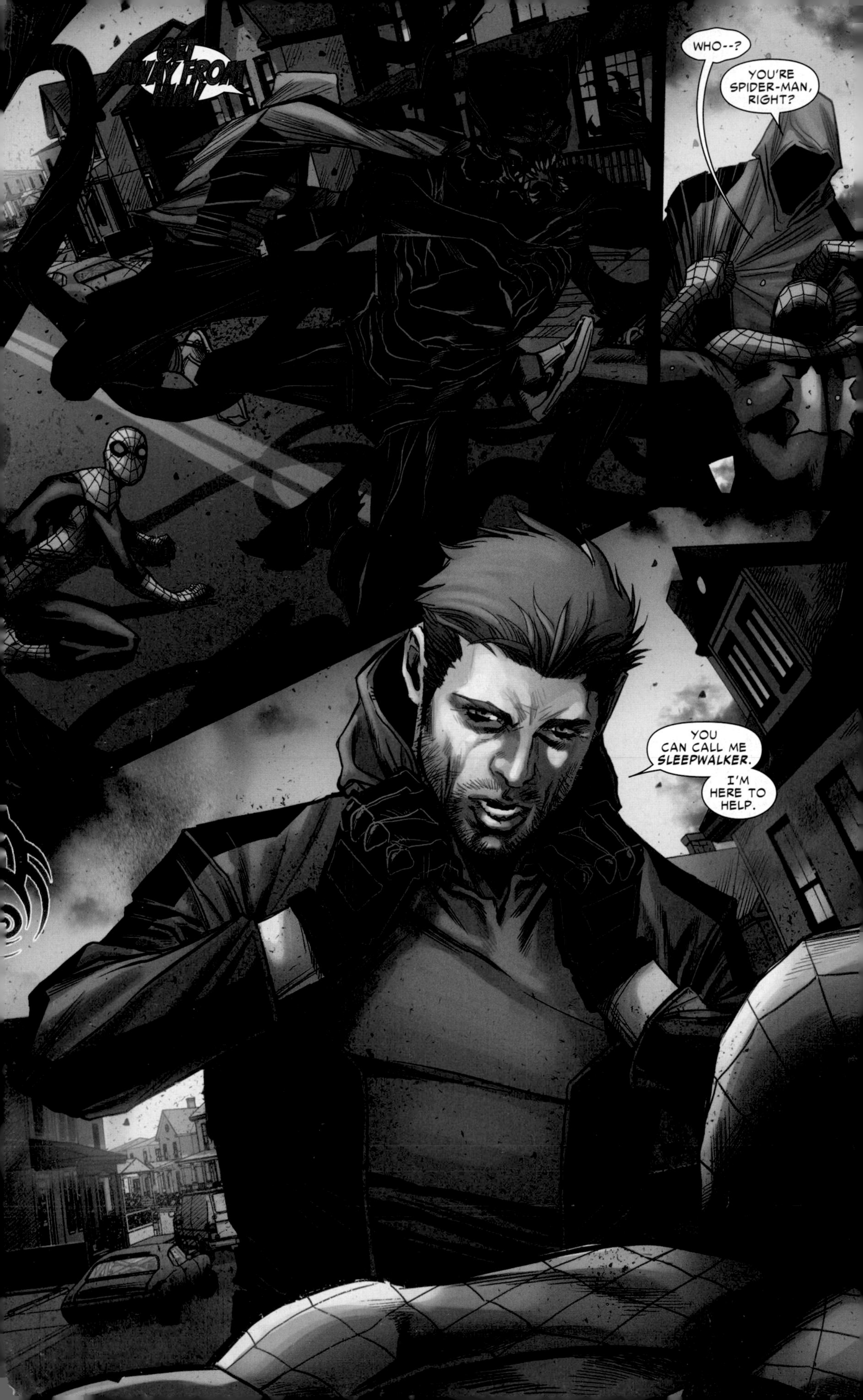
GET AWAY FROM HIM!
WHO--?
YOU'RE SPIDER-MAN, RIGHT?
YOU CAN CALL ME *SLEEPWALKER*.
I'M HERE TO HELP.

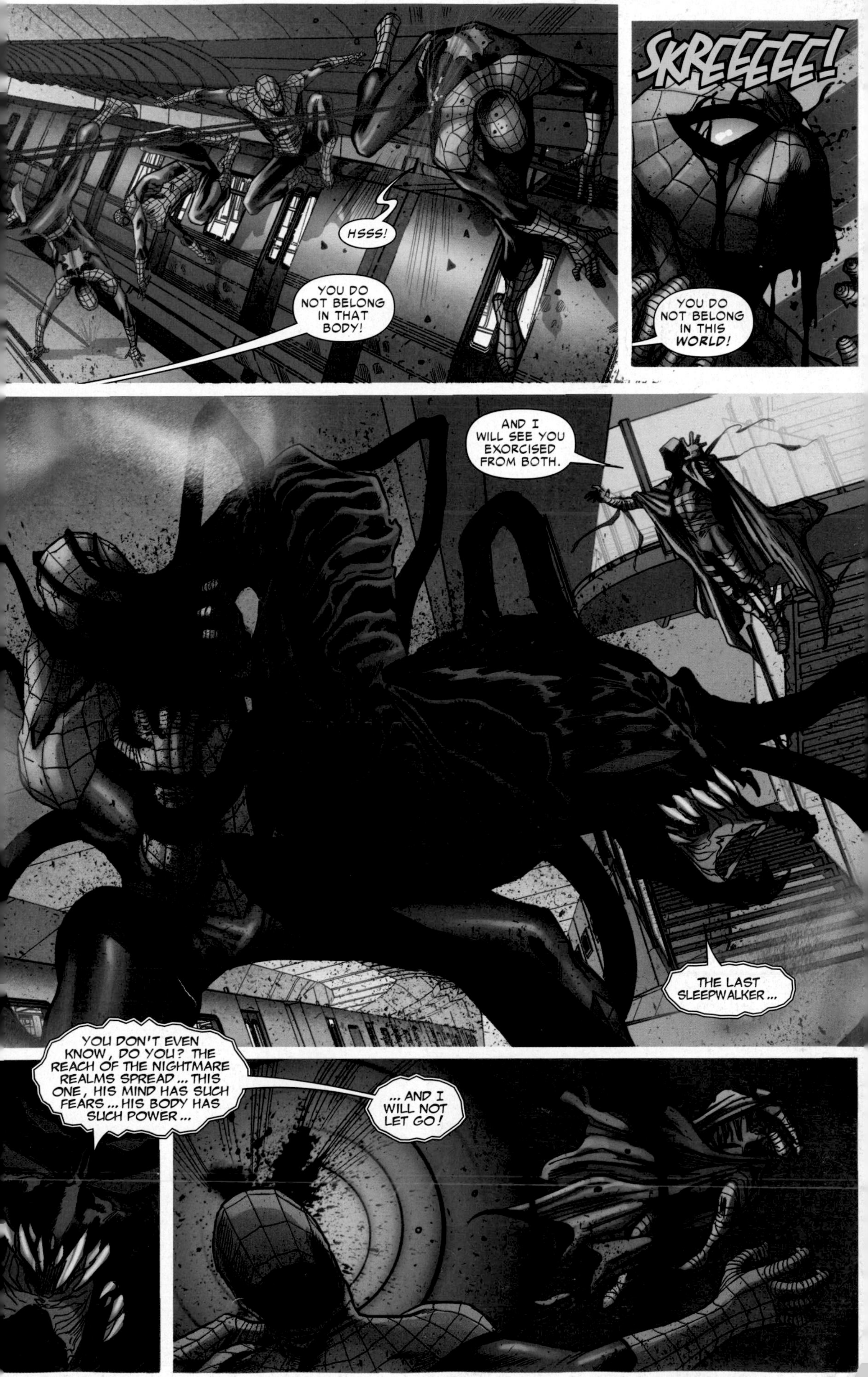
HSSS!
YOU DO NOT BELONG IN THAT BODY!
SKREEEEEE!
YOU DO NOT BELONG IN THIS WORLD!
AND I WILL SEE YOU EXORCISED FROM BOTH.
THE LAST SLEEPWALKER...
YOU DON'T EVEN KNOW, DO YOU? THE REACH OF THE NIGHTMARE REALMS SPREAD... THIS ONE, HIS MIND HAS SUCH FEARS... HIS BODY HAS SUCH POWER...
...AND I WILL NOT LET GO!

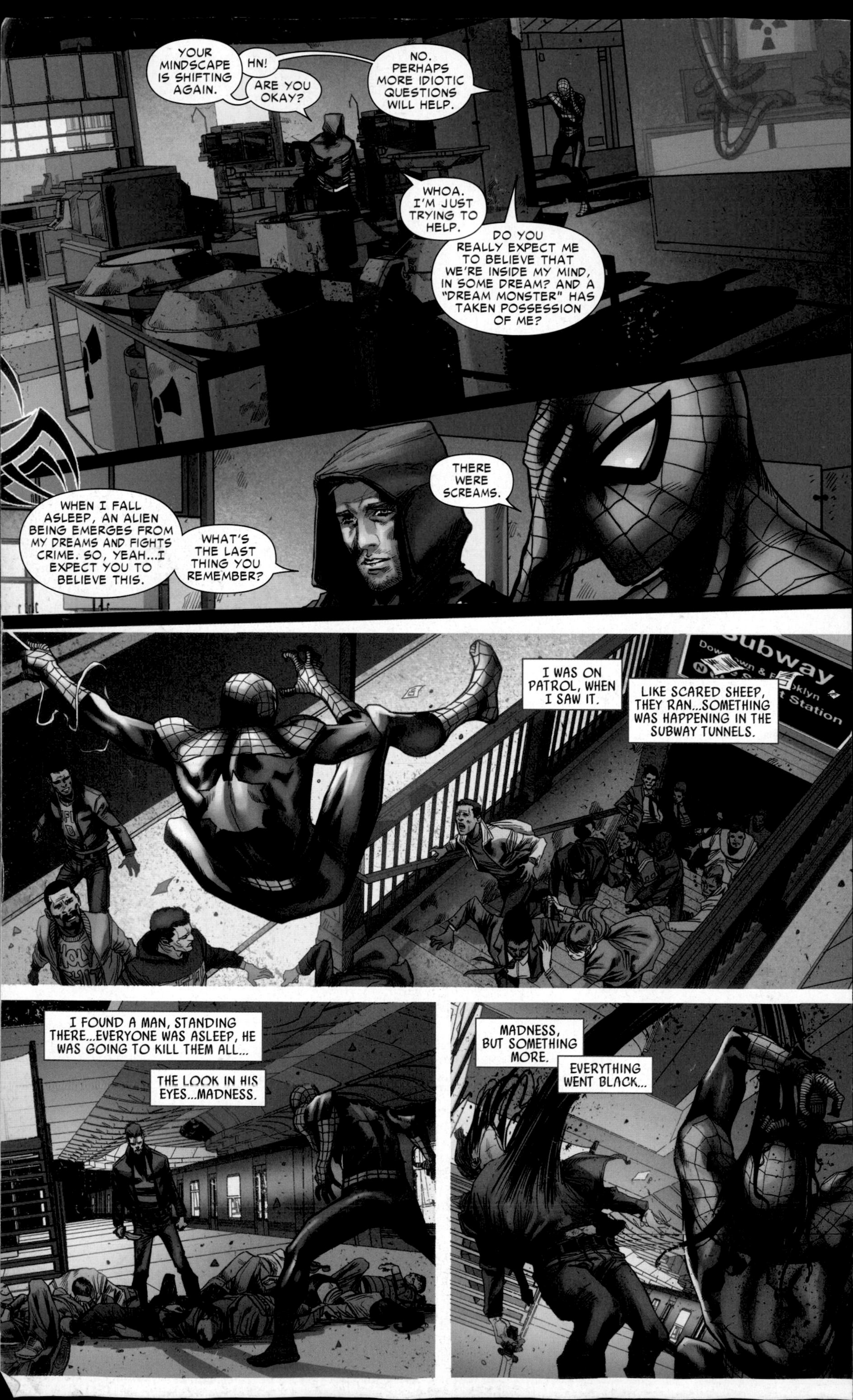
YOUR MINDSCAPE IS SHIFTING AGAIN.
HN!
ARE YOU OKAY?
NO. PERHAPS MORE IDIOTIC QUESTIONS WILL HELP.
WHOA. I'M JUST TRYING TO HELP.
DO YOU REALLY EXPECT ME TO BELIEVE THAT WE'RE INSIDE MY MIND, IN SOME DREAM? AND A "DREAM MONSTER" HAS TAKEN POSSESSION OF ME?
WHEN I FALL ASLEEP, AN ALIEN BEING EMERGES FROM MY DREAMS AND FIGHTS CRIME. SO, YEAH...I EXPECT YOU TO BELIEVE THIS.
WHAT'S THE LAST THING YOU REMEMBER?
THERE WERE SCREAMS.
I WAS ON PATROL, WHEN I SAW IT.
LIKE SCARED SHEEP, THEY RAN...SOMETHING WAS HAPPENING IN THE SUBWAY TUNNELS.
I FOUND A MAN, STANDING THERE...EVERYONE WAS ASLEEP, HE WAS GOING TO KILL THEM ALL...
THE LOOK IN HIS EYES...MADNESS.
MADNESS, BUT SOMETHING MORE.
EVERYTHING WENT BLACK...

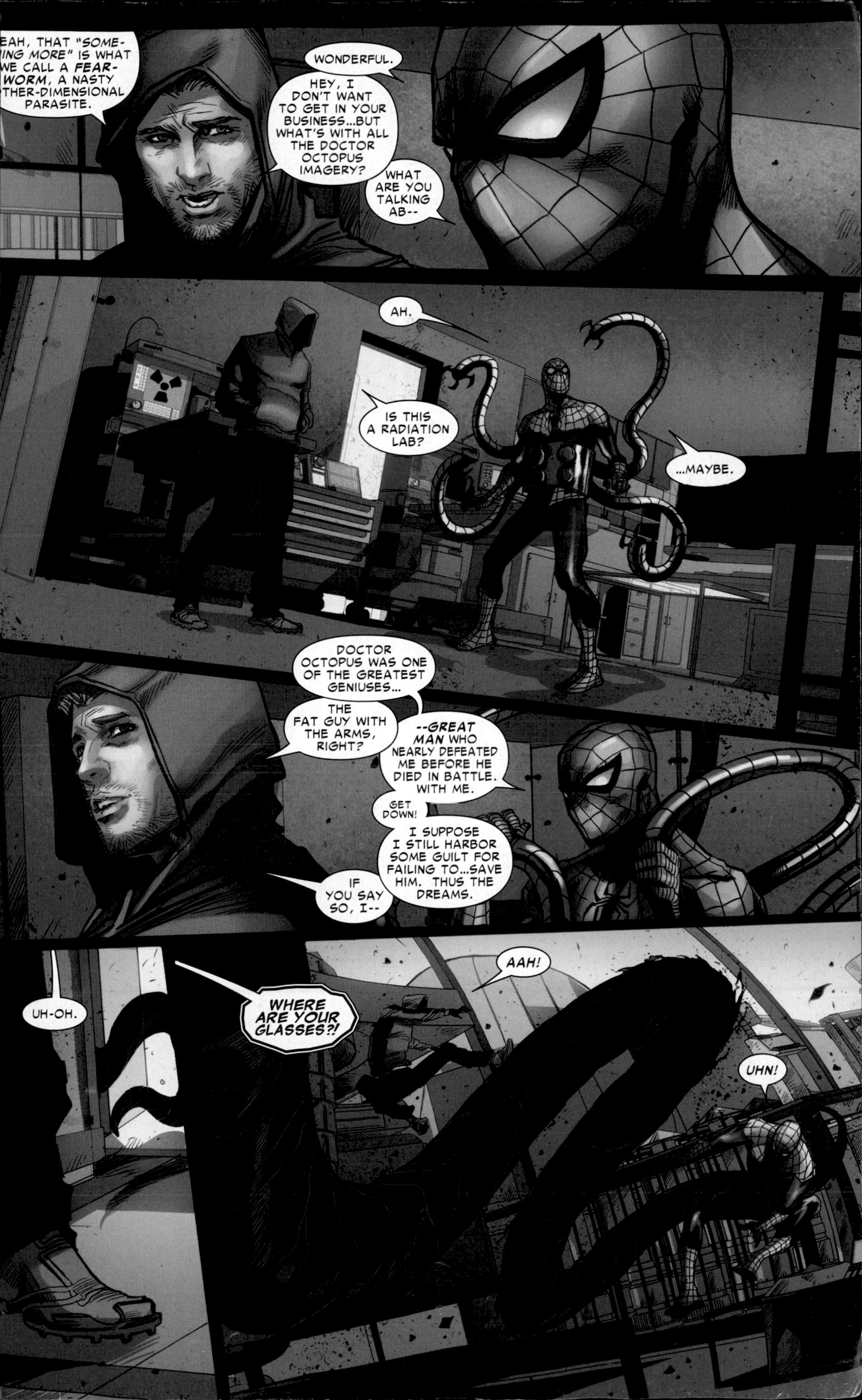
EAH, THAT "SOME-ING MORE" IS WHAT WE CALL A FEAR-WORM, A NASTY OTHER-DIMENSIONAL PARASITE.
WONDERFUL.
HEY, I DON'T WANT TO GET IN YOUR BUSINESS...BUT WHAT'S WITH ALL THE DOCTOR OCTOPUS IMAGERY?
WHAT ARE YOU TALKING AB--
AH.
IS THIS A RADIATION LAB?
...MAYBE.
DOCTOR OCTOPUS WAS ONE OF THE GREATEST GENIUSES...
THE FAT GUY WITH THE ARMS, RIGHT?
--GREAT MAN WHO NEARLY DEFEATED ME BEFORE HE DIED IN BATTLE. WITH ME.
GET DOWN!
I SUPPOSE I STILL HARBOR SOME GUILT FOR FAILING TO...SAVE HIM. THUS THE DREAMS.
IF YOU SAY SO, I--
UH-OH.
WHERE ARE YOUR GLASSES?!
AAH!
UHN!

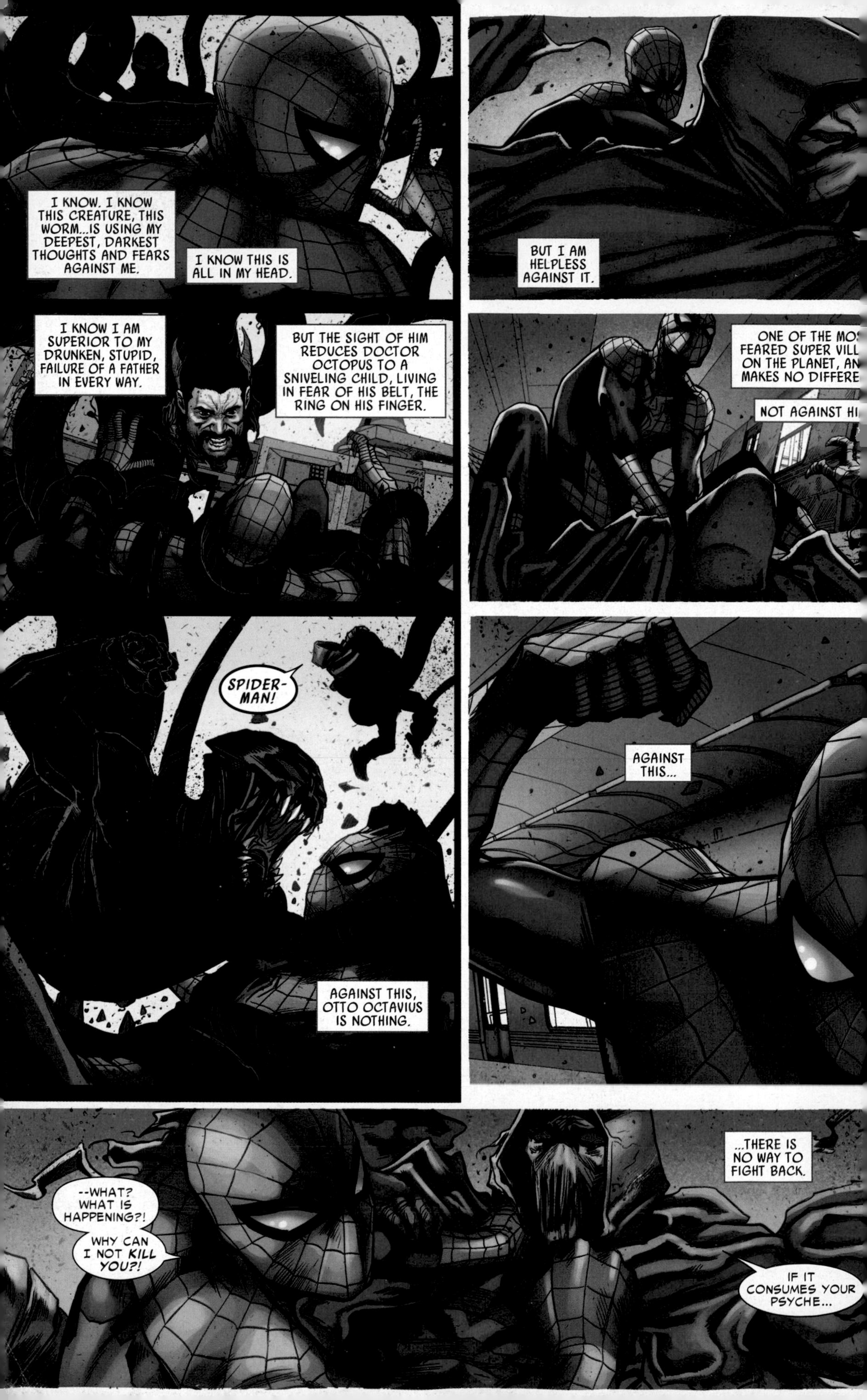
I KNOW. I KNOW THIS CREATURE, THIS WORM...IS USING MY DEEPEST, DARKEST THOUGHTS AND FEARS AGAINST ME.
I KNOW THIS IS ALL IN MY HEAD.
BUT I AM HELPLESS AGAINST IT.
I KNOW I AM SUPERIOR TO MY DRUNKEN, STUPID, FAILURE OF A FATHER IN EVERY WAY.
BUT THE SIGHT OF HIM REDUCES DOCTOR OCTOPUS TO A SNIVELING CHILD, LIVING IN FEAR OF HIS BELT, THE RING ON HIS FINGER.
ONE OF THE MOS FEARED SUPER VILL ON THE PLANET, AN MAKES NO DIFFERE
NOT AGAINST HI
SPIDER-MAN!
AGAINST THIS, OTTO OCTAVIUS IS NOTHING.
AGAINST THIS...
--WHAT? WHAT IS HAPPENING?!
WHY CAN I NOT KILL YOU?!
...THERE IS NO WAY TO FIGHT BACK.
IF IT CONSUMES YOUR PSYCHE...

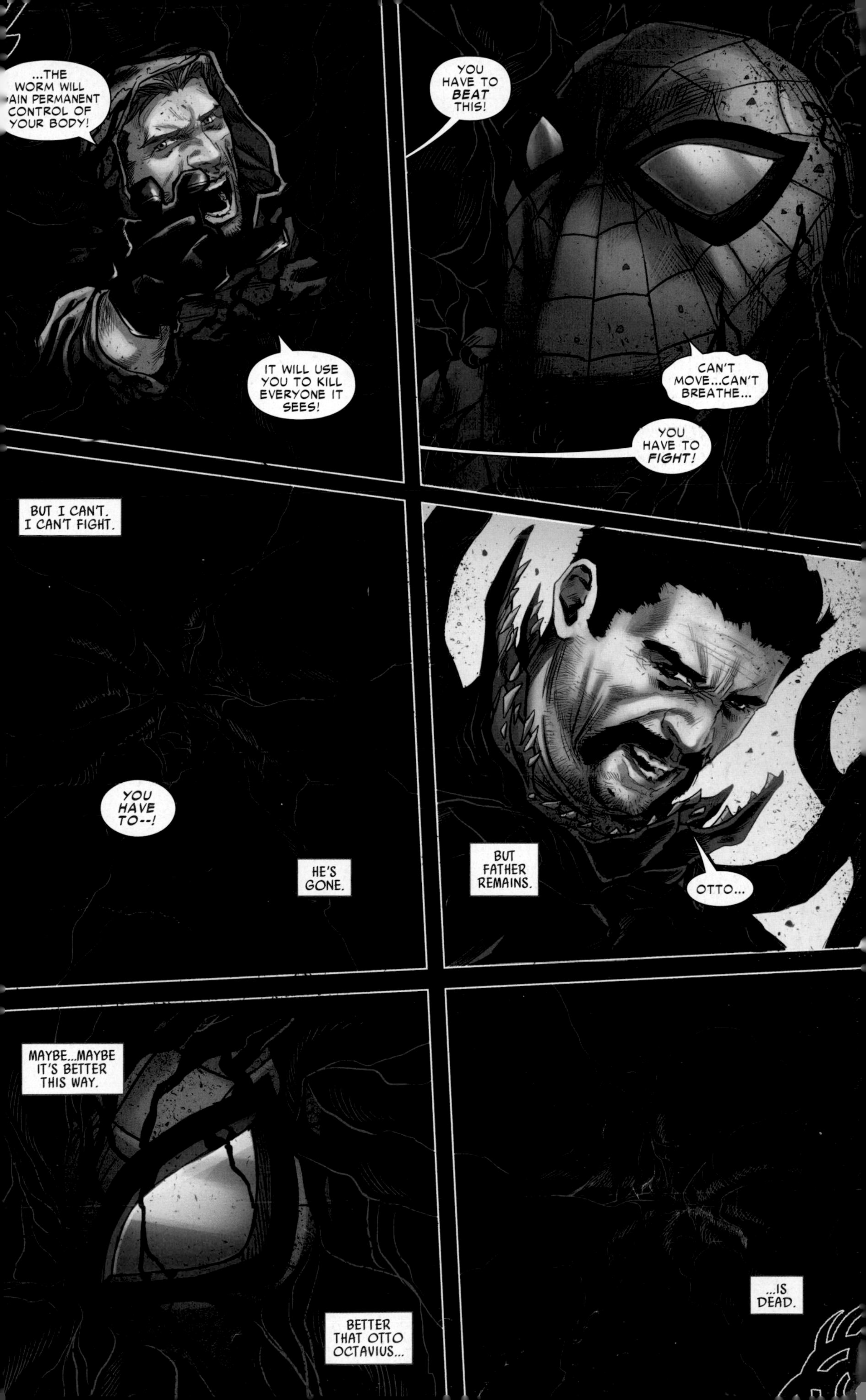

...THE WORM WILL GAIN PERMANENT CONTROL OF YOUR BODY!
IT WILL USE YOU TO KILL EVERYONE IT SEES!
YOU HAVE TO BEAT THIS!
CAN'T MOVE...CAN'T BREATHE...
YOU HAVE TO FIGHT!
BUT I CAN'T. I CAN'T FIGHT.
YOU HAVE TO--!
HE'S GONE.
BUT FATHER REMAINS.
OTTO...
MAYBE...MAYBE IT'S BETTER THIS WAY.
BETTER THAT OTTO OCTAVIUS...
...IS DEAD.

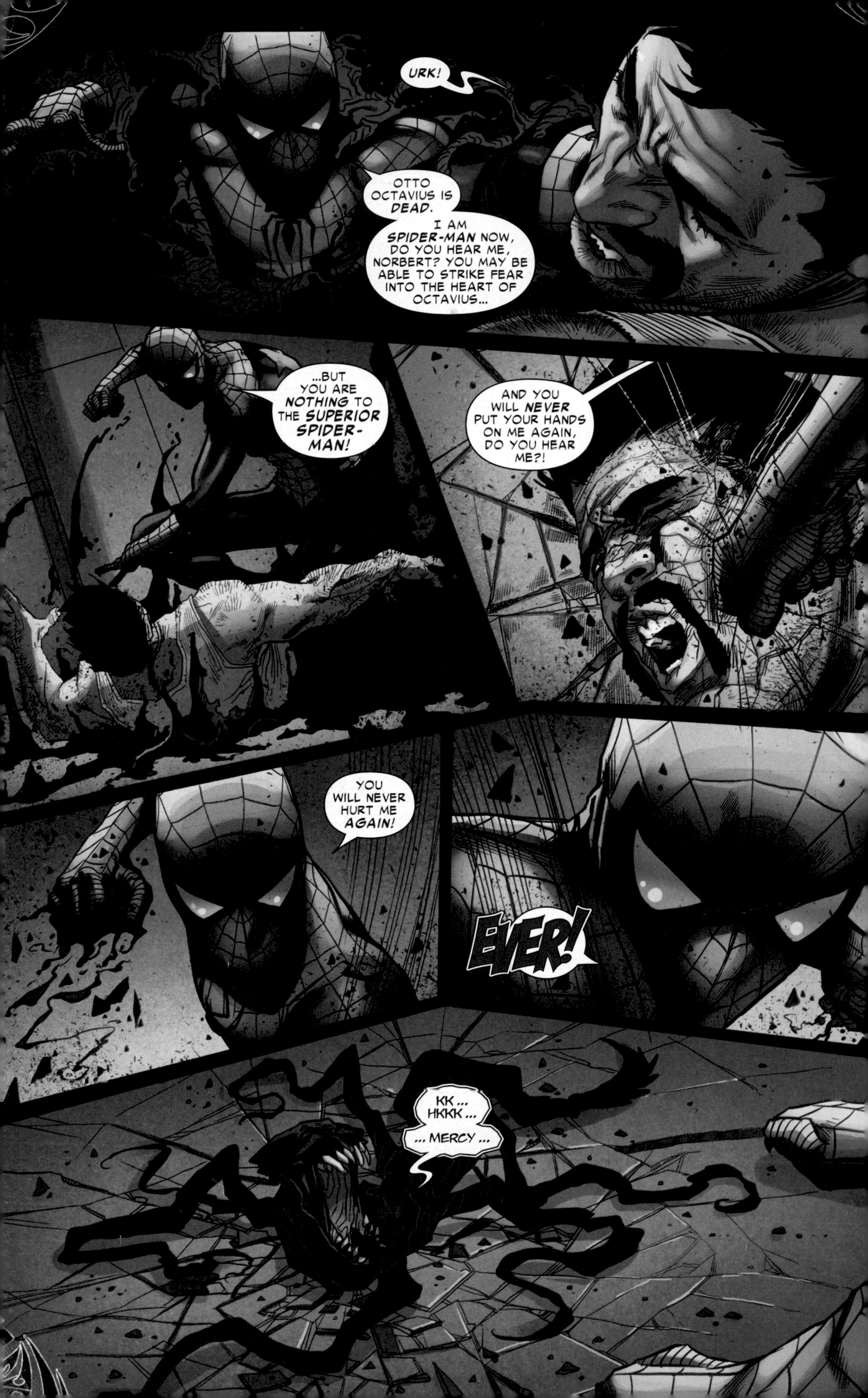
URK!
OTTO OCTAVIUS IS DEAD.
I AM SPIDER-MAN NOW, DO YOU HEAR ME, NORBERT? YOU MAY BE ABLE TO STRIKE FEAR INTO THE HEART OF OCTAVIUS...
...BUT YOU ARE NOTHING TO THE SUPERIOR SPIDER-MAN!
AND YOU WILL NEVER PUT YOUR HANDS ON ME AGAIN, DO YOU HEAR ME?!
YOU WILL NEVER HURT ME AGAIN!
EVER!
KK... HKKK...
...MERCY...

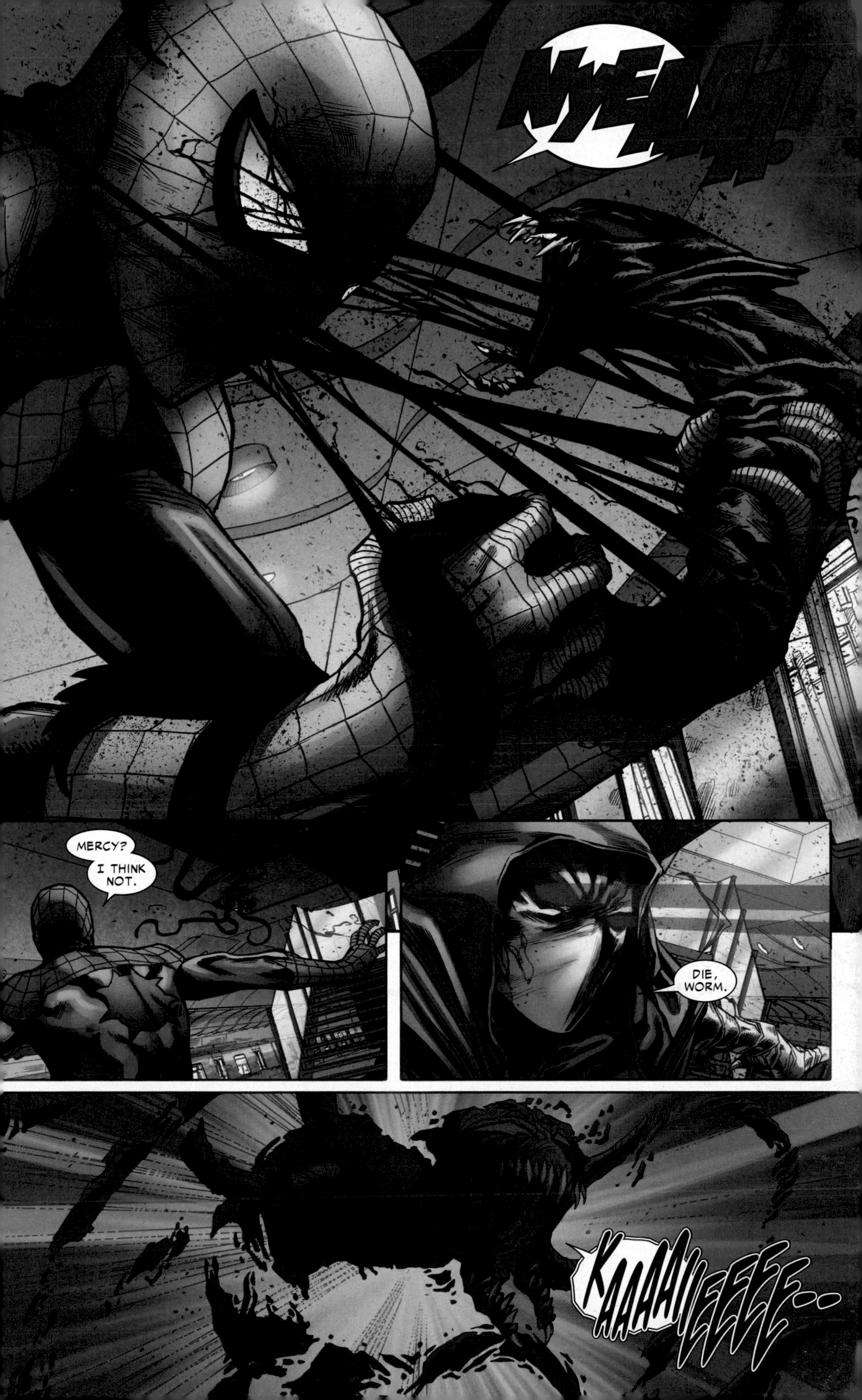
MERCY?
I THINK NOT.
DIE, WORM.
KAAAAIEEEEE..

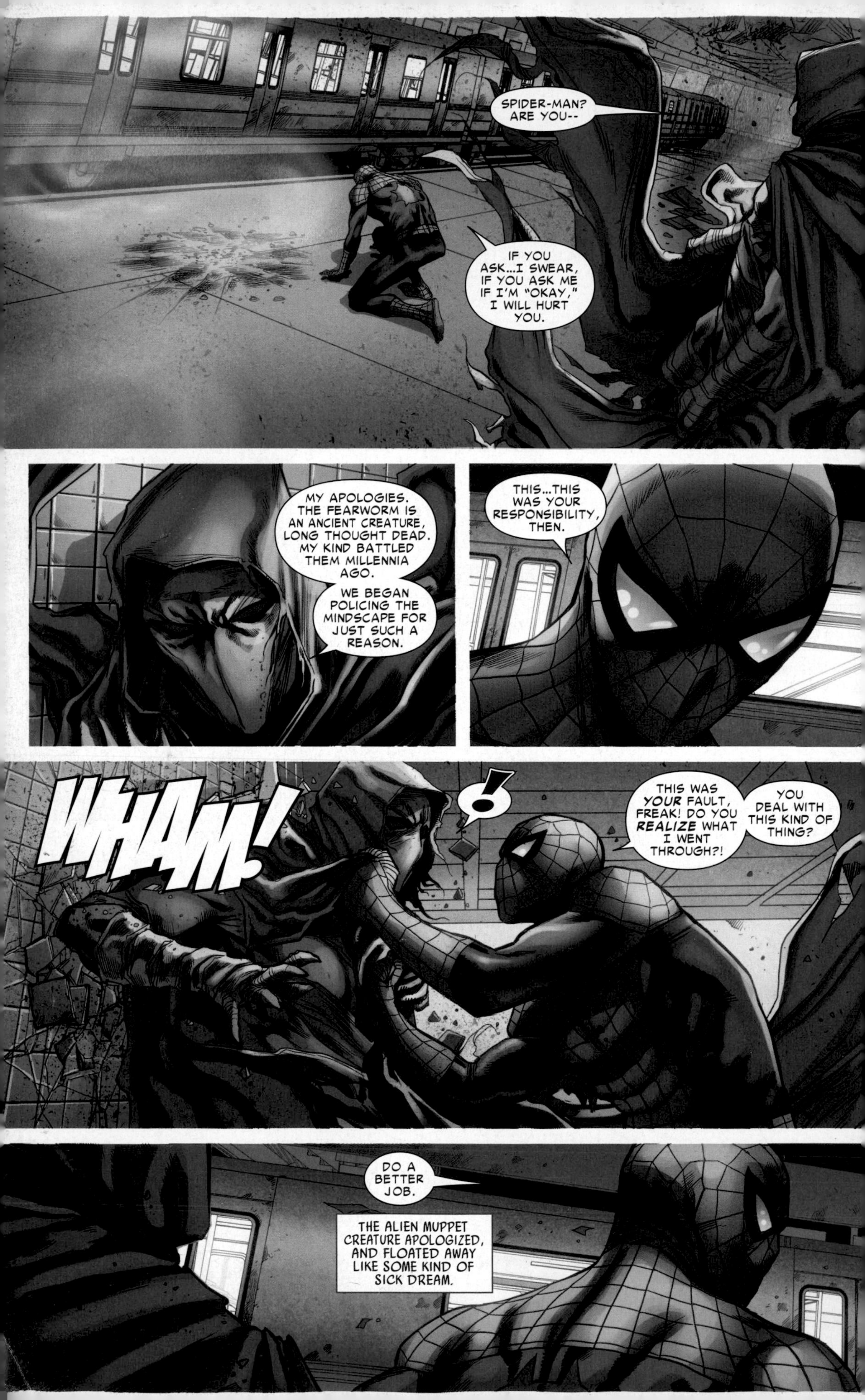
SPIDER-MAN? ARE YOU--
IF YOU ASK...I SWEAR, IF YOU ASK ME IF I'M "OKAY," I WILL HURT YOU.
MY APOLOGIES. THE FEARWORM IS AN ANCIENT CREATURE, LONG THOUGHT DEAD. MY KIND BATTLED THEM MILLENNIA AGO.
WE BEGAN POLICING THE MINDSCAPE FOR JUST SUCH A REASON.
THIS...THIS WAS YOUR RESPONSIBILITY, THEN.
WHAM!
!
THIS WAS *YOUR* FAULT, FREAK! DO YOU *REALIZE* WHAT I WENT THROUGH?!
YOU DEAL WITH THIS KIND OF THING?
DO A BETTER JOB.
THE ALIEN MUPPET CREATURE APOLOGIZED, AND FLOATED AWAY LIKE SOME KIND OF SICK DREAM.

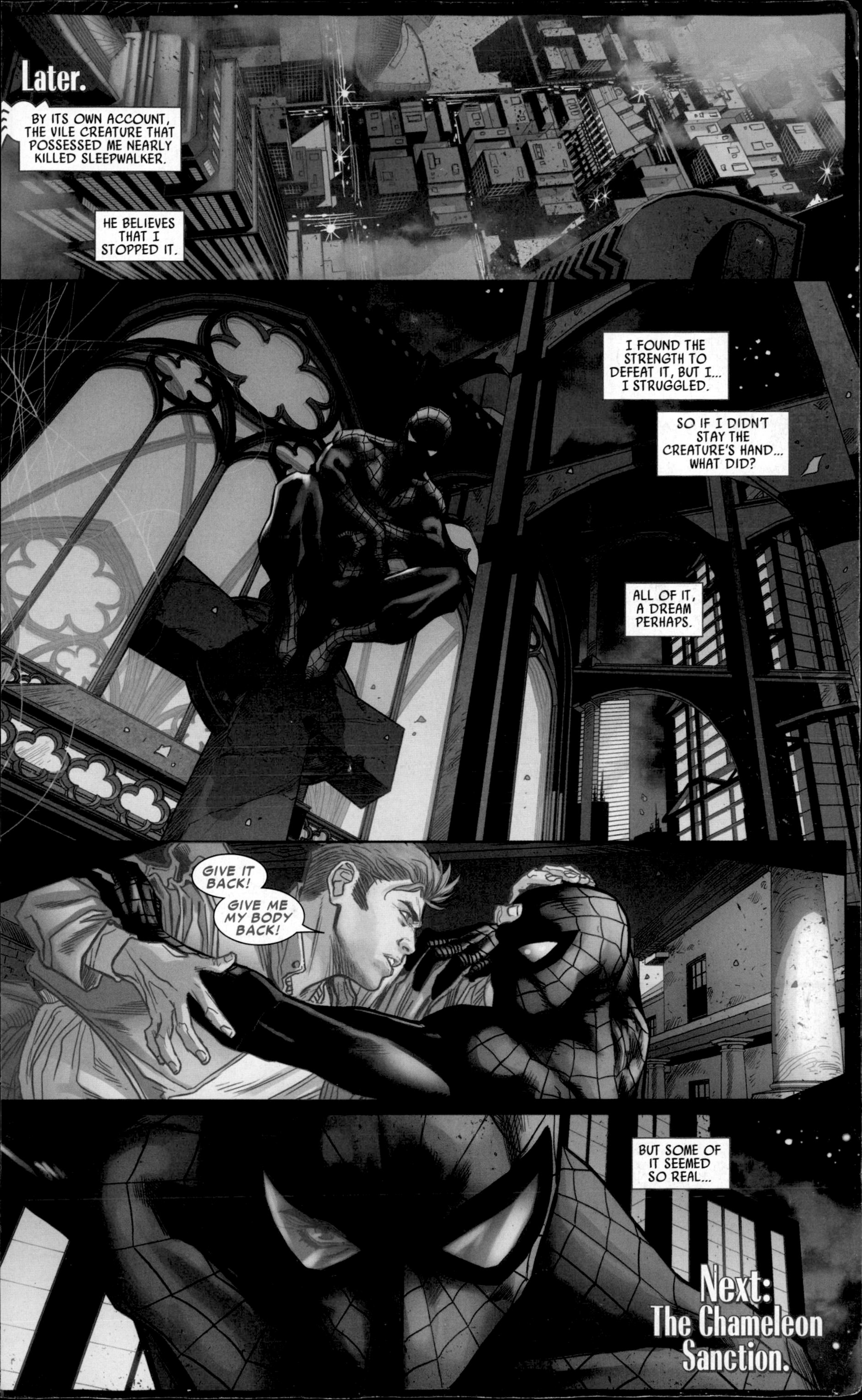
Later.
BY ITS OWN ACCOUNT, THE VILE CREATURE THAT POSSESSED ME NEARLY KILLED SLEEPWALKER.
HE BELIEVES THAT I STOPPED IT.
I FOUND THE STRENGTH TO DEFEAT IT, BUT I... I STRUGGLED.
SO IF I DIDN'T STAY THE CREATURE'S HAND... WHAT DID?
ALL OF IT, A DREAM PERHAPS.
GIVE IT BACK!
GIVE ME MY BODY BACK!
BUT SOME OF IT SEEMED SO REAL...
Next: The Chameleon Sanction.

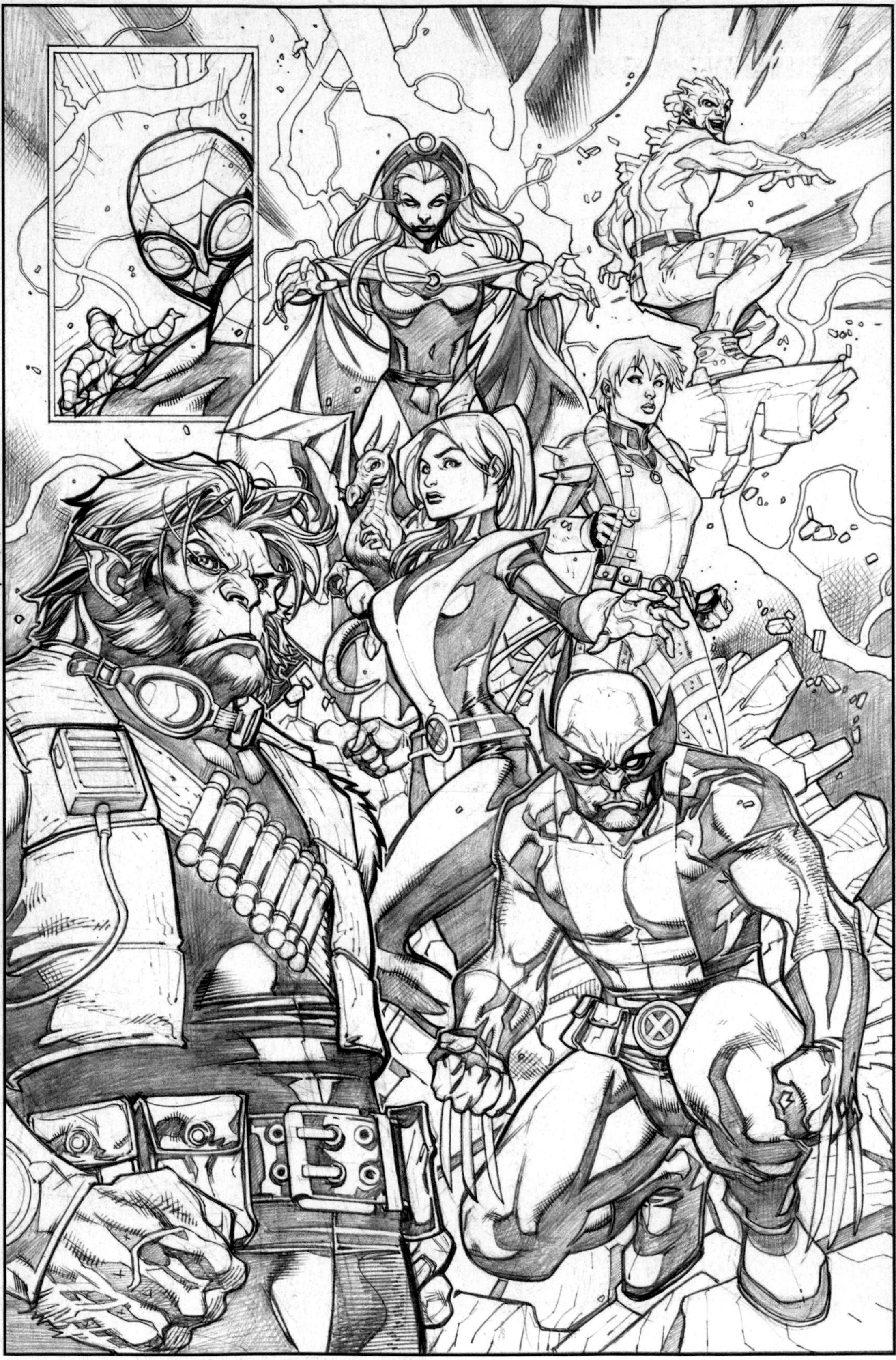

## #16, PAGE 6 ART PROCESS
PENCILS BY PACO MEDINA

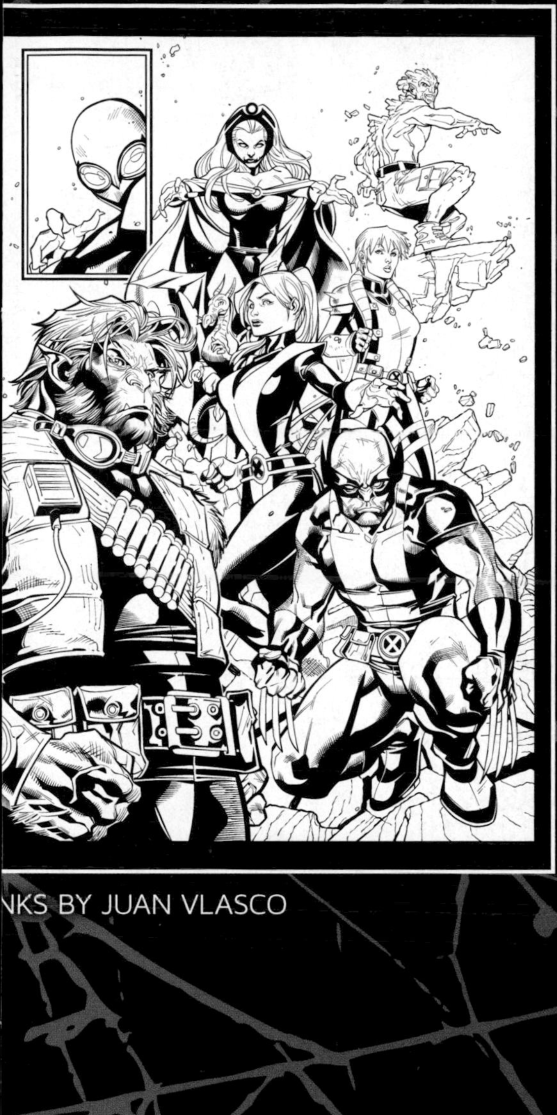

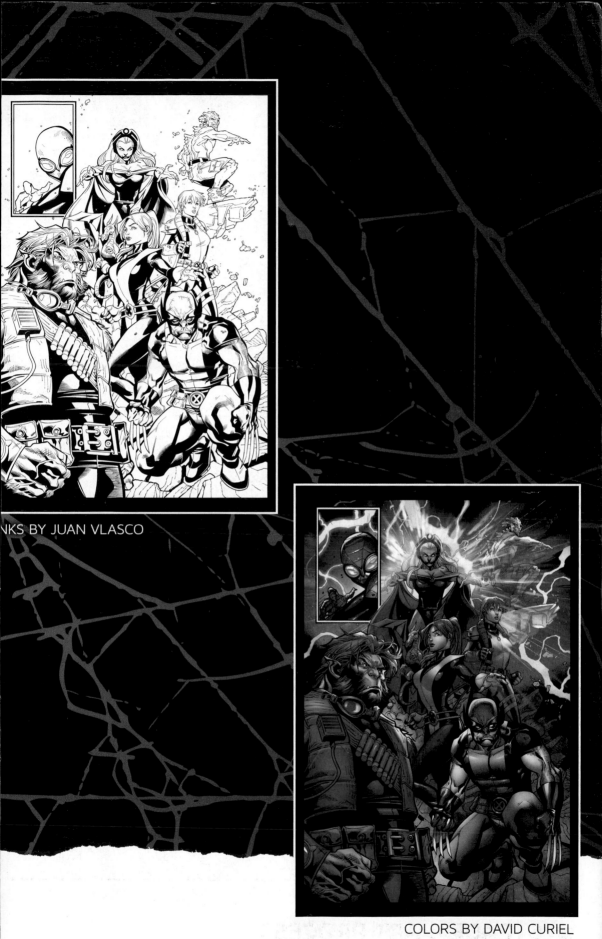

NKS BY JUAN VLASCO

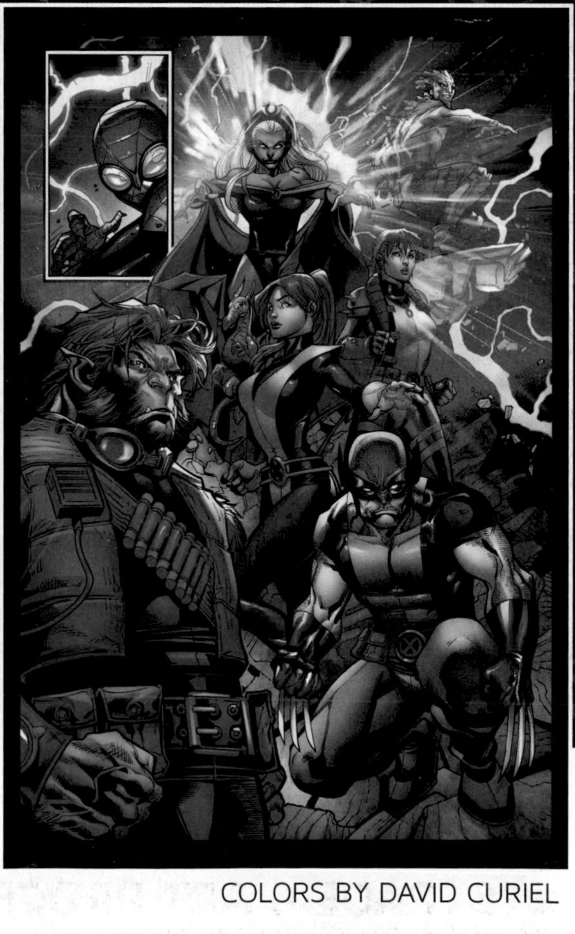

COLORS BY DAVID CURIEL

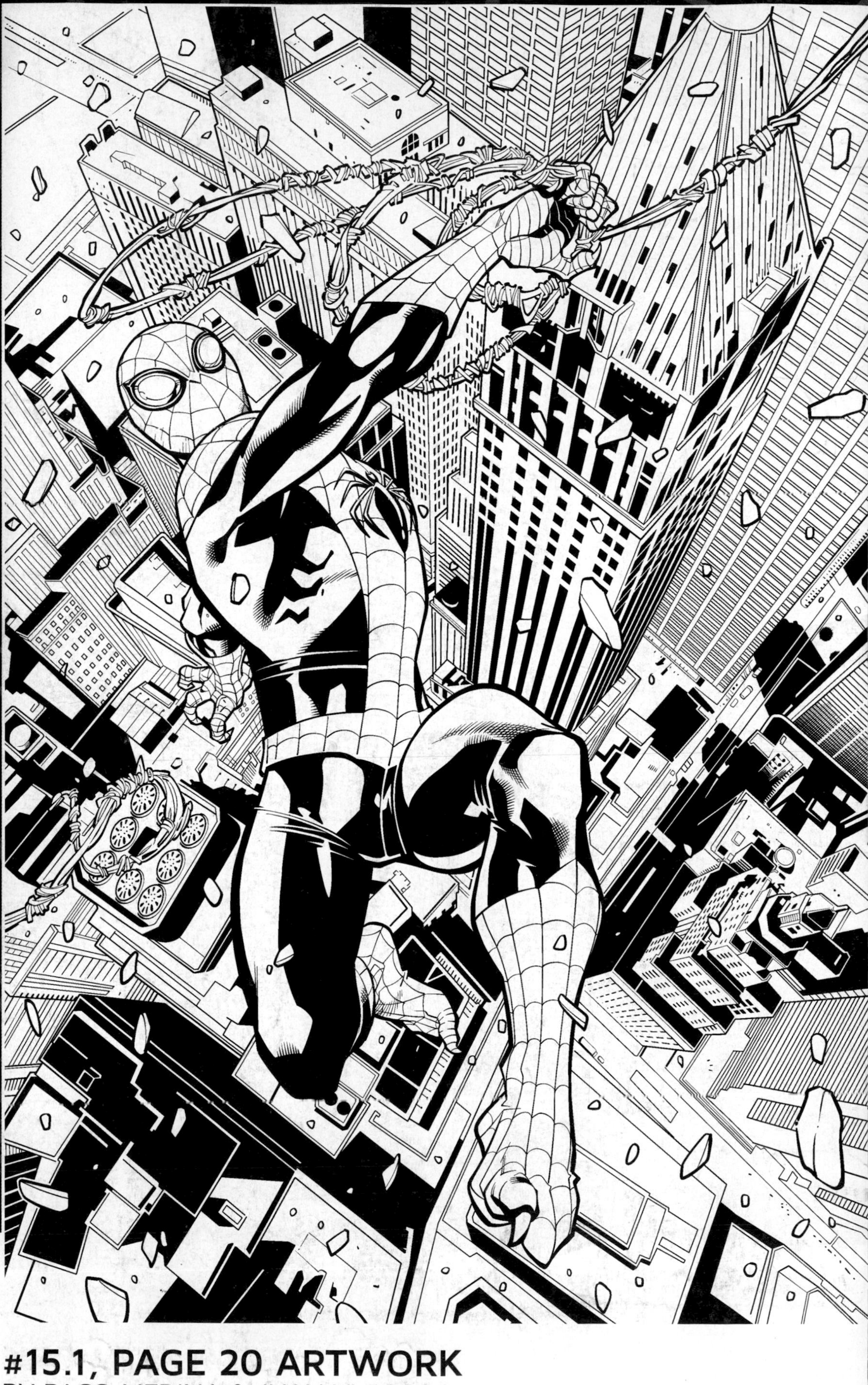

#15.1, PAGE 20 ARTWORK
BY PACO MEDINA & JUAN VLASCO

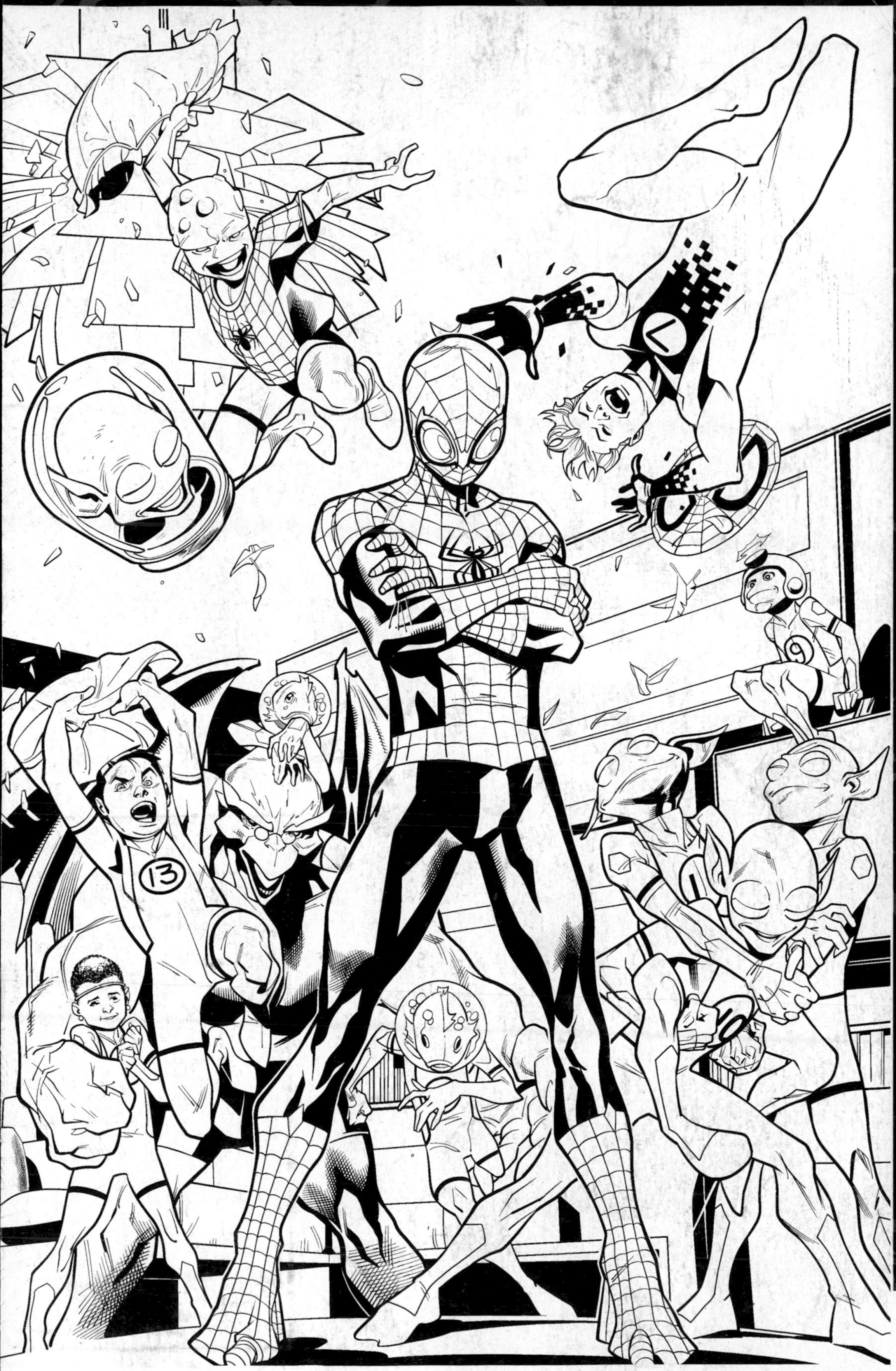

**#17, PAGE 4 ARTWORK**
BY PACO MEDINA & JUAN VLASCO

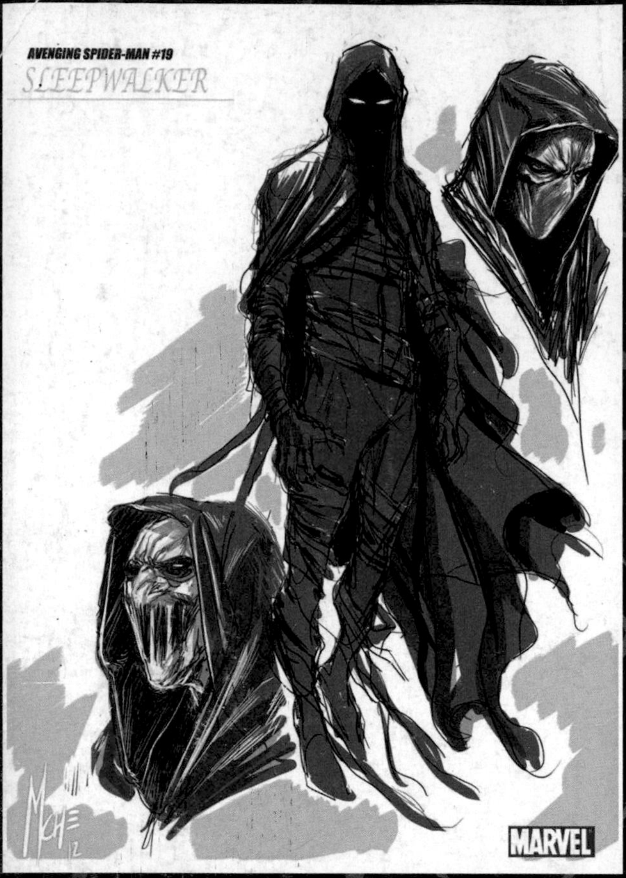
AVENGING SPIDER-MAN #19
SLEEPWALKER

**SLEEPWALKER SKETCH**
BY MARCO CHECCHETTO

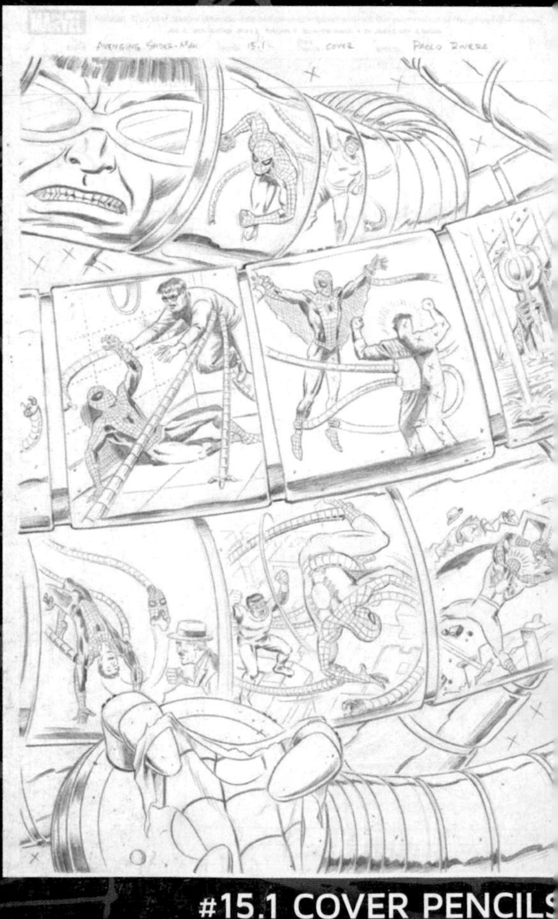
AVENGING SPIDER-MAN
15.1
COVER
PAOLO RIVERA

**#15.1 COVER PENCILS**
BY PAOLO RIVERA